Spain, the United States, and Transatlantic Literary Culture throughout the Nineteenth Century

The relationship between the United States and Spain evolved rapidly over the course of the nineteenth century, culminating in hostility during the Spanish–American War. However, scholarship on literary connections between the two nations has been limited aside from a few studies of the small coterie of Hispanists typically conceived as the canon in this area. This volume collects essays that push the study of transatlantic connections between U.S. and Spanish literatures in new directions. The contributors represent an interdisciplinary group including scholars of national literatures, national histories, and comparative literature. Their works explore previously understudied authors as well as understudied works by better-known authors. They use these new archives to present canonical works in new lights. Moreover, they explore organic entanglements between the literary traditions, and how those traditions interface with Latinx literary history.

John C. Havard is Professor of early American literature at Kennesaw State University. His research focuses on hemispheric studies and religious studies. His book *Hispanicism and Early US Literature: Spain, Mexico, Cuba, and the Origins of US National Identity* was published by the University of Alabama Press in 2018.

Ricardo Miguel-Alfonso is Associate Professor of American Studies and Literary Theory at the University of Castilla-La Mancha, Spain. He is the author of *La idea romántica de la literatura en Estados Unidos* (*American Romanticism and the Idea of Literature*, Verbum, 2018), and he recently coedited with David LaRocca *A Power to Translate the World: New Essays on Emerson and International Culture* (Dartmouth, 2015). He has written journal essays and book chapters on figures such as Ralph Waldo Emerson, Robert Coover, Eliza Haywood, Lydia Sigourney, and Nathaniel Hawthorne. He has also translated into Spanish Ralph Waldo Emerson's *Essays* (2001) and George Santayana's *Reason in Art* (2008), among others. He is currently at work on a book manuscript on Emerson's career as the American symbol of modern disenchantment.

Routledge Transnational Perspectives on American Literature
Edited by Susan Castillo, King's College London

Masculinity in Contemporary New York Fiction
Peter Ferry

Ethnic Literatures and Transnationalism
Critical Imaginaries for a Global Age
Edited by Aparajita Nanda

Gender and the Self in Latin American Literature
Emma Staniland

Navigating the Transnational in Modern American Literature and Culture
Edited by Tara Stubbs and Doug Haynes

Richard Wright and Transnationalism
New Dimensions to Modern American Expatriate Literature
Mamoun Alzoubi

Transatlantic Footholds
Turn-of-the-Century American Women Writers and British Reviewers
Stephanie Palmer

Ambivalent Transnational Belonging in American Literature
Silvia Schultermandl

Spain, the United States, and Transatlantic Literary Culture throughout
the Nineteenth Century
Edited by John C. Havard and Ricardo Miguel-Alfonso

For more information about this series, please visit: www.routledge.com/
Routledge-Transnational-Perspectives-on-American-Literature/book-
series/SE0701

Spain, the United States, and Transatlantic Literary Culture throughout the Nineteenth Century

Edited by
John C. Havard and
Ricardo Miguel-Alfonso

NEW YORK AND LONDON

First published 2022
by Routledge
605 Third Avenue, New York, NY 10158

and by Routledge
2 Park Square, Milton Park, Abingdon, Oxon OX14 4RN

Routledge is an imprint of the Taylor & Francis Group, an informa business

© 2022 Taylor & Francis

The right of John C. Havard and Ricardo Miguel-Alfonso to be identified as the authors of the editorial material, and of the authors for their individual chapters, has been asserted in accordance with sections 77 and 78 of the Copyright, Designs and Patents Act 1988.

All rights reserved. No part of this book may be reprinted or reproduced or utilised in any form or by any electronic, mechanical, or other means, now known or hereafter invented, including photocopying and recording, or in any information storage or retrieval system, without permission in writing from the publishers.

Trademark notice: Product or corporate names may be trademarks or registered trademarks, and are used only for identification and explanation without intent to infringe.

Library of Congress Cataloging-in-Publication Data
A catalog record for this title has been requested

ISBN: 978-1-03-210840-7 (hbk)
ISBN: 978-1-03-211345-6 (pbk)
ISBN: 978-1-00-321946-0 (ebk)

DOI: 10.4324/9781003219460

Typeset in Sabon
by Newgen Publishing UK

Contents

List of Contributors   vii

1   Introduction   1
JOHN C. HAVARD AND RICARDO MIGUEL-ALFONSO

2   Spain and Washington Irving's Global America   10
JEFFREY SCRABA

3   Moriscos and Mormons: Captivity Literature on the
Spanish and American Frontiers   29
ELIZABETH TERRY-ROISIN AND RANDI LYNN TANGLEN

4   The Writings of U.S. Hispanists and the Malleability
of the U.S. Empire's Spanish Past   55
GREGG FRENCH

5   Sketches of Spain: The Traveling Fictions of Frances
Calderón de la Barca's *The Attaché in Madrid*   79
NICHOLAS SPENGLER

6   "Benito Cereno," Spaniards, and Creoles   96
JOHN C. HAVARD

7   Inspiration or Coincidence? Guadalupe Gutierrez and
María Berta Quintero y Escudero's *Espinas y rosas* as
Discursive Doubles   111
VANESSA OVALLE PEREZ

8   Spain, U.S. Whiteness Studies, and María Amparo
Ruiz de Burton's "Lost Cause"   132
MELANIE HERNÁNDEZ

vi   *Contents*

9 Future and Past in Nilo María Fabra's Science Fiction
Stories on Spain versus the United States   159
JUAN HERRERO-SENÉS

10 George Santayana's Transatlantic Literary Criticism
and the Potencies of Aesthetic Judgment   175
DAVID LAROCCA

   Index   197

Contributors

Gregg French is an assistant professor in the Department of History at the University of Prince Edward Island. His research explores identity formation and projections of power in colonial spaces. His current book project examines how the relationships that developed between representatives of the U.S. and Spanish empires influenced the American imperial experience in North America, the Caribbean Basin, and the Philippines.

John C. Havard is Professor of early American literature at Kennesaw State University. His research focuses on hemispheric studies and religious studies. His book *Hispanicism and Early US Literature: Spain, Mexico, Cuba, and the Origins of US National Identity* was published by the University of Alabama Press in 2018.

Melanie Hernández is Associate Professor and Chair of the English Department at Fresno State, where she teaches courses in U.S. literature and cultural production. She specializes in nineteenth-century U.S. literature, with an emphasis on comparative African American and Chicanx studies. She has held research fellowships at the American Antiquarian Society and LLILAS Benson Latin American Studies and Collections at the University of Texas, Austin, and was a volunteer composition instructor for University Beyond Bars, in collaboration with the Washington State Reformatory and Shoreline Community College. Prior to teaching, she worked in television and radio, including the Oxygen network, ABC's *The View*, radio station K-EARTH 101, *Saturday Night Live!*, *E! News Daily*, *The Howard Stern Show*, and *Eyewitness News*. She prefers teaching.

Juan Herrero-Senés is Associate Professor of Spanish at the University of Colorado Boulder. His main areas of research are early science fiction, modernist intellectual networks, and the peninsular avant-garde. His latest books are *Mensajeros de un tiempo nuevo: modernidad y nihilismo en la literatura de vanguardia (1918–1936)* (Anthropos, 2014) and *Mundos al descubierto: Antología de ciencia ficción de la Edad de Plata (1898–1936)* (Renacimiento, 2021). He has published

viii *List of Contributors*

critical editions of Benjamín Jarnés and Miguel de Unamuno, among others, and articles in journals such as *Anales de Literatura Española Contemporánea, Revista Hispánica Moderna, Bulletin of Spanish Studies, Revista Canadiense de Estudios Hispánicos, Hispanic Review, Studies in the Novel,* and *Hispanófila.*

David LaRocca is the author, editor, or coeditor of a dozen books, including *Emerson's English Traits and the Natural History of Metaphor, The Bloomsbury Anthology of Transcendental Thought,* and *Inheriting Stanley Cavell.* His articles have appeared in journals such as *Afterimage, Conversations, Epoché, Estetica, Film and Philosophy, Liminalities, The Midwest Quarterly, Nineteenth-Century Prose, Post Script, The Senses and Society, Transactions of the C.S. Peirce Society, The Journal of Religion and Business Ethics, Journalism, Media and Cultural Studies, The Journal of Aesthetic Education,* and *The Journal of Aesthetics and Art Criticism.* Formerly Harvard's Sinclair Kennedy Fellow in the United Kingdom, and a participant in an NEH Institute and the School of Criticism and Theory, he has held visiting research and teaching positions at Binghamton, Cornell, Cortland, Harvard, Ithaca College, the School of Visual Arts, and Vanderbilt. Information about his work may be found at www. DavidLaRocca.org.

Ricardo Miguel-Alfonso is Associate Professor of American Studies and Literary Theory at the University of Castilla-La Mancha, Spain. He is the author of *La idea romántica de la literatura en Estados Unidos (American Romanticism and the Idea of Literature,* Verbum, 2018), and he recently coedited with David LaRocca *A Power to Translate the World: New Essays on Emerson and International Culture* (Dartmouth, 2015). He has written journal essays and book chapters on figures such as Ralph Waldo Emerson, Robert Coover, Eliza Haywood, Lydia Sigourney, and Nathaniel Hawthorne. He has also translated into Spanish Ralph Waldo Emerson's *Essays* (2001) and George Santayana's *Reason in Art* (2008), among others. He is currently at work on a book manuscript on Emerson's career as the American symbol of modern disenchantment.

Vanessa Ovalle Perez is an assistant professor of English at California State University, San Bernardino. Currently, she is writing a book exploring the social and poetic aspects of texts published by Latinas in Spanish-language, California newspapers of the nineteenth and early twentieth centuries. Her writing has appeared in *Letras Femeninas* and *J19: The Journal of Nineteenth-Century Americanists,* and her podcast episode on Latina dedication poetry is available on the C19 Podcast.

Jeffrey Scraba is Associate Professor and Director of Graduate Studies at the University of Memphis. He has published several other articles

List of Contributors ix

on Washington Irving, as well as articles on Walter Scott, Edgar Allan Poe, Raymond Chandler, and the HBO series *Deadwood*.

Nicholas Spengler is currently Associate Lecturer (Teaching) in English Literature at University College London. He holds a BA from Middlebury College and an MA and PhD from the University of Edinburgh. His first book, *Melville's Americas: Hemispheric Sympathies, Transatlantic Contagion*, is a study of Herman Melville's literary representations of and engagements with Spanish America, forthcoming from Edinburgh University Press in 2022. He also has published articles in *Leviathan: A Journal of Melville Studies* and *Textual Practice*.

Randi Lynn Tanglen is executive director of Humanities Montana and an independent scholar based in Missoula, Montana. She was previously professor of English and director of the Robert and Joyce Johnson Center for Faculty Development and Excellence in Teaching at Austin College in Texas. Her work has appeared in *Western American Literature* and several edited volumes, and she is coeditor of *Teaching Western American Literature* (University of Nebraska Press, 2020). The research for her coauthored article in this volume was made possible by a fellowship from the Charles Redd Center for Western Studies at Brigham Young University in Provo, Utah.

Elizabeth Terry-Roisin has a PhD in History from the University of California-Berkeley and an AB in History from Dartmouth College. She is currently Assistant Professor of History at Florida International University and has also taught at Austin College. She is an historian of early modern Europe and medieval Europe with an emphasis on Spain, Italy, and the Mediterranean world. Her research in the cultural and social history of Spain has focused on the Spanish Renaissance, noble culture and chivalric culture, and the experiences of religious minorities, such as the Moriscos. Her research has been supported by a Franklin Grant from the American Philosophical Society, and her coauthored essay with scholar of Spanish literature Ignacio Navarrete, "Nobles and Court Culture," has appeared in Brill's *Companion to the Spanish Renaissance* (2019).

1 Introduction

John C. Havard and Ricardo Miguel-Alfonso

Between the American Revolutionary War (1775–1783) and the Spanish–American War (1898), the relations between the United States and Spain went through different phases, from initial trust and mutual interest to suspicion and open confrontation. The process is long and sometimes convoluted, but what began as an attempt to defeat common enemies ended up in a clash of empires that would put an end to what was by then understood as the old aristocratic Spanish imperial power in favor of the new American technological, commodity-based one. Changing along with the international images of the two countries were their literary relations.

Those relations were often easier than the political ones. Although literature was informed by stereotypes dating back to the colonial period, the overt friendships and antagonisms that characterized political struggles did not always enter the artistic field, and more often than not the literary relations between both countries remained outside political strife until the end of the century. Their respective literatures found common points of inspiration in each other, and their literary relations quickly materialized in two different ways.

On the one hand, we have what we may call the *literary* integration of Spanish culture in the United States. By the 1820s, U.S. publishers—mainly in Boston but also in New York—began to pay serious attention to the Spanish classics, so that English translations soon began to reach the general public. Although the American public was only rudimentarily acquainted with the history of Spain, its culture and character began to appeal to different writers in such a way that by the late 1830s the history and landscapes of Spain had found a way into the works of writers such as Washington Irving (*Tales of the Alhambra*, 1832), Henry Wadsworth Longfellow (*Outre Mer*, 1835), and James Fenimore Cooper (*Mercedes of Castile*, 1840). However idealized their visions of Spain were, their influence was so enduring that influential critical studies of Spanish–U.S. relations routinely group them as a sort of "canon" of Spain-influenced writers (Kagan 2002, Jakšić 2007).

On the other hand, the nineteenth century also witnessed the rise of Hispanism as an *academic* discipline in the United States, mostly

DOI: 10.4324/9781003219460-1

2 John C. Havard and Ricardo Miguel-Alfonso

thanks to figures such as George Ticknor and William H. Prescott. Their respective works (in literature and history) opened the history and culture of Spain to American readers. The culmination of this process was the publication in 1849 of the first edition of George Ticknor's *History of Spanish Literature*, the first modern and comprehensive literary history of Spain ever published, which was shortly after translated into Spanish and French. Ticknor's work, together with that of the historian William H. Prescott, helped to make Spanish culture and literature available in the United States and opened new paths of study and recognition between both countries. Despite the political turmoil of the last decade of the century, this exchange continued in the twentieth century in the works of writers such as John Dos Passos and Ernest Hemingway among others.

There is, however, another story to be told—one to which this volume is a contribution. Although writers such as Irving, Longfellow, and Cooper (and, later, William Cullen Bryant) originated literary Hispanism and Ticknor and Prescott its academic iteration, an entire generation of U.S. writers contributed to the knowledge of Spain in a variety of other ways, including travelogues, political pamphlets, and religious writings. From James Cheetham's *Letters on Our Affairs with Spain* (1804) and Alexander S. MacKenzie's *A Year in Spain. By a Young American* (1829) to James Pettigrew's *Notes on Spain and Spaniards* (1861), the acquaintance with Spain and its culture materialized in forms that are not only literary or academic. Many nonliterary and nonacademic writers took Spain as their object of observation throughout the century and produced works that offer relevant insights into the mutual interests and vision of both countries. The list of writers includes names that are for the most part forgotten now, but whose importance remains crucial for understanding our subject: for instance, Caleb Cushing, Alexander Everett Hale, S. Teackle Wallis, Nicholas Thieblin, and James Albert Harrison.

The chapters in this volume are meant to expand and find more alternatives to the "canonical" twofold (literary/academic) narrative about Spanish–U.S. literary relations. They do so in three different ways: first, by looking at traditionally overlooked writers and works; second, by exploring some of the well-known writers under a different light; lastly, by considering Spanish-language responses to U.S. culture and literature. In doing so, they provide us with alternative views of a relationship that has been long underrepresented in the literary history of both countries. Each one of them opens a new theoretical way of looking at texts that dramatize the exchange between both countries, from a renewed consideration about the global character of Irving's vision to the fluid national character of Santayana as a Spanish (and/or American) critic.

For example, in "Spain and Washington Irving's Global America," Jeffrey Scraba argues that Washington Irving's *A History of the Life and Voyages of Christopher Columbus* is a global prehistory of the United States. The chapter illuminates how *Life of Columbus* stresses the role of contingency in shaping historical trajectories. The work presents

Introduction 3

Columbus as a foundational American hero, but it also illustrates the roles chance and external influences played in Columbus' story, with examples ranging from Prince Henry of Portugal's accidental discovery of lost navigational knowledge to Columbus' timely appeal to the Spanish sovereigns in the wake of the Conquest of Granada. In reflecting on the contingent fall of the Nasrid state in Spain as a necessary precondition in the rise of the Spanish empire, *Columbus* invites reflection on the decline of the Spanish empire as a chance precondition in the rise of the United States as the dominant power in the Western Hemisphere. The work thus emphasizes Spanish imperialism as the foundation for American empire and state building. As such, Irving demonstrates that the United States is not an exceptional religious and political experiment, but rather an effect and cause in the history of the vicissitudes of global power. Irving stresses that assumption of this global perspective draws readers out of provincial thinking and revolutionizes their knowledge. Scraba resuscitates Irving's reputation from tendentious arguments charging him with an uncomplicated criticism of Spanish empire and celebration of American empire; *Columbus*' emphasis on contingency in the transmission of power, as well as similarities between the United States and Spain, shows a nuanced perspective consistent with Irving's criticisms of Indian Removal in "Philip of Pokanoket." More generally, the chapter demonstrates the role of reflection on transnational connections between the United States and Spain in the shaping of U.S. literature.

In "Moriscos and Mormons: Captivity Literature on the Spanish and American Frontiers," Elizabeth Terry-Roisin and Randi Lynn Tanglen argue that comparing early modern Spanish captivity narratives and both colonial and nineteenth-century U.S. narratives reveals similarities between Spanish and New World frontier spaces as well as the role of religious difference in the formation of the American captivity genre. Whereas Spanish captivity narratives are understood to clearly focalize religious difference, American captivity narratives are often thought to explore American conceptions of racial difference, such as the racialization of Native Americans. However, religion and race were often conflated in early American literature, which initially presented Native Americans, Muslims, Catholics, and Mormons as the religious other of Protestant Anglo-America, and only came to focalize specifically racial difference over the course of the nineteenth century. The comparative framing with Spanish literature allows us to see the importance of religion and the overlapping nature of religious and racial othering in the U.S. narratives.

In "The Writings of U.S. Hispanists and the Malleability of the American Empire's Spanish Past," Gregg French highlights how and why Spanish–American War U.S. military and later colonial administrators enforced their rule by appropriating the Whiggish narratives developed by Hispanists such as Washington Irving and William H. Prescott that had celebrated the role of Spanish "discoverer" figures as civilizing forces. These leaders recognized they were building upon the foundation laid by

4 *John C. Havard and Ricardo Miguel-Alfonso*

their imperial predecessors and consciously sought to draw connections between past and present. The chapter charts this process in the cases of Puerto Rico, Guam, and the Philippines. After Puerto Rican annexation, General Nelson A. Miles placated Puerto Rican elites for remaining part of the Spanish empire by declaring that the U.S. military government would not interfere with Spanish laws it found palatable. U.S. colonial administrators later looked to education to continue this work, drawing connections between the United States, Spain, and Puerto Rico. The curriculum they developed was based on the nineteenth-century Hispanists' Whiggish celebrations of Columbus and Ponce de León. In Guam and the Philippines, the U.S. military and colonial administrations faced a lack of knowledge about the islands and their cultures. Needing to justify colonial rule in this cultural vacuum, they turned to venerating Spanish figures in the islands' histories as predecessors to U.S. leadership in the Pacific, principally Ferdinand Magellan, but also Andrés de Urdaneta and Miguel López de Legazpi. Magellan Day Celebrations have been important sites for drawing connections between Guam's present and its colonial past throughout the history of U.S. rule, and the 1921 Manila Carnival provides a striking example of the same in the case of the Philippines. The chapter concludes by placing current tensions regarding the legacies of these European colonizers in the context of the removal of Confederate monuments in the United States.

Whereas Frances Calderón de la Barca is best known for *Life in Mexico* (1843), in "Sketches of Spain: The Traveling Fictions of Frances Calderón de la Barca's *The Attaché in Madrid*," Nicholas Spengler argues for the importance of Calderón's lesser-known work, *The Attaché in Madrid* (1856). Although like *Life in Mexico* in that *The Attaché in Madrid* is based on the author's experiences traveling as a diplomat's wife, in the latter work Calderón assumes a more substantial textual guise by creating a German *attaché* as a narrator. According to Spengler, this guise allows Calderón to write a work that is not only a travel narrative but also an intertextual and meta-narrative engagement with transatlantic writing on Spain. The work is, in fact, a riposte to such writing, especially writing engaged in figurative simplifications of national character. Taking a cue from the work's subtitle, "Sketches of the Court of Isabella II," Spengler places the work in the sketch tradition of narrative fiction about Spain, exemplified by Washington Irving's writings working out the romantic idea of Spain. Although Irving's works serve as a literary model for Calderón, Calderón also resisted Irving's mystifications of Spanish life and culture. In this sense, Spengler demonstrates that Calderón was more than a travel writer. *The Attaché in Madrid* represents her engagement in a complex fictional project.

In "'Benito Cereno,' Spaniards, and Creoles," John C. Havard investigates Herman Melville's choice to reposition the historical Benito Cerreno, who was Spanish, as a Chilean creole in "Benito Cereno." Cerreno's Spanish origins placed him at odds with Juan Martínez de

Introduction 5

Rozas, the acting colonial governor of Chile, during Cerreno and Amasa Delano's legal proceedings to settle the finances of the *Tryal* affair. That affair would become the basis for Melville's classic novella. Rozas would later become a leading figure in Chilean independence efforts. Even though some of this context, such as Rozas' disdain for Cerreno, was unavailable to Melville, Melville's choice to figure Cereno as a Chilean creole is striking because Cereno's historical prototype was an object of contempt to a leading creole precisely due to his Spanish ancestry. Melville did so to emphasize, against Delano's pretensions to moral differentiation from Cereno, that the two captains shared "creole" status as men of power engaged in New World economic processes of racialized labor exploitation.

In "Inspiration or Coincidence? Guadalupe Gutierrez and María Berta Quintero y Escudero's *Espinas y rosas* as Discursive Doubles," Vanessa Ovalle Perez examines connections between two novels titled *Espinas y rosas*, one authored by a Latina, Guadalupe Gutierrez, and published in the nineteenth century, the other by a Spaniard, María Berta Quintero y Escudero, and published in the twentieth century. Gutierrez's *Espinas y rosas* is a rarity in nineteenth-century Spanish-language literature as a published Latina novel, but unfortunately most of it has been lost. While the fragmentary archival record makes it difficult to prove that the novels' similarities are more than coincidence, Ovalle Perez argues that they are in fact related. Quintero's adaptation provides a glimpse into the "lived reality" of Gutierrez's roman a clef. Moreover, Ovalle Perez illuminates transnational points of contact and shared literary choices that are evident in the authors' respective use of the *bildungsroman*. In both works, female characters are included in the traditionally all-male mentorship dynamic: in Gutierrez's novel, this comes in the form of two sisters taking on the mentee role, and in Quintero, in a traditional masculine mentee coming under the mentorship of his aunt, who convinces him to reconsider his uncle's recommendation that he join the clergy. Her recommendation leads him to choose to be a professor at a regional teachers college instead, a choice outside the traditional Spanish norm of rural farmer and urban professional. For her part, in her novel's surviving fragments, Gutierrez stages a complex reflection on the American Dream, in which her protagonists desire class mobility but from a Latina perspective express their skepticism regarding its availability. Both works ultimately suggest that education is more valuable than material gain. In these respects, reading the works together provides insights into the gendered possibilities of the mentorship relationship in Spanish and Latinx societies. Similarly, from these perspectives they reformulate the social narratives upheld by the *bildungsroman*, interrogating the American Dream narrative of American examples and the class stratification of European examples. These similarities as well as attendant differences speak to social, cultural, and literary entanglements of Mexican, American, and Spanish women writers.

6 *John C. Havard and Ricardo Miguel-Alfonso*

In "Spain, U.S. Whiteness Studies, and María Amparo Ruiz de Burton's 'Lost Cause,'" Melanie Hernández places María Amparo Ruiz de Burton's response to Anglo-American racialization of Mexicans in the wake of the U.S.-Mexican War in the context of whiteness studies. Hernández positions her reading both against scholars who read Ruiz de Burton's work as resisting the racialization of Mexicans generally in order to posit a filial claim to Ruiz de Burton as a precursor to twentieth- and twenty-first-century Chicanx resistance literature, as well as against those who describe this resistance message to be contradicted by the author's racialization of non-white characters. Such readings only make sense, Hernández stresses, if we ignore the fact that Ruiz de Burton's fiction, especially *Who Would Have Thought It?*, resists the racialization of Spanish *Californios* specifically. This resistance was not meant to speak for racially mixed and laboring class Mexicans, whose subjugation Ruiz de Burton accepted as a matter of course. Ruiz de Burton's work is best situated in the context of a mid-nineteenth-century era in which racial categories were in flux and several races vied to differentiate themselves as white against African and Native Americans. Ruiz de Burton's fiction urged that Spanish-descended Mexicans be so differentiated. Although in Anglo-America's eyes *Californios* would eventually be weeded out of this process and instead lumped together with all Mexican Americans, that process was not yet complete at the time of Ruiz de Burton's authorship. Hernández's reading highlights how Ruiz de Burton subtly deploys several contemporaneous genres—especially the captivity narrative and the passing novel—both to contend that her protagonist Lola represents a culturally superior form of whiteness that deserves to be incorporated within the U.S. body politic and to reveal the hypocrisy of white U.S. northern claims to superiority. To make this claim in the context of Reconstruction, Ruiz de Burton embraces U.S. anti-Black sentiment and affiliates *Californios* with the U.S. South. Hernández's reading serves to remind modern readers that nineteenth-century Mexican Americans were not a monolith; Ruiz de Burton's protest was not for all Mexican Americans but specifically for her class.

In "Future and Past in Nilo María Fabra's Science Fiction Stories on Spain versus the United States," Juan Herrero-Senés examines two early science fiction short stories by Spanish writer Nilo Maria Fabra. The stories were critical of American society and politics, particularly in the context of affairs with Spain. Herrero-Senés argues that the tales "synthesized the official, prevalent, and conservative viewpoint on the United States, while simultaneously registering global geopolitical alterations." The stories appeared in *La Ilustración Española y Americana* alongside news reports and scientific and historical pieces. They were written in an objective, direct, and journalistic style, rather than being based around character plots, which invited readers to consider them as hypotheticals rather than as literary pieces. Herrero-Senés contextualizes the tales in light of Fabra's political leanings: He was a technocrat, a

Introduction 7

bourgeois liberal, and had an interest in speculating on the course of nations. He viewed Americans as materialistic, exploitative, and racist. Regarding the tales themselves, Herrero-Senés describes them as "future wars" fictions, which was a popular genre in the late nineteenth century. In "La guerra de España con los Estados Unidos," Fabra predicts Spanish victory in the Spanish–American War. After Spain's defeat, he published "La Yankeelandia. Geografía e historia en el siglo XXIV," which predicts a more distant future in which the United States' victory in the Spanish–American War precipitates its conquest of the Western Hemisphere as well as other parts of the globe, which it proceeds to ruthlessly exploit. Whereas the first text was overly optimistic that Spain's spirit and colonial experience would overpower U.S. inexperience and materialism, the latter cynically cedes the future to U.S. values but preserves dignity for Spain by presenting Spain's defense of traditional values as well-meaning and tragic. In these respects, the texts are valuable records of prevailing Spanish interpretations of the war and its aftermath. Herrero-Senés concludes that the contradictions of Fabra's texts reflect the futility of blind patriotism.

In "George Santayana's Transatlantic Literary Criticism and the Potencies of Aesthetic Judgment," David LaRocca examines the impact of George Santayana's cosmopolitan perspective on his philosophy and literary criticism. LaRocca does not argue that Santayana, who was born in Spain, who was educated and began his career in the United States, and who in middle age resigned his academic position and then lived as an itinerant writer in Europe, brought a specifically Spanish perspective to his work, but that Santayana's outsider sensibility endowed him with an acute sensitivity to nonnormative perspectives in literature and the history of philosophy. LaRocca details this perspective by analyzing Santayana's remarks on Emerson's and Tom Sawyer's respective "poetic" sensibility and "adolescence." Moreover (and similar in this respect to Tanglen's and Terry-Roisin's analysis of the captivity trope), LaRocca demonstrates Emerson's and Twain's transatlantic genealogies by drawing aesthetic parallels between Emerson, Sawyer, and Don Quijote's "madness." Emerson's philosophy explores the bounds of reason and common sense; his eschewal of doctrine favors a "poetic" approach to achieving insight through experience. Similarly, Santayana figures Don Quijote's "madness" as a search for the literary in the everyday, as Alonso Quixano seeks to live out the adventures he has read about in romances. Much as Quijote's romances shaped hallucinations regarding mystical experiences of penance and martyrdom, Tom Sawyer's mad "adolescence" and mischief involve a love for overly elaborate ceremony and exacting labors. The parallels are between the child's romantic quest, the hidalgo's quest to right wrongs, and the philosopher's ideational quest, all "mad" but at the same time virtuous. LaRocca poses the possibility that Santayana's insight into these surprising connections owes to his cosmopolitan perspective of someone who was both at home everywhere and nowhere.

8 *John C. Havard and Ricardo Miguel-Alfonso*

As can be seen from these chapter descriptions, in addition to putting understudied texts in dialogue with more canonical ones to generate a fuller picture of nineteenth-century transatlantic literary dialogue, we have another goal: to avoid decontextualizing comparisons between the two literatures by exploring entanglements. We seek to identify organic literary dialogues that reveal new dimensions in the evolution of the sociocultural interactions between the two nations. The chapters achieve this aim by carefully historicizing the literature and working from insights provided by theoretical methods such as critical race studies, religious studies, and gender studies. In this sense, the collection both incorporates but also adds to some of the past two decades' most significant statements in the field. For instance, María DeGuzmán's *Spain's Long Shadow* (2005) remains critical for understanding the idea of the Spanish empire and its afterlives in U.S. culture. However, in positing that the construction of the Spanish empire as an illiberal contrast to a benevolent U.S. empire for liberty defines U.S. literary dialogue with Spain, the study underemphasizes both the nuances of some of this literature and the variety of interests it displays.

One such interest to which we were especially drawn are the intersections between U.S., Spanish, and Latinx literatures, which did not evolve as self-contained traditions. In this respect, our book responds to recent works in hemispheric studies, such as Kirsten Silva Gruesz's *Ambassadors of Culture* (2002), Raúl Coronado's *A World Not to Come* (2013), and Rodrigo Lazo's *Letters from Filadelfia* (2020). These explorations of the cultural construction and development of Latinx literatures in the eighteenth and nineteenth centuries instructively focus on concrete entanglements between various U.S. and Spanish-speaking transatlantic worlds. They achieve this goal through expanded archives, such as Coronado's focus on oral traditions and Lazo's focus on translations. Their approach demonstrates the value in thinking beyond decontextualized comparative readings of canonical texts or similarly decontextualized analyses of the role images of one nation played in the culture of the other. They similarly demonstrate that the myriad sociocultural interactions between Spain and the Spanish-speaking Americas ensure that any work analyzing connections between Spanish and U.S. literature will necessarily include discussion of the role transatlantic processes played in the emergence of Latinx literatures. We engage this dynamic intersection between hemispheric and transatlantic contexts while maintaining an explicit Spain–U.S. framing that highlights the complex mediating roles each nation played in the other's processes of literary construction.

In this respect, this book responds to Gruesz's and Lazo's charge that "the hemispheric turn that began more than two decades ago has not significantly altered an epistemology of scholarship that separates Anglo from Latin America" (2018, 641). They argue that scholars must continue to labor to recover Latinx literary histories, and that in doing so they must attend to "entanglement": "intertwined ... economic relations, technological exchanges, transculturation, and language interactions" (Gruesz and Lazo 2018, 652). Rather than positioning fixed spaces with presumed static, hierarchized cultures against each other, entanglement highlights "communication across boundaries" (Gruesz and Lazo 2018, 652). Our book achieves this aim by placing Latinx, Spanish, and U.S. literary traditions in dialogue.

Such transnational scholarship remains timely. In the contemporary geopolitical context, nationalist sentiment is rising throughout the world. The unlearning of the discursive practices informing this state of affairs may be spurred by scholarship that lends clarity to the cultural history of U.S.–Hispanophone relations.

Works Cited

Coronado, Raúl. 2013. *A World Not to Come: A History of Latino Writing and Print Culture*. Cambridge: Harvard University Press.

DeGuzmán, María. 2005. *Spain's Long Shadow: The Black Legend, Off-Whiteness, and Anglo-American Empire*. Minneapolis: University of Minnesota Press.

Gruesz, Kirsten Silva. 2002. *Ambassadors of Culture: The Transamerican Origins of Latino Writing*. Princeton: Princeton University Press.

Gruesz, Kirsten Silva and Rodrigo Lazo. 2018. "The Spanish Americas: Introduction." *Early American Literature* 53, no. 3: 641–664.

Jakšić, Iván. 2007. *The Hispanic World and American Intellectual Life, 1820–1880*. New York: Palgrave.

Kagan, Richard, editor. 2002. *Spain in America: The Origins of Hispanism in the United States*. Urbana-Champaign: University of Illinois Press.

Lazo, Rodrigo. 2020. *Letters from Filadelfia: Early Latino Literature and the Trans-American Elite*. Charlottesville and London: University of Virginia Press.

2 Spain and Washington Irving's Global America

Jeffrey Scraba

Taking up Paul Giles' recent challenge to examine how Washington Irving's texts "deliberately realign themselves in relation to a welter of global affairs" (2012, 24), I will explain how Irving structures *A History of the Life and Voyages of Christopher Columbus* as a global prehistory of the United States. Using a popular approach to history that has frequently been misunderstood by readers, the *Life of Columbus* foregrounds contingency in shaping events. Explicitly, Irving's narrative constitutes a reflection on the decline of the Muslim Nasrid dynasty in the wake of the Spanish *Reconquista*. Implicitly, it likewise constitutes a meditation on the decline of imperial Spain in the wake of the development of the New World. More speculatively, the *Life of Columbus* considers the future of the United States as an emerging empire, especially considering that Spanish influence on the Americas was dwindling in the early nineteenth century. Emphasizing Spanish imperialism as the founding influence for American development in the *Life of Columbus*, Irving recasts America not as an exceptional religious and political experiment but as an effect and cause of global mobility and power.

American Columbus

Looking for new material after the relative failure of *Tales of a Traveller* in 1824, Irving jumped at Alexander Everett's invitation to travel to Spain in 1826 in order to translate a cache of documents related to the exploration of the New World. These documents were unearthed and compiled by Martín Fernández de Navarrete, as the Spanish crown sought to reassess its historical role in exploring the New World. Rather than simply translating this archive, Irving decided to use it as the basis for a new biography of Columbus. Irving's 1828 text was the first full biography of Columbus in English (and the most comprehensive account of his life and voyages at the time), and it went through 175 editions in Europe and the Americas in the nineteenth century.[1] As Lindsay DiCuirci argues, "Irving secured the Spanish archive for American purposes in a cultural transaction" (2013, 179).[2] Andrew Burstein observes that "[a]ccording to a recent survey of the contents of American libraries, rural and urban alike,

DOI: 10.4324/9781003219460-2

in the mid-nineteenth century, Irving's *Life of Columbus* was the most commonly owned book" (2007, 196). Not only did this work launch a new phase of Irving's career as a historian,[3] but it also launched his new project to situate the founding and development of America in a global context.

In a diary entry for December 1828, Irving expresses satisfaction at the reception of *Columbus* and anticipates his reception on returning to the United States:

> the literary success of the Hist of Columb has been greater than I anticipated and gives me hopes that I have executed something which may have greater duration than I anticipate for my works of mere imagination. ... The only future event from which I promise myself any extraordinary gratification is the return to my native country, which I trust will now soon take place.
>
> (Penney 1930, 90)

Irving obviously meant his biography of Columbus to be a nationalist project. It was published shortly after the acquisition of Florida in 1821 and the declaration of the Monroe Doctrine in 1823. And it clearly positions America as the imperial inheritor of Spain, especially considering that Spanish hemispheric influence was waning sharply in the wake of independence movements in Central and South America in the eighteen-teens and twenties. In the preface to the *Life of Columbus*, Irving explains that he decided to compose a new biography of Columbus instead of merely translating Navarrete's documents, because Navarrete's "disconnected papers and official documents" would be "repulsive to the general reader," and a narrative history would be "a more acceptable work to [his] country" (Irving 1981, 3).[4] He closes the preface by declaring his intention to suture European and American history through the *Life of Columbus*: "The narrative of his troubled life is the link which connects the history of the old world with that of the new" (Irving 1981, 10).

Irving also took especial pleasure in the biography's American reception, as he wrote to Henry Breevort in 1828: "Columbus has succeeded beyond my expectations, and I am particularly gratified by the Success it has had in America" (Irving 1979, 366). Some contemporaneous American reviewers (like many twentieth- and twenty-first-century critics) objected to Irving's heroic portrayal of Columbus and what they perceived to be the generic confusion of the work. For example, an assessment in the *Monthly Review* for April 1828 concedes that Irving has produced a "very amusing and elegant book," but complains about the "author's extravagant partiality for his hero," which "has imbued his pages with far more of the colouring of mere romance, than that of authentic narration" (1828, 419). More typical of the American reception of the work was Alexander Everett's own evaluation that the *Life*

12 *Jeffrey Scraba*

of Columbus was "on the whole, more honorable to the literature of the country, than any one [work] that has hitherto appeared among us" (1829, 103). Identifying Irving with his subject, Everett praises the innovation of the history: "Mr. Irving shares, in some degree, the merit and the glory that belong to the illustrious hero of his present work, that of leading the way in a previously unexplored and untrodden path of intellectual labor" (1829, 104). Controversy over Irving's originality that has perpetually dogged the work also emerges in these first reviews, with the *Monthly Review* unable to "recognize … pretentions to any remarkable historical value" (1828, 419), while Everett claims that "[b]efore the publication of the work before us, there was not satisfactory account of Columbus in any language" (1829, 128).[5] In contrast to the *Monthly Review*'s lukewarm assessment, Everett applauds Irving's representation of the "towering sublimity," "bold creative genius," and "high religious feeling" of Columbus (1829, 131). As Rolena Adorno explains, disputes over what Irving added to the documents published by Navarrete were closely tied to the positioning of Columbus as a distinctly American hero, as Everett and others felt that "*Columbus* was … capable of building the [American] national reputation in the field of letters" (2002, 66).[6]

While Columbus was obviously already an important figure in the American cultural imaginary, Andrew Burstein points out that Revolution-era Americans, such as Joel Barlow and Jeremy Belknap, had created a "merely mythic" version of Columbus. In Burstein's terms, Irving therefore "undertook to locate Columbus the historical actor and render him flesh and blood," and to describe him "as a well-mannered, well-intended visionary" (2007, 197). Adorno carefully traces the lasting influence of this Anglo-American Columbus, especially through Irving's one-volume abridgement of his own work, arguing that "Irving's extraordinarily influential biography gave Columbus to the United States and made the admiral a staple of nineteenth-century U.S. culture that filters into the teaching of basic U.S. history to this day" (2002, 51). While Irving's Columbus has clearly been recognized as a proto-American hero, we have yet to attend closely to the global context of Irving's transatlantic appropriation of New World exploration. The figure of Columbus not only allows Irving to create a nationalist hero, but he also allows Irving to recreate a global history of empire.

Global Vision

While Irving clearly saw Columbus as "national forefather and founder" and "succeeded in creating a historical foundation for the United States that extended further back than the 1609 settlement at Jamestown" (Adorno 2002, 65), he elaborates his history in a complex global (rather than restrictively national) context. Irving opens the *Life of Columbus* with what he calls "matters of vague and visionary speculation" (1981, 9). Before he begins his serious account of Columbus' history, Irving

Spain and Washington Irving's Global America   13

invokes "old times ... beyond the reach of history or tradition," in which "arts may have flourished to a degree unknown to those whom we term the Ancients" and there may have been "an intercourse between the opposite shores of the Atlantic" (1981, 9). He discusses Viking exploration of the New World, and he entertains the idea that Plato's Atalantis "was indeed no fable, but the obscure tradition of some vast country, engulphed by one of those mighty convulsions of our globe" (Irving 1981, 9). Invoking what Irving elsewhere calls "regions of doubt and fable," the *Life of Columbus* thus begins by asking the reader to imagine vanished cultures and lost knowledges. Before leaving this familiar territory, Irving intriguingly turns to a twelfth-century Arabic writer, "Xerif al Edrizi" [al-Idrisi], to illustrate medieval "ignorance" of geographical knowledge, even among the Almoravids, who were "the boldest navigators of the middle ages, and possessed all that was then known of geography" (1981, 9). Irving's citation from al-Idrisi emphasizes the medieval impossibility of navigating the ocean and discovering what is beyond it, "on account of its great obscurity, its profound depth, and frequent tempests; through fear of its mighty fishes, and its haughty winds" (1981, 10). By turning to an Arabic authority at this point, Irving both establishes the non-European knowledge that was necessary to Columbus' discoveries and emphasizes how Columbus was able to supersede that knowledge. The geographic knowledge necessary to Columbus' voyages was neglected by European nations, but "it had taken refuge in the bosom of Africa" (Irving 1981, 12): while "the pedantic schoolmen of the cloisters were wasting time and talent," "the Arabian sages ... were taking the measurement of a degree of latitude, and calculating the circumference of the earth" (Irving 1981, 12).

However, while this passage establishes both the intellectual preeminence and limitations of medieval Muslim knowledge, Irving does not include al-Idrisi's following account of a voyage that supposedly took place in spite of all these obstacles. In an article titled "Muslim Discovery of America before Columbus," Mohammed Hamidullah paraphrases this account. According to al-Idrisi, an expedition sponsored by the twelfth-century Almoravid king Ali ibn Yusef departed from Lisbon with the goal of finding out what lay beyond the "ocean of fogs" (1968, 8). After a voyage of several weeks in unknown waters, the Almoravid expedition was captured by a fleet of barks and transported to an unknown coast. There they found "*people with red skin*; there was not much hair on their body, the hair of their head was straight, and they were of high stature. Their women were of an extraordinary beauty" (Hamidullah 1968, 8; emphasis in original). According to Hamidullah, this account has long been adduced as evidence that the Berbers discovered America well before Columbus. So, while Irving uses this excerpt to emphasize the relative paucity of geographical knowledge before Columbus, it also winks at the "vague and visionary" tradition that Arab cultures discovered America before the Europeans.

14   *Jeffrey Scraba*

Whether or not Irving expected his audience to catch this allusion, his use of an Almoravid writer in the opening section introduces what contemporaneous audiences would have called "Moorish" culture as a vital part of the "welter of global affairs" in fifteenth-century Europe. The Moors not only preserved the geographic and navigational knowledge that was crucial to Columbus' success, but they also figured in vital conflicts that spurred European imperial exploration. The first key Arab-European exchange in the *Life of Columbus* is embodied in the person of Prince Henry of Portugal, who for Irving was the "master mind" of the period's "grand impulse to discovery," "from whose enterprizes the genius of Columbus took excitement" (Irving 1981, 18). Prince Henry's passion for exploration was kindled during an expedition to Africa against the Moors, which culminated in the taking of Ceuta in the northeast part of Morocco. While in Ceuta, Henry eagerly gathered information from the conquered Moors about the interior of Africa, then unknown to Europeans. On his return, Henry gathered "men eminent in science" and dedicated himself to study of "all the astronomy known to the Arabians of Spain" (Irving 1981, 18), from which he concluded that Africa must be circumnavigable. Henry was incited to explore this route not simply through scientific curiosity, but so he could rival the Italians in trading Silk Road goods: "the silks, the gums, the perfumes, the precious stones and other luxurious commodities of Egypt and southern Asia" (Irving 1981, 19). As with Columbus' future expeditions, Henry buttressed his explorations with religious sanction:

> To secure the quiet prosecution and full enjoyment of his discoveries, Henry obtained the protection of a papal bull, granting to the crown of Portugal sovereign authority over all the lands it might discover in the Atlantic ... at the same time menacing with the terrors of the church, all who should interfere in these Christian conquests.
>
> (Irving 1981, 20)

In Prince Henry, Columbus found a template for his own ambitions, merging scientific discovery, commercial potential, and religious authority. And in a pattern that characterizes the narrative throughout, this advance emerges from Henry's accidental discovery of lost knowledge.

This recovered knowledge then led Henry to contemplate and plan numerous expeditions along the Western coast of Africa. In turn, according to Irving, these expeditions awakened an intense interest in exploration among all maritime and commercial nations, most particularly the Genoese. "To these circumstances," Irving explains, "may we ascribe the enthusiastic devotion which Columbus imbibed in his childhood for cosmographical studies, and which influenced all his after fortunes" (1981, 13). To Prince Henry's campaigns against the Moors, then, can be attributed the geographical knowledge that fueled the so-called age of discovery, and to the spirit of this age can be attributed Columbus' passion and knowledge that led to the discovery of the New World.

Inspired by Prince Henry, Columbus' own "strong passion for geographical knowledge" was also awakened by Arabic preservation of Latin and Greek texts, along with the writings of "Averroes, Alfraganus, and other Arabian sages, who had kept the sacred fire of science alive, during the interval of European darkness" (Irving 1981, 13). In particular, Columbus' theories about the circumference of the globe derive from *Elements of Astronomy on the Celestial Motions* by "Alfraganus the Arabian" (Abū al-ʿAbbās Aḥmad ibn Muḥammad ibn Kathīr al-Farghānī), a ninth-century astronomer from the Abbasid Caliphate (though Columbus failed to understand that Alfraganus' calculations were in Arabic miles, not Roman).[7] Soon after his first overture to Ferdinand and Isabella of Spain, armed with these theories, Columbus tries to contend with the scholarly council at Salamanca who had anachronistic views of the shape and nature of the world: they "opposed figurative texts of scripture" to Columbus' "simplest proposition, the spherical form of the earth" (Irving 1981, 50). Although several recent commentators see the story as apocryphal (e.g., Sale 1990, 344; Bushman 1992, 110), Columbus' arguments with the council at Salamanca are crucial in developing Irving's global vision. Columbus' literal vision of the globe echoes Irving's transnational perspective on historical events. As Irving explains, such global perspectives revolutionize our knowledge:

> The practicability, therefore, of finding land by sailing to the west, was one of those mysteries of nature which are considered incredible while matters of mere speculation, but the simplest things imaginable when they have once been ascertained.
>
> (1981, 29–30)

The *Reconquista* and the New World

More directly, the Spanish campaigns against the Moors in the fifteenth century were vital in the fruition of Columbus' plans. This was the period of what Spain came to call the "*Reconquista*," resulting in victory over the last Muslim kingdom on the Peninsula and the expulsion of Spain's Jews. More specifically, the final military victories of the *Reconquista*, in which *los Reyes Católicos*, Ferdinand and Isabella, retook the Kingdom of Granada from the Nasrid king Boabdil, ultimately led to the funding of Columbus' voyages. Prior to his first appeal to Ferdinand and Isabella in 1486, Columbus approached the courts of Genoa, Venice, and England to finance his explorations, but political conditions at each court precluded supporting such a speculative venture. But Spain, by contrast, had "consolidated the Christian power in the Peninsula" through the marriage of Ferdinand and Isabella, and "[t]he

16 *Jeffrey Scraba*

whole force of united Spain was now exerted in the chivalrous enterprise of the Moorish conquest" (Irving 1981, 41). The *Reconquista*, in Irving's view, prepares Spain militarily and culturally to expand its dominion: "the various petty kingdoms of Spain began to feel and act as one nation, and to rise to eminence in arts as well as arms" (1981, 42). In the balance of power between the two monarchs, Spain takes the shape of a proto-empire: "Ferdinand and Isabella, it has been remarked, lived together, not like man and wife, whose estates are common, under the orders of the husband, but like two monarchs strictly allied" (Irving 1981, 42). As the expansion of European exploration is dependent on appropriating knowledge preserved in the Arabic world, the expansion of the Spanish empire is dependent on conquering the remnants of the Moorish presence on the Peninsula. In a gesture that reifies this connection, part of the first gold brought back by Columbus "was employed in gilding the vaulted ceilings of the royal saloon on the grand palace of Saragossa ... anciently the Aljaferia, or abode of the Moorish kings" (Irving 1981, 65). Just as Spain will provide a prehistory for U.S. development, so *al-Andalus* provides a prehistory for the development of imperial Spain.

Columbus first approaches *los Reyes Católicos* for support as they are garrisoned in Cordova, preparing for their campaign against Granada. Because they are preoccupied with the prosecution of the war, Ferdinand and Isabella are only able to give Columbus passing attention, though they do periodically encourage him to continue his suit. Not only does Columbus follow the court through several years of campaigns, but Irving also maintains that Columbus' ultimate success was at least partially due to his active participation in some of the key battles of the *Reconquista*. Unusually for Irving, he directly cites "an old chronicler of the place," Diego Ortiz de Zúñiga, that "Columbus was found fighting [in a campaign against the town of Baza], giving proofs of the distinguished valour which accompanied his wisdom and his lofty desires" (1981, 55). Setting off this claim from his narrative by quotation, Irving suggests that he is skeptical about the story but is attentive to the processes through which stories of the past, such as Columbus fighting in the *Reconquista*, gain currency.

Columbus is finally given his commission shortly after, and as a result of, the final Spanish victory at Granada, which ended over 700 years of Muslim rule in *al-Andalus*. To emphasize the symbiosis between these two events, Irving stresses the "similar purport" of the Nasrid surrender and authorization of Columbus' voyage:

> The capitulations [of the Nasrid Emirate of Granada] were signed by Ferdinand and Isabella at the city of Santa Fe, in the Vega or plain of Granada, on the 17th of April, 1492. A letter of privilege or commission to Columbus, of similar purport, was drawn out in form, and issued by the sovereigns in the city of Granada, on the thirtieth of the same month.
>
> (1981, 67)

Spain and Washington Irving's Global America 17

Irving emphasizes that the exploration of the New World was immediately contingent on the success of the *Reconquista*: the end of one empire makes way for the development of the next. But this was not a logical and inevitable sequence of events. Columbus happened to be on the scene when *los Reyes Católicos* develop their plans for Christian power, and he frames his own ambitions in the same terms in order to finance his exploration.

According to Elise Bartosik-Vélez, the commission stipulated that Columbus' expedition was "strictly a commercial venture that had nothing to do with either religious matters or territorial expansion" (2014, 22), but in the journal of his first voyage (the *Diario*), Columbus shifted the rhetorical terms of his project. This *Diario* was one of the key documents made available to Irving through Navarrete's research. In the preface to the *Diario*, crafted as a letter addressed to Ferdinand and Isabella, Columbus himself confirms the intimate connection between the Conquest of Granada and the discovery of the New World. Columbus begins his preface by recalling the end of the campaign against Granada, when he

> saw the royal banners of your highnesses placed by force of arms on the towers of the Alhambra ... and beheld the Moorish king sally forth from the gates of the city, and kiss the royal hand of your Highnesses.
>
> (Irving 1981, 73)

Immediately following, in Columbus' account, Ferdinand and Isabella, as "lovers and promoters of the holy Christian faith, and enemies of the sect of Mahomet,"

> determined to send me, Christopher Columbus, to the said parts of India, to see the said princes, and the people and lands, and discover the nature and disposition of them all, and the means to be taken for the conversion of them to our holy faith.
>
> (Irving 1981, 73–74)

Not only is Columbus' voyage facilitated by the successful conclusion of the war against the Moors, but he contextualizes his enterprise in the same terms of Christian domination used to justify the expulsion of Muslims and Jews from Spain. The discovery of the New World, in other words, is an ideological counterpart of the *Reconquista* and the Inquisition. In the preface to his *Diario*, claims Bartosik-Vélez, Columbus "first used the language of the reconquest, a language which drew from the Spanish discourse of universal Christian empire" (2014, 23). In Bartosik-Vélez' reading, Columbus himself was responsible for linking the campaigns of Granada with his own speculative ventures (2014, 17). Irving, like many historians since, follows Columbus' lead in linking the *Reconquista* and his voyages.

18   *Jeffrey Scraba*

Irving also follows Columbus in linking the *Reconquista* and the conversion of people in India to the renewal of the Crusades in the Holy Land. Irving's version conflates the campaigns in Andalusia and Columbus' dream of a new crusade against Jerusalem. At the end of the campaign in which Columbus is alleged to have fought against Baza, Columbus witnesses the surrender of Muley Boabdil, one of the two rival rulers of Granada. Just as the siege of Baza is reaching its culmination, two friars from the holy sepulchre at Jerusalem arrive to bring a message from the Sultan of Egypt, "threatening to put to death all the Christians in his dominions ... and to destroy the sepulchre, if the sovereigns [Ferdinand and Isabella] did not desist from the war against Granada" (Irving 1981, 56). The coincidence of these events, in Irving's version, caused Columbus to make a "kind of mental vow" that if his voyage proved successful, he would "devote the profits arising from his anticipated discoveries, to a crusade for the rescue of the holy sepulchre from the power of the infidels" (1981, 56). Echoing Columbus in the preface to his *Diario*, Irving connects the experience of the Grenadine war and the idea of Christian empire.

Narrative History and Contingency

Columbus' rhetorical capitalization on the fortunate concurrence of his appeal to Ferdinand and Isabella and the victory in Granada is not the only serendipity in Irving's narrative. In fact, while Columbus himself continually interprets events as a fulfillment of divine destiny, Irving takes pains to show that most of the key events in Columbus' story are the result of error, coincidence, or sheer chance. Unlike contemporaneous philosophical histories, which attempted to establish unvarying principles of social and intellectual development, Irving's narrative methodology in the *Life of Columbus* allows him to stress the contingency of social and political change. This narrative approach facilitates an exploration of the global causes and conditions of national development. Rather than exemplifying the laws of historical development, Irving's text stresses that chance plays a huge role in history: things could always have been otherwise.

One of the first adventitious steps in Columbus' career was his arrival in Portugal, where he was inspired by the explorations of Prince Henry, as discussed previously. Irving speculates that Columbus may have been "drawn thither by liberal curiosity, and the pursuit of honourable fortune," but it is more likely that he was "thrown there, as has been asserted, by the fortuitous result of a desperate adventure" (1981, 21)—a failed attempt at pirating a Venetian galley led by his nephew, from which disaster Columbus swum to the Portuguese shore, according to the biography composed by Columbus' son Fernando. Fernando Colón's biography of his father, which was first published in 1571, was an important source for Irving's narrative. But as Adorno emphasizes, while Fernando

Spain and Washington Irving's Global America   19

"claimed that his father had discovered unknown lands that he had knowingly sought," Irving's seminal contribution "was to initiate the modern view of the discovery of America as an accident" (2002, 61). The accidental discovery of America, in Irving's version, was grounded in "two happy errors": "the imaginary extent of Asia to the east, and the supposed smallness of the earth; both errors of the most learned and profound philosophers, but without which Columbus would hardly have ventured upon his enterprize" (1981, 29). Though Columbus is painted as a visionary by Irving, his "enterprize" was based on lost knowledges that turned out to be wrong about the configuration and size of the planet.

Columbus' errors ultimately prove fortuitous, which is especially remarkable given the state of geography in his time. While Prince Henry and others did recover lost geographical knowledge from the Arab world, this revival of knowledge was blended with (as Irving opens the history with) "matters of vague and visionary speculation." Though "emerging from the darkness that had enveloped it for ages," geography was a jumble of science and folklore: "The maps of the fifteenth century display a mixture of truth and error, in which facts handed down from antiquity, and others revealed by recent discoveries, are confused with popular fables, and extravagant conjectures" (Irving 1981, 23). As Giles comments, in the *Life of Columbus* "the chain of cause and effect is turned on its head, with geographical discoveries being dependent on fundamentally mistaken assumptions" (2012, 18). If Columbus was taken as the enterprising hero of the prehistory of the United States, the country was essentially founded on faulty understanding.

There are numerous examples of happenstance in the narrative, but one sequence of events is worth tracing. According to Irving, after many years of unsuccessful petitioning of Ferdinand and Isabella, Columbus finally determined to give up his suit to the Spanish crown and travel to France. On his journey by foot, Columbus stops to ask for food at the convent of Santa María de La Rábida. Impressed by Columbus' bearing, the prior of the convent, Juan Pérez de Marchena, engages him in conversation and learns about his project. The prior summons his most scientifically knowledgeable friend, a local physician, to hear Columbus' plans, and the physician is similarly impressed. Discussions among the three are attended by "several of the veteran mariners" of nearby Palos, among whom is the wealthy Martín Alonzo Pinzón (Irving 1981, 60). Pinzón, along with his brothers, will eventually provide the Pinta and the Niña for the first voyage, and the family will be critical in impressing reluctant sailors in the expedition, which will embark from their home port of Palos. As Irving explains, Columbus' reception at the convent reanimates his ambition: "Columbus' project was treated with a deference in the quiet cloisters of La Rabida, and among the seafaring men of Palos, which had been sought in vain among the sages and philosophers of the court" (1981, 60). The impromptu community at La Rábida convinces Columbus to stay in Spain and make one more attempt to convince the

20 *Jeffrey Scraba*

sovereigns to back his venture. Prior Juan Pérez, having formerly been confessor to the queen, sends an emissary to Isabella, who summons Pérez to the provisional court at Santa Fe. Pérez pleads the "cause of Columbus with characteristic enthusiasm, speaking, from actual knowledge, of [Columbus'] honourable motives, his professional knowledge and experience, and his perfect capacity to fulfill the undertaking" (Irving 1981, 61). Isabella, having "never heard the proposition urged with such honest zeal and impressive eloquence," and "being naturally more sanguine and susceptible than the king, and more open to warm and generous impulses," sends money to Columbus so that he may journey to Santa Fe and renew his appeals (Irving 1981, 61).

As it happens, Columbus arrives at the court just in time for the surrender of Boabdil, last ruler of Granada, when *los Reyes Cátolicos* are ready to turn their thoughts to empire: "The war with the Moors was at an end, Spain was delivered from its intruders, and its sovereigns might securely turn their views to foreign enterprize" (Irving 1981, 62). Newly inspired with an "ardent imagination" about his "contemplated discoveries," Columbus forgets "his present obscurity" and his "present indigence" and "[feels] himself negociating [sic] about empire" (Irving 1981, 64). While Isabella is also newly excited about the potential of Columbus' voyage ("for the first time, the subject broke upon her in its real grandeur" [Irving 1981, 65]), Ferdinand is more cautious, and the treasury has been depleted by the war. Seemingly disappointed one last time, Columbus once again departs for France, but Isabella pledges her crown jewels to fund the expedition, and a courier is sent to catch up with Columbus. Columbus is intercepted at the bridge of Pinos, not coincidentally "famous in the Moorish wars for many a desperate encounter between the Christians and infidels" (Irving 1981, 65). As the infidels were defeated in this strategic location, so Columbus' new crusade was launched from the same place. This series of fortunate coincidences— Columbus' chance stop at the convent, the mariners' faith in his project, Juan Perez's personal connection to the queen, Columbus' arrival at the surrender of Granada, Pinzon's willingness to provide ships for the voyage, Isabella's inspiration, and the providential meeting at the bridge of Pinos—is the proximate cause of Columbus' discovery of the New World. Against Columbus' and the Spanish crown's (and by implication the United States') narratives of manifest destiny, Irving juxtaposes this series of happenstances.

The *Life of Columbus* clearly illustrates what Giles calls Irving's "paradigm of romantic irony," in which "the advance of civilization is paradoxically predicated on ignorance and loss, and where Enlightenment is systematically bound up with delusion" (2012, 18). To extend this paradigm identified by Giles, I would argue that Irving situates Columbus' exploration in a context of lost knowledges and failed cultures. The *Life of Columbus* not only back projects U.S. history into the Spanish past, but it reconstructs that Spanish past as shaped by the rediscovery

Spain and Washington Irving's Global America   21

of knowledge preserved in the Arabic world, the European exploration of Africa, and the *Reconquista* of the Peninsula from the Muslim *taifas*. As Irving himself explains in the 1828 version of the text, the culture of exploration that gave rise to Columbus' voyages was predicated not on new advances in science but on "revisiting some long neglected region of knowledge, and exploring and reopening its forgotten paths" (1828, 10). For "thought" to take "some sudden and general direction," it requires "an ardent and imaginative genius, catching the impulse of the day," who "outstrips all less gifted contemporaries ... and presses forward to achievements, which feebler spirits would never have ventured to attempt" (Irving 1981, 10). Thought accidentally taking a new direction and the imaginative genius of Columbus are the intertwining threads that comprise Irving's narrative. Columbus' construction of the theories that led to the discovery of the New World, it might be said, is analogous to Irving's construction of history: "it is interesting to notice from what a mass of acknowledged facts, rational hypotheses, fanciful narrations and popular rumours, his grand project of discovery was wrought out by the strong workings of his vigorous mind" (Irving 1981, 26). While Irving clearly intended to write an authoritative and factual history (and has been widely credited for doing so), he was not above including popular rumors and fanciful stories if they fit the thematic goals of his text.

Columbus and U.S. Empire

As I discussed earlier, from the earliest reviews, nineteenth-century readers of Irving's *Life of Columbus* frequently criticized it as mere narrative rather than rigorous philosophical history. Many recent readers also misconstrue the historiographic approach of Irving's *Columbus*, applying anachronistic standards to his text. For example, Kirkpatrick Sale accuses Irving of a "glaring abdication of the responsibility of the historian in favor of the license of the novelist" (1990, 344). (He goes on to list "[a]t least ten serious and substantial biographies [that] followed Irving's in the course of the rest of the century" (Sale 1990, 345), although he fails to explain why Irving's version of the story remained the most influential account.) Other critics have been more sympathetic to Irving's project. John H. McElroy, the editor of the definitive edition of *Columbus*, maintains that Irving was the "first of the so-called 'literary historians,' because in his *Columbus* he took fully into consideration the work's value both as literature and as history" (1981, lxxvii). In *Popular History and the Literary Marketplace*, Gregory Pfitzer counts Irving as a pioneer of popular history, which flourished from the 1840s to the end of the century:

> Of all the established literary and poetic figures who dabbled in history writing in the mid-nineteenth century, Washington Irving came closest to embodying the spirit of the wide-reaching and

22 *Jeffrey Scraba*

> comprehensive popularity ... that defined the genre in its later nineteenth-century iterations.
>
> (2008, 35)

Pfitzer explains that the genre of popular history "was concerned more with recovering the pervasive spirit of an age than with accuracy of minute detail" (2008, 39). Irving in particular, argues Pfitzer,

> constructed stories that offered moral visions to a nation in need of guidance. For [Irving], popular history was a 'moral science' whose task was not so much to re-create the past for its own sake as to convey an appreciation for the way in which history could be used to encourage an ethically responsible present.
>
> (2008, 39–40)

Irving's own perspective emerges most clearly in *Columbus* when he is dispelling what he considers absurd rumors about how Columbus had "previous information of the lands which he had pretended to discover":

> There is a certain meddlesome spirit which, in the garb of learned research, goes prying about the traces of history, casting down its monuments, and marring and mutilating its fairest trophies. Care should be taken to vindicate great names from such pernicious erudition. It defeats one of the most salutary purposes of history, that of furnishing examples of what human genius and laudable enterprize may accomplish.
>
> (1981, 31)

Clearly contemplation of Columbus' character was meant to encourage ethical responsibility in Irving's readers. But so was reflecting on chance and accident in the shaping of events: for Irving, history is not a matter of manifest destiny but of unanticipated circumstances and unforeseen rediscoveries.

As several critics have observed, Irving paints Columbus as American hero with a nineteenth-century palette, emphasizing his independence, enterprise, and vision (e.g., Bartosik-Vélez 2014, 86; Adorno 2002, 61). Irving frequently touts Columbus' self-reliance, determination, and ambition, qualities that are of course supposed to characterize citizens of a nation looking toward Westward expansion:

> He was one of those men of strong natural genius, who from having to contend at their very outset with privations and impediments, acquire an intrepidity in encountering and a facility in vanquishing difficulties ... Such men learn to effect great purposes with small means, supplying this deficiency by the resources of their own energy and invention.
>
> (1981, 13)

Spain and Washington Irving's Global America   23

As Irving's mode of history teaches, though, energy and invention are subject to a complex interconnection of events:

> In tracing the early history of a man like Columbus, whose actions have had a vast effect on human affairs, it is interesting to notice how much has been owing to external influences, how much to an inborn propensity of his genius.
>
> (1981, 11)

The narrative reveals that this is an irresolvable question, for individuals and societies alike. While Irving positions Columbus as founding American hero, he also registers the unlimited influence of external influences.

The tension between these two narrative imperatives generates an equivocal moral vision for Irving's native land, which was gradually emerging as a hemispheric empire. Like their nineteenth-century counterparts, recent critics have frequently had difficulty in understanding Irving's aims for the history. For example, John Hazlett sees a deep ambivalence in Irving's representation of Columbus. On the one hand, Irving creates a character "to meet the demands of literary nationalism," a Columbus whose qualities of innate nobility, leadership, pragmatism, and vision make him a prototypical American hero (Hazlett 1983, 564). On the other hand, Irving also represents a "darker Columbus," one whose sense of cultural superiority "corrupts and infects everything it touches," making the *Life of Columbus* ultimately an anti-imperialist text (Hazlett 1983, 564). Unfortunately, like many of Irving's readers, Hazlett attributes this ambivalence to the author's incompetence, rather than understanding this deliberate complexity as *The Life of Columbus*' strength. In a similar vein, Claudia Bushman asserts that "[i]f Columbus had wanted to become an American hero and had mounted a campaign for the position, he could not have chosen a better biographer than Washington Irving," but that even Irving "could not conceal Columbus' failings and the havoc he wrought on the native population of America" (1992, 107). In Bushman's view, Irving also appears to have failed in his purposes.

Other critics of Irving fault him for *not* addressing the havoc Columbus wrought in the New World. Building on Hazlett, Richard McLamore argues that the *Life of Columbus* positions Spain "as an emblematic ancestor of the United States" and thus "counter[s] the nation's Anglophilic cultural reliance" (1993, 30). By positioning "Columbus as *the* American Adam," McLamore suggests, Irving ignored the "shared heritage" of European "confrontation with and eradication of savage heathens" (1993, 30). María DeGuzmán mines a similar vein in the service of a larger argument that the

> image of Spain as a great imperial power in decline losing its grip on the Americas was a gratifying one. Such an image provided not

24   Jeffrey Scraba

simply a convenient foil, but a truly significant foil to the growing prosperity and power of the United States.

(2005, 79)

For DeGuzmán, histories such as *Columbus* "provided US readers with … both a model and an antitype for empire": they "implicitly identified the nineteenth-century United States with discovery, exploration, and triumph while disavowing and displacing Anglo-Americans' own extermination of Native Americans and expropriation of their lands back onto the early decades of Spanish empire in the Americas" (2005, 76).[8] These tendentious arguments assume that because Irving is critical of Spanish colonization, he sees English colonization, which is not addressed in *Columbus*, as relatively unproblematic. When looking at Irving's oeuvre as a whole, this claim does not hold water. To pick one example among many, in "Philip of Pokanoket" from the *Sketch-Book* (the work which made Irving famous and is still his best known), Irving reflects on his perusal of "a volume of early [U.S.] colonial history":

It is painful to perceive, even from these partial narratives, how the footsteps of civilization may be traced in the blood of the aborigines; how easily the colonists were moved to hostility by the lust of conquest; how merciless and exterminating was their warfare. The imagination shrinks at the idea how many intellectual beings were hunted from the earth.

(1822, 213)

Clearly this is not a writer who wants to whitewash the U.S. colonial past.

For me, it is more useful to think of Irving using the example of the Spanish empire as a salutary example for the emerging U.S. empire. In fact, the final chapter of *The Life and Voyages of Christopher Columbus*, titled "Observations on the character of Columbus," might be taken, in Pfitzer's terms, as a specific "moral vision" for the United States in the late 1820s. Irving is indeed critical of Spain's administration of her American colonies, wishing that later colonists had possessed the "sound policy and liberal views" of Columbus: "The new world, in such case, would have been settled by peaceful colonists, and civilized by enlightened legislators, instead of being overrun by desperate adventurers, and desolated by avaricious conquerors" (1981, 566). While this is definitely an indictment of Spanish corruption and greed, it makes more sense to read it as a warning about the course of empires and the potential degeneration of the American character: would that they should be enlightened legislators rather than avaricious opportunists.

In contrast to the "desperate adventurers" who followed him, Columbus' "conduct as a discoverer was characterized by the grandeur of his views, and the magnanimity of his spirit": "He was desirous …

Spain and Washington Irving's Global America   25

of building cities, introducing the useful arts, subjecting everything to the control of law, order, and religion, and thus of founding regular and prosperous empires" (Irving 1981, 565). Observing the strengths of Columbus' character, Americans might likewise establish a regular and prosperous empire. While Irving makes Columbus into the prototypical American hero whose liberal character helps him avoid the pitfalls of his successor Spanish imperialists, he also thinks that his readers can learn from the limitations of Columbus' character. Columbus' most grievous character deficiency was that although he was commendable in his religious devotion, his "piety was mingled with superstition, and darkened by the bigotry of the age" (Irving 1981, 567). This superstition and bigotry is especially evident in his treatment of the native populations:

> In this spirit of bigotry he considered himself justified in making captives of the Indians, and transporting them to Spain to have them taught the doctrines of Christianity, and in selling them for slaves, if they pretended to resist his invasions. In so doing he sinned against the natural benignity of his character, and against the feelings which he had originally entertained and expressed towards this gentle and hospitable people.
>
> (Irving 1981, 567)

Not only is this criticism of Columbus a pointed commentary on the treatment of native North Americans by all European colonizers, but as William Shurr points out, it is also a condemnation of the system of slavery upon which the U.S. empire is founded: "Irving ends his Life of Columbus as if the whole of his endeavor as biographer has been to trace the origin of the American institution of Slavery and to condemn it as it existed in the American 1820s" (1992, 242). The bigotry of Irving's own age is exposed by reflecting on the bigotry of Columbus', and the complex Atlantic triangular system of the slave trade is one of the "external influences" that might control American destiny.

These final reflections again emphasize a central point of Irving's account of imperial development: cultures are not products of manifest destiny but of contingency and human action. The chapter and the history end on a note of hopefulness, as Irving imagines that Columbus' "magnanimous spirit [would] have been consoled, amidst the chills of age and cares of penury, the neglect of a fickle public, and the injustice of an ungrateful king," if he were able to anticipate "the splendid empires which were to spread over the beautiful world he had discovered; and the nations, and tongues, and languages which were to fill its lands with his renown, and bless his name to the latest posterity!" (Irving 1981, 569). On this closing note, Irving offers a prospect of a multicultural North America shaped by his global vision, a New World of multiple nations and languages that all embrace Columbus as ancestor. And as Bartosik-Vélez has shown, this vision proved to be prophetic, as Columbus later

26 *Jeffrey Scraba*

appeared "as an imperial figure in New-World republics that claimed political independence from Old-World empires" (2014, 2).

For twenty-first-century readers, attending to the "welter of global affairs" that produce the conditions of Columbus' voyages to the New World is a precondition for understanding not only the *Life of Columbus*, but Irving's overall body of work. As in *Columbus*, an ambivalence toward contact between Europe and its others marks Irving's global vision in general. If the *Life of Columbus* could be and was read as a celebration of the European discovery of the New World and the first American hero, Irving's next two Spanish texts work toward a much more complex view of this imperialist history. As he explored the archives of Spanish exploration of the New World, Irving was captivated by the history and culture of the Moors who had been defeated by Ferdinand and Isabella. *A Chronicle of the Conquest of Granada* (1829), describing the *Reconquista* from the perspective of the fictional xenophobic Catholic monk Fray Antonio Agapida, shows how ideologies inevitably refract the description of historical events. *The Alhambra* (1832) describes Irving's empathetic identification with Boabdil, the last Muslim ruler in Spain, to explore what was lost in the triumph of *los Reyes Católicos* and the expansion of the Spanish empire to the New World. Taken together with the *Life of Columbus*, these Spanish texts probe the problems and possibilities of empire, and they raise profound questions about the emergence of U.S. power in the early nineteenth century.

Notes

1 In the remaining thirty-one years of his life, three Latin American editions of the full work by three different publishers appeared, thirty-nine imprints and editions of the full work and the abridgement were published by nine American and three British houses, and twenty-nine publishers on the Continent brought out fifty-one imprints and editions of the full and abridged texts in Spanish, Dutch, French, German, English, Greek, Italian, Polish, Swedish, and Russian. The posthumous editions and imprints after 1859 to the end of the nineteenth century in all languages (including, besides the ten already given, Catalan and Czech) were 82 in the total of 175 editions and imprints of *The Life and Voyages of Christopher Columbus* between 1828 and 1900. To date, in all languages, the full and abridged editions and imprints of the work total no fewer than one hundred and ninety-three.

(McElroy 1981, lxxvi)

2 In DiCiurci's (2013, 175–176) view, the *Life of Columbus* reflects the recent " 'global turn' in American literature and history" by "illustrating how nineteenth-century writers were themselves interrogating the 'boundaries' of US history and literature, the role of international cooperation in producing historical narratives, and the duties of the historian to convey the 'truth' of history, including its darker episodes."

3 As Adorno (2002, 65) explains, *Columbus* earned Irving transatlantic acclaim:

Spain and Washington Irving's Global America   27

With Navarrete's blessing as its president, Spain's Real Academia de la Historia elected Irving corresponding member on December 12, 1828. In the name of King George IV he was awarded a gold medal from England's Royal Society of Literature in 1830. Oxford University granted him an honorary doctor in civil law (D.C.L.). ... Columbia University awarded him an honorary doctor of laws (L.L.D.) in 1829, and Harvard University did the same in 1831.

4 Except for one passage quoted later in the essay, all citations are from the text in *The Complete Works of Washington Irving*, edited by John Harmon McElroy (Irving 1981).

5 In several numbers of the *Southern Literary Messenger* from 1840 to 1843, Severin Teackle Wallis accused Irving of plagiarizing Navarrete, a charge that has long stuck with the work, despite being thoroughly disproven (McElroy 1981, lxx–lxxv).

6 Adorno (2002, 66) further explains that in his ... encomium to Irving's new work in the *North American Review*, Everett virtually proclaimed the birth of a national literature whose effect would be to end the decades-long European dismissal of the new country's feeble literary and scientific pursuits.

7 "Columbus wrongly assumed that [al-]Farghani had presented his measurements in Roman miles rather than Arab miles. This caused him to understate the actual circumference of the earth by 25 per cent" (Starr 2013, n.p.).

8 Building on the arguments of Adorno and Bushman, Jaksić (2007, 16) also sees Spain as an antitype to the United States in Irving's Spanish works, emphasizing two principle themes: "his view of a rapidly decaying Spanish character, as exemplified by new extremes of chivalry and religious fanaticism, and the emerging theme of Spanish despotism, as exemplified by the cruel neglect and mistreatment of Columbus by King Ferdinand."

Works Cited

Adorno, Rolena. 2002. "Washington Irving's Romantic Hispanism and Its Columbian Legacies." *Spain in America: The Origins of Hispanism in the United States*, edited by Richard L. Kagan. Urbana: University of Illinois Press, 49–105.

Bartosik-Vélez, Elise. 2014. *The Legacy of Christopher Columbus in the Americas: New Nations and a Transatlantic Discourse of Empire*. Nashville: Vanderbilt University Press.

Burstein, Andrew. 2007. *The Original Knickerbocker: The Life of Washington Irving*. New York: Basic.

Bushman, Claudia L. 1992. *America Discovers Columbus: How an Italian Explorer Became an American Hero*. Hanover: University Press of New England.

DeGuzmán, María. 2005. *Spain's Long Shadow: The Black Legend, Off-Whiteness, and Anglo-American Empire*. Minneapolis: University of Minnesota Press.

DiCuirci, Lindsay. 2013. "The Spanish Archive and the Remapping of U.S. History in Washington Irving's *Columbus*." *Urban Identity and the Atlantic World*, edited by Elizabeth Fay and Leonard Morzé. New York: Palgrave Macmillan, 175–192.

28   *Jeffrey Scraba*

Everett, Alexander. 1829. Review of *The Life and Voyages of Christopher Columbus*. *North American Review* 28, no. 62: 103–134.

Giles, Paul. 2012. "Antipodean American Geography: Washington Irving's 'Globular' Narratives." *The Oxford Handbook of Nineteenth-Century American Literature*, edited by Russ Castronovo. Oxford: Oxford University Press, 11–26.

Hamidullah, Mohammed. 1968. "Muslim Discovery of America before Columbus." *Journal of the Muslim Students' Association of the United States and Canada* 4, no. 2: 7–9.

Hazlett, John D. 1983. "Literary Nationalism and Ambivalence in Washington Irving's *The Life and Voyages of Christopher Columbus*." *American Literature* 55, no. 4: 560–575.

Irving, Washington. 1822. *The Sketch-Book of Geoffrey Crayon, Gent.* London: John Murray.

———. 1828. *The Life and Voyages of Christopher Columbus*. Paris: A. and W. Galignani.

———. 1979. *Letters: Volume II, 1823–1838*. Edited by Ralph M. Aderman, H. L. Kleinfield, and Jenifer S. Banks. Boston: Twayne.

———. 1981. *The Life and Voyages of Christopher Columbus*. Edited by John H. McElroy. Boston: Twayne.

Jaksić, Iván. 2007. *The Hispanic World and American Intellectual Life, 1820–1880*. New York: Palgrave Macmillan.

McElroy, John H. 1981. Introduction to *The Life and Voyages of Christopher Columbus*, edited by John H. McElroy. Boston: Twayne, xvii–xcvii.

McLamore, Richard. 1993. "Postcolonial Columbus: Washington Irving and *The Conquest of Granada*." *Nineteenth-Century Literature* 48, no. 1: 26–43.

Penney, Clara L., ed. 1930. *Diary of Washington Irving, Spain 1828–1829*. New York: Hispanic Society of America.

Pfitzer, Gregory M. 2008. *Popular History and the Literary Marketplace, 1840–1920*. Amherst: University of Massachusetts Press.

Review of *The Life and Voyages of Christopher Columbus*. 1828. *Monthly Review* 7, no. 32: 420–433.

Sale, Kirkpatrick. 1990. *The Conquest of Paradise: Christopher Columbus and the Columbian Legacy*. New York: Knopf.

Shurr, William H. 1992. "Irving and Whitman: Re-Historicizing the Figure of Columbus in Nineteenth-Century America." *American Transcendental Quarterly* 6, no. 4: 237–250.

Starr, S. Frederick. 2013. "So, Who Did Discover America?" *History Today* 63, no. 12: n.p.

3 Moriscos and Mormons
Captivity Literature on the Spanish and American Frontiers

*Elizabeth Terry-Roisin and
Randi Lynn Tanglen*

Raúl Coronado, in the conclusion to *A World Not to Come: A History of Latino Writing and Print Culture*, writes that "narrative histories ... can enrich our own imaginaries by reintroducing concepts that had been discarded or perhaps, more accurately, existed only liminally" (2013, 395). While Coronado is concerned with the transnational epistemological struggle between Spanish-Americans and Anglo-Americans in the U.S. Southwest, his insistence that by diving into the "fleeting" and seemingly "irrelevant" pasts "we may learn new, more capacious ways of empathizing and thinking of our present" is relevant to those of us seeking trans-Atlantic and postsecular approaches to understanding the global rise of anti-immigrant and Islamophobic rhetoric (2013, 395). To that end, in this chapter, we argue that analyzing the unexpected connections, or what Coronado calls the "fleeting liminality," between the cultural work of captivity literature in early modern Spain and the nineteenth-century United States can bring greater understanding to the historiography and literary history of both nations. Coronado's work, which spans oceans, continents, languages, genres, languages, and disciplines, is also instructive for our comparative analysis of early modern Spanish and nineteenth-century American captivity literature.

Bringing together our fields of nineteenth-century American literature and the history and literature of early modern Spain, we contribute to a more complete understanding of Spain's role in the United States' colonial and modern development, which works by art historian M. Elizabeth Boone and historians Richard Kagan and Carrie Gibson have recently emphasized (Boone 2019; Gibson 2019; Kagan 2019). Specifically, we argue that two seemingly disparate contexts, the nineteenth-century American frontier, and late medieval and early modern Spain (1400–1650), and its empire, share many elements in common, including a genre of literature known as the captivity narrative. The captivity narrative makes way for and follows the expansion of empire and the spread of imperial religion, both Catholic and Protestant, in early modern Spain and the nineteenth-century United States.

Early modern Spain, like the United States in the nineteenth century, was an expansive state. It had just completed its Reconquista, conquering

DOI: 10.4324/9781003219460-3

30 *Elizabeth Terry-Roisin et al.*

Muslim Granada in 1492 and closing its frontier with Islam on the peninsula. It then looked to its next frontier, North Africa, and engaged in numerous campaigns to conquer it throughout the sixteenth century. Spain added Mexico, Peru, and other parts of the New World to its dominions in this same period. After the Conquest of Granada, Moriscos (Muslims who had converted to Christianity) remained in Christian Spain, subject to the oversight of the Spanish Inquisition. In 1609–1614, King Philip III of Spain expelled the Morisco community, concerned that they would open the borders to the Ottoman Turks. The United States in the nineteenth century was also pressing against its frontiers, conquering and expelling native peoples, including Creeks and Cherokees, and facing the challenge of assimilating religious minorities, like Mormons and Catholics.

In this chapter, we propose that the literatures that came out of Golden Age Spain and the United States in the nineteenth century have more in common than have been recognized by current scholarship. According to a number of scholars, the Indian captivity narrative in the United States was a new genre, and a new, uniquely American national literature, with Mary Rowlandson's seventeenth-century captivity narrative as its Ur-text (Pearce 1947, 1–20; Slotkin 1973; Kolodny 1993, 184–195; Derounian-Stodola 1998). We will show, through an analysis of Golden Age poetry and literature, including the *novella morisca*, or Morisco novel, and Miguel de Cervantes' "Captive's tale," that similar tropes of captivity had already been employed in early modern Spain, to express anxieties about religious others, on constantly shifting Mediterranean and Atlantic frontiers. In the captivity literature of early modern Spain and that of the nineteenth-century United States, captivity was a malleable metaphor that carried within it orientalist assumptions and exposed the fluidity of religion, gender, race, and ethnicity on the ever-moving frontier.

It is important to note that the Catholic Spanish and Protestant British forged different types of relationships with the native peoples whom they encountered as they built their Atlantic empires. According to historian Carla Pestana, "Protestantism, with its emphasis on deep knowledge of Scripture and (in some cases) its insistence on the need of believers to convey a conversion experience to gain access to church membership, raised the bar for conversion," marriage, and assimilation (2010, 71). Uneasy trading relationships were established with the inhabitants of New England, but British settlers focused mainly on moving Native tribes out of the way of their settlements, rather than converting them. On the other hand, in the Spanish empire, Pestana explained,

> Catholicism was understood as a universal church, which was supposed to unite all the peoples of the world, and that understanding may have made church officials and lay people more open to accepting

Moriscos and Mormons 31

the native people they encountered both as church members and as marriage partners.

(2010, 71)

Religion shaped the way the Atlantic and American empires developed. The frontier of empire was a place of religious anxiety and conflict. Pestana argues that "The entry of England into the colonization business was framed in terms of confronting and displacing papist Spain" (2010, 65).

The European age of religious wars played out on American soil. For example, in 1565, the Spanish commander Pedro Menéndez de Aviles massacred a group of French Protestants, or Huguenots, in North Florida at Ft. Caroline and what is now called the Matanzas inlet (Gannon 1983, 28–29; Bennett 2001, 37–39). In New England, when Puritan Protestants wrote accounts of captivity among Catholic-influenced Native Americans, they emphasized their resistance to religious conversion (Demos 1994).

Spanish and American Frontiers

An integrated comparison between the literatures and histories of the frontier with Islam in the late medieval and early modern Mediterranean world, and on the American frontier, is revealing. What is a frontier? Physical frontiers can stand in between states but also between ideas and religions. Frederick Jackson Turner argued in 1893 that the

peculiarity of American institutions is the fact that they have been compelled to adapt themselves to the changes of an expanding people—to the changes involved in crossing the continent, in winning a wilderness, and in developing at each area of this progress out of the primitive economic and political conditions of the frontier into the complexity of city life.

(1994, 35)

While Turner believed the American frontier to be "ly(ing) on the hither edge of free land," fundamentally different from Europe's "fortified boundary line" (Turner 1994, 36), scholars of medieval Europe will find a great deal of commonality with his idea of the frontier, particularly in the "Great Age of Clearing" from 1000 to 1300, when Europeans brought more land under cultivation. In late medieval Spain, the frontier was a porous zone, a place of cultural, economic, and religious exchange, constantly moving and never fixed. The frontier was also a place of war, of bloody conflict, of a moving political boundary line, of outposts and raids, and occasionally of pitched battle—a place of difference.[1] In Spain, the military orders of Santiago, Calatrava, and Alcántara, which were founded in the twelfth century, were the guardians of the frontier. These "ecclesiastical knights" stood guard in their castles against the raids

32   *Elizabeth Terry-Roisin et al.*

coming north from Muslim lands and sent raids of their own, burning the orchards and olive trees of the south.[2]

After the Reconquest, and the fall of Granada in 1492, the frontier moved to North Africa and the New World, yet as David Coleman has shown, places like the city of Granada were still "frontier societies," in that they were physically places of tension and violence between Christian immigrants and the former Muslim inhabitants of the city. According to Coleman,

> Postconquest Granada obviously long remained a cultural and religious frontier zone in which elements of traditional Iberian Islamic and Christian faith and practices met, coexisted, blended, and frequently clashed ... postconquest Granada long housed a particularly fluid and dynamic frontier society distinct from the more established social orders of many of Spain's other major cities ... like many frontier communities, Granada not only suffered from political instability, but it also offered many of its residents a variety of possibilities for social and economic advancement.
>
> (2003, 3)

There were opportunities for many Christian settlers and for elite Moriscos, or Muslim converts to Christianity to stake political and economic claims in Christian Granada.

Scholars do not agree about the nature of the history of the Spanish frontier. Should it be defined by the "Reconquista," the 700-year advance of Christians into the Muslim south, as Joseph O'Callaghan (2003) has argued, and part of the history of the European crusades, due to the papal indulgences offered for both? Or, was the Spanish frontier better defined by the living together, or *convivencia* of Jews, Christians, and Muslims? In *The Arts of Intimacy: Christians, Jews and Muslims in the Making of Castilian Culture* (2008), building on Américo Castro's *España en su historia: cristianos, moros y judíos* (1948), Jerrilynn D. Dodds, María Rosa Menocal, and Abigail Krasner Balbale focus on the city of Toledo under the rule of the Christian king Alfonso VI, arguing that even in a time of religious and political conflict, Jews, Christians, and Muslims in Toledo shared a culture, which included architectural styles, learning, and language. The horseshoe arch, for instance, was not just an Islamic style, but a local Toledan style that the people of the three religions shared (Dodds, Menocal, and Balbale 2008). These authors agree with Américo Castro (1948), for whom *convivencia* was the peaceful interchange between the three religions that defined medieval Spain, and that interchange was brutally ripped apart by the Catholic Kings' conquest of Granada and the subsequent agenda of religious uniformity in Habsburg Spain. Neither "Reconquista" (a term now tainted for the political "work" it did for Francisco Franco in the twentieth century)[3] nor *convivencia* adequately

Moriscos and Mormons 33

describe the fluid and hybrid nature of the frontier, which was periodically a place of both friendship and violence.

For Claudio Sánchez-Albornoz (1956), an émigré like Castro from Franco's Spain, the real Spain had been founded by the Christian Visigoths in Late Antiquity, and there were elements of this essential Spanish culture that remained, despite centuries of *convivencia* and conflict with other religions. A belief that late medieval Spain was defined by Reconquista is consistent with Albornoz's argument, because the fifteenth-century propagandists of the Reconquista themselves were claiming to be returning to a lost Christian past, reconquering, not conquering a land, and removing the Muslim population that had taken it unjustly. With this desire to return to an imagined past, it is obvious to see how the Reconquista became a Renaissance project under Ferdinand and Isabella, and why building churches in Granada over mosques was not enough—they needed to be in the Palace of Charles V and the Cathedral of Granada, Vitruvian architectural statements that the Roman Empire, under a new Christian Constantine, had been revived.[4]

There is abundant evidence that the late medieval frontier between the kingdoms of Castile, Aragon, and Nasrid Granada was a place of exchange, and even a place where the lines between religions became blurred, because of a shared chivalric and noble culture. The king of Castile had a Moorish guard to protect him, and some of his Moorish knights remained Muslim though others ultimately converted. A poem that best expresses this connection between Nasrid and Castilian culture is the anonymous frontier ballad, *Abenamar, Abenamar* from the mid-fifteenth century, which describes a meeting between Castilian king Juan II and Abenalmao, Sultan Yusuf IV, in 1431, in which it is clear the Christian king admires the Muslim Sultan and considers him a "good Moor" (Arié 1992, 64–65).[5] *Abenamar, Abenamar* also refers to the captivity of a Christian princess who remained true to her ancestral religion, and who taught her son, a Muslim prince, not to lie.

The admiration Spanish and Nasrid nobles had for each other in the fifteenth century spilled into something that literary scholar Barbara Fuchs has called "maurophilia—the idealization of Moors in chivalric and romance texts," which ironically takes place at a time when Muslim culture "was officially denounced." Barbara Fuchs argues that the best examples of this are the anonymous "Abencerraje" (1561) and Mateo Alemán's "Ozmín y Daraja," which is a tale contained in his *Guzmán de Alfarache* (1599) (Fuchs et al. 2014, 1). In these *novelas moriscas*, the Moorish characters often displayed even greater nobility than the Christians but ultimately converted. In "Ozmín y Daraja," Daraja is a Muslim woman taken captive by Christians, whose fiancé Ozmín follows her and disguises himself as a gardener and also as an Aragonese knight to find her. In one scene, he explains to her Christian suitor that they both want the same thing, to marry Daraja and share her religion. This

34 *Elizabeth Terry-Roisin et al.*

story, written by a Christian Spaniard, ends by Ozmín's status as a noble Muslim knight being revealed, and by Ozmín y Daraja converting to Christianity, marrying, and taking on the Christian names of Fernando y Isabel, their sovereigns (Fuchs 2009, 131–135; Fuchs et al. 2014).

The Captive's Tale

In a nineteenth-century American captivity narrative, the captive is successful when they hold fast and do not leave Protestant Christianity. In these early modern Catholic stories, Moors are highly praised when they *do* convert to Christianity, and the writers of these narratives are sure to point out when Christians remain steadfast, like Spanish soldier Alvar Nuñez Cabeza de Vaca, who wrote in 1542 his account of his experiences as a captive and slave of Native Americans, offering to the Spanish crown the knowledge he gained on his journey as his "service," because he was naked and had no gold to show for his sufferings (2002, 4).

One of the most famous Spanish captivity narratives from the Siglo de Oro is the "Captive's tale" contained in Cervantes' *Don Quixote* (1605). This captive began his life as a Christian in the region of León, in the north of Castile. His brothers and he soon left home to seek their fortune, and he decided to become a soldier and a sailor and joined the navies of Don Juan de Austria, fighting in the famous Battle of Lepanto (1571). Despite the Christian victory, he was captured by the Ottomans. While in captivity in Algiers, he met a "Spanish soldier named Saavedra," and the captive remarks that "I'd tell you of this soldier's exploits, and they would entertain and amaze you much more than my own story." Miguel de Cervantes Saavedra himself was a captive in North Africa, and so this is his way of inserting himself into the fictional story (2001, 370).

The fictional captive ended up imprisoned in a courtyard adjacent to a rich Muslim's house. There, a woman signaled to him through a window, tossing him a small packet of coins and a note. He and the other prisoners thought she could have been a Christian woman, or a renegade (a Christian who had converted to Islam), but the woman was actually the daughter of a rich Muslim merchant, who, as she explained to them in the note, had learned about Christian worship, and Lela Marien (the Virgin Mary) from her father's female slave, who was a Christian.

> The Christian slave died, and I know that it wasn't to the fire that she went to Allah, because since then I have seen her twice, when she told me to go to the land of the Christians to see Lela Marien, who loved me very much.
>
> (Cervantes 2001, 373)

The lady then told the man that she was young and beautiful, and that he was the first Christian captive she had seen who seemed a gentleman, and if he helped her escape, she would be his wife. The lady's note was translated by a Christian renegade (who was also a captive), who then declared that he would help this plan come to fruition, and then "he would achieve what he so desired: to be restored to the bosom of our Holy Mother Church, from which, like a gangrenous limb he had been cut off because of his ignorance and sinfulness." He said this with "many tears" and "repentance" (Cervantes 2001, 373). The captive managed to escape with his bride to Spain, though there was a tense scene between her and her angry father, whom they left stranded on a beach (Cervantes 2001, 389).

The "Captive's tale" in *Don Quixote* contains a number of the same themes we observe in later American captivity narratives—remaining true to one's religion, converting others, and helping other coreligionists escape. Ultimately, the lady, whose name was Zoraida, was able to enter a church and find the truth she had been seeking, as did the renegade:

> As Zoraida walked in(to the church), she said that there were faces there that looked like Lela Marien's faces (the Virgin Mary). We told her that they were images, and the renegade explained the best he could what they signified, so that she could worship them as if each one really were the very same Lela Marien who'd spoken to her. Zoraida had a good mind and a clear and ready understanding, and immediately grasped what she was told about the images ... We stayed for six days in Vélez Málaga, at the end of which the renegade, having made his formal declaration of intentions to the authorities, went to the city of Granada to be restored to the sacred bosom of the Church through the good offices of the Holy Inquisition.
>
> (Cervantes 2001, 394)

The Veneration of images and the intercession of the Virgin Mary were two of the major doctrinal and cultural hurdles for Muslims to surmount when they converted to Christianity. Zoraida's embrace of these elements of early modern Catholicism is used by Cervantes to show her sincerity. *Don Quixote* is a rich and complicated work by a former captive. According to some scholars, *Don Quixote* can only be understood within the context of North Africa, captivity, the history of Spain's Moriscos, and the integration of religious minorities (López-Baralt 1992).

Morisco and Cherokee Expulsions

Moriscos had been living in Spain since the fall of Nasrid Granada to Ferdinand and Isabella in 1492 and in more Northern parts of the peninsula for many years prior. There had been almost a decade, from 1492 to 1500, in which it seemed they would be allowed to remain Muslim, but as the efforts to convert them increased, the Moriscos revolted against the crown, in 1500, and thus many Muslims were forced to convert or leave Granada in 1501. Some of their cultural practices, such as speaking

36   Elizabeth Terry-Roisin et al.

Arabic, writing in *Aljaimado* script, wearing traditional dress, dancing the *Zambra*, or practicing particular bathing rites, were outlawed by state and church authorities, though between 1526 and 1566 in Granada these rules were rarely enforced, due to an arrangement that was made with Emperor Charles V.[6]

In 1569, a second Morisco revolt broke out in Granada, which failed. King Philip II then expelled the Moriscos of Granada into the rest of Castile, hoping their isolation would cause them to assimilate. Ultimately, his son Philip III chose to expel the Moriscos from all of Spain. Not all of these people were still crypto-Muslims who practiced Islam in secret. Some had been Christians for generations. Regardless, between 1609 and 1614, over 300,000 Moriscos were expelled from their homes, forced onto boats at Andalucian beaches, some reaching North Africa, France, and Italy, and suffering loss of property, injury, or death (Vincent 2014, 23, 31).[7] Philip III made this decision in the context of the Dutch Revolt—a conflict he was losing—possibly because he hoped a hard line on Catholic orthodoxy would offset the damage done to Spain's prestige by military defeats (Prada 2009).[8] It is in this political context that many of the captivity narratives in Spanish literature were written.

One of the closest American parallels to the experience of Spain's Moriscos is that of the Cherokee Nation. Many Cherokees, by the 1820s, had assimilated into the culture of their encroaching white neighbors. In the Moriscos' case, by 1609, many had assimilated into the culture of their new Castilian rulers, and yet still both communities were expelled. In the early nineteenth century, many Cherokee Indians converted to Christianity, becoming Presbyterians, Baptists, and Methodists (Conley 2005, 104). They established "a bicameral legislature, a national police force, a Supreme Court, an elective system of representation ... and in 1828, a written constitution patterned after that of the U.S. federal government" (Strum 2002, 52–53). Some Cherokees even owned plantations with black slaves (Strum 2002, 68). They bought a printing press and published the first edition of the *Cherokee Phoenix* newspaper in 1828 (Conley 2005, 105). And yet still, the state of Georgia pursued numerous draconian anti-Cherokee laws. According to a thoroughly assimilated Cherokee, Elias Boudinot:

> The Cherokees have been reclaimed from their wild habits—instead of hunters they have become the cultivators of the soil—instead of wild and ferocious savages, thirsting for blood, they have become the mild "citizens," the friends and brothers of the white man— Instead of the superstitious heathens, many of them have become the worshippers of the true God ... No sooner was it known that they had learned the proper use of the earth, and that they were now less likely to dispose of it for a mess of pottage, than they came in conflict

with the cupidity and self-interest of those who ought to have been their benefactors ...

(1983, 141–142)

There is a parallel here to Francisco Nuñez Muley, an elite Morisco who wrote to Granada's Chancery Court in 1567 on behalf of his fellow Moriscos, saying that

In their reports, the prelates contend that the preservation of the traditional style of dress and footwear of the natives of this kingdom is tantamount to a continuation of the ceremonies and customs of the Muslims. I can only say, My Lord, that in my modest judgement (which has nonetheless helped me reach old age) these reports are wholly without merit, because the style of dress, clothing, and footwear of the natives cannot be said to be that of Muslims, nor is it that of Muslims. It can more rightly be said to be clothing that corresponds to a particular kingdom and province.

(2007, 69–70)

Moriscos had religiously assimilated, he argued, and their clothing was merely cultural, not a sign of their lack of loyalty to the new regime. Nuñez Muley's argument is similar to what the authors of *Arts of Intimacy* observed, that it was possible for members of the three religions of Toledo to share culture and aesthetics (Dodds, Menocal, and Balbale 2008).

In both Nuñez Muley and Boudinot's cases, their concern for their communities fell on deaf ears. In 1830, President Andrew Jackson passed his act of "Indian Removal," expelling the Cherokees from their homes in today's Georgia and Tennessee, sending them to Oklahoma, leading to an estimated 4000 Cherokee people dying first in concentration camps and then along the Trail of Tears (Conley 2005, 157). As noted earlier, Spain expelled religious "others" in the Jewish expulsion of 1492 and the Morisco expulsion of 1609–1614.[9] While some elite Moriscos, like the Granada Venegas family, managed to assimilate into the Spanish nobility, gaining titles and honors like memberships in the military orders that helped them avoid Philip III's expulsion (Terry 2015), this was not the case for elite Cherokees. Sadly for the Cherokees, even their most assimilated leaders were also forced to "remove" to Oklahoma.

In the context of the early stages of "Indian Removal," in 1832, American author Washington Irving went on a pleasure trip into Oklahoma and then wrote and published his account, *A Tour of the Prairies*, in 1833. At that point in his career, Irving had traveled in Europe and had even enjoyed an extended stay in Granada's Alhambra Palace in 1829. He had already served as a diplomat to Spain, with access to rare books in Madrid when he wrote his *Life and Voyages of Christopher Columbus*

38 *Elizabeth Terry-Roisin et al.*

(1728), *Alhambra* (1832), and other works. Irving was an enthusiastic lover of Spanish history and literature and was a central crafter of the cultural phenomenon which Richard Kagan has called "Sunny Spain." His writings helped to create an American fascination with Spain and to inspire other travelers (Kagan 2019, 134–143).

Back at home, Irving drew on his knowledge of Spain's frontier with Islam, chivalric romance, and Spanish Golden Age fiction to aid him in grappling with the real American frontier. Two of his companions on his Oklahoma trip, a young Swiss Count and a French Creole named Tonish, Irving described in this way,

> emerging from a forest, we beheld our raw boned, hard winking, knight errant of the frontier, descending the slope of a hill, followed by his companion in arms. As he drew nearer to us the gauntness of his figure and ruefulness of his aspect, reminded me of the descriptions of the hero of La Mancha …
>
> (2004, 26)

Thus, Irving's own wanderings on the American frontier reminded him of those of *Don Quixote*. Irving and his companions were on this journey to hunt buffalo, accompanied by a commissioner from Washington who occasionally made a speech to the local tribes "assuring them that he was sent to the frontier to establish a universal peace," which to readers in Irving's day may have originally been humorous (Irving 2004, 118).

Creek Indians had had a similar experience to the Cherokees and had assimilated into settled life. Irving describes the Creeks in their farms as having "adopted, with considerable facility, the rudiments of civilization, and to have thriven in consequence" (2004, 25).

Yet he also saw them as "quite oriental in appearance," dressed in "brilliant colours" and with "gaudy handkerchiefs tastefully bound round their heads" (Irving 2004, 20). Drawing images from his Spanish travels, considering that the horses of the West came from Arabia by way of the Spanish empire, Irving wrote that

> The habits of the Arab seem to have come with the steed. The introduction of the horse on the boundless prairies of the Far West changed the whole mode of living of their inhabitants. It gave them that facility of rapid motion and of sudden and distant change of place so dear to the roving propensities of man … on horseback, on vast flowery prairies and under cloudless skies.
>
> (2004, 91)

In addition to the Creeks, Irving wrote of the

> trappers, half breeds, creoles, negroes of every hue; and all that other rabble rout of nondescript beings that keep about the frontiers,

Moriscos and Mormons 39

between civilized and savage life, as those equivocal birds the bats, hover about the confines of light and darkness.

(Irving 2004, 21)

Irving shows some admiration for the human diversity of the frontier, and yet there are other troubling places in his text where he says he "had been taught to look upon all half breeds with distrust" (2004, 22).

Irving's younger British contemporary, Joseph Conrad, also wrote about the anxieties that affect the edges of empire, though like many nineteenth-century European authors, Conrad framed the conflict more directly as the struggle between "Civilization and Barbarism," while using similar language to Irving of light and darkness. The frontier he described in Africa was a frontier with self-control, a frontier with sanity, and a voyage into that frontier was to "penetrate deeper and deeper into the heart of darkness." His main character, Kurtz, though there to spread "Civilization" (while actually stealing ivory) became more barbarous in the end than any of the African peoples he had previously condemned (Conrad 1990, 31).

For Dominican priest and settler Bartolomé de las Casas and Spanish soldier Alvar Nuñez Cabeza de Vaca, in the sixteenth century, the frontier of the Spanish empire was less a metaphor for the corruption of the soul and more an ever-moving political and religious boundary. The two Spaniards also described how the conquistadors and settlers of the frontier acted far worse than those they condemned as pagan or barbarous. Las Casas wrote:

I know beyond any shadow of a doubt that they [the native peoples] had, from the very beginning, every right to wage war on the Europeans, while the Europeans never had a just cause for waging war on the local peoples. The actions of the Europeans, throughout the New World, were without exception wicked and unjust; worse in fact than the blackest kind of tyranny.

(2004, 23)

While Cabeza de Vaca did not criticize his fellow Spaniards to the same extent as Las Casas, he wrote that after his long journey through Florida, Louisiana, and Texas, being enslaved by Indians as well as living with them as a healer, when he met up with his countrymen again, naked, in Mexico, "we had many and bitter quarrels with the Christians, for they wanted to make slaves of our Indians" (2002, 95). Cabeza de Vaca wrote to the king that "in order to bring those people to Christianity and obedience unto Your Imperial Majesty, they should be well treated, and not otherwise" (2002, 90).

With Cabeza de Vaca's account of his time in the new world, the Mediterranean captivity narrative crossed the Atlantic. He described how he maintained his Christianity while held captive by heathen others, some

40 *Elizabeth Terry-Roisin et al.*

of whom he healed, by using the sign of the cross (Cabeza de Vaca 2002, 57). The captivity narrative was a part of the cultural imaginary of the Catholic Spanish when they encountered indigenous cultural and religious difference in the New World, and would also be a part of how the Protestant English and Protestant Americans grappled with their frontier, in the early Puritan context, as well as in the nineteenth century when these captivity literatures functioned to project Protestant concerns about the role of the West in the United States' putative millennial destiny and promoted a unified, white, and thoroughly Protestant national identity. Popular and best-selling American accounts of captivity and "life among the Indians" reflect some of the same concerns regarding imperial power and religious and racial mixing in European literatures from the frontier with Islam in the Mediterranean world.

This chapter finds commonalities within the sixteenth and the nineteenth centuries, but it still needs to acknowledge some of the historical gaps and transformations separating these two time periods. The adoption of race-based slavery in the American colonies by the mid-seventeenth century was one of these transformations. According to historian Peter H. Wood, previous Mediterranean slavery had contained a "loophole," that religious conversion could lead to freedom, as it was not lawful for Christians to enslave Christians and Muslims to enslave Muslims. But in the Spanish Caribbean, in search of higher profits, landholders began making a dark-skinned appearance and African origin the basis for slavery. In 1662, Virginia also made slavery hereditary, based on the status of the mother, not their father, as it had been previously (Wood 2003). While this transformation would have dramatic and devastating consequences for the Africans brought to this country, it did not necessarily remove the central role of religion from the American frontier. We argue that despite this change, religion and anxiety about religious conversion were central to both early modern Spanish and nineteenth-century American empire building and their captivity narratives (Tanglen 2016, 65–75). What we also argue is that both Catholics and Protestants shared this anxiety about conversion, and it can be seen in both early modern and nineteenth-century texts.

American Captivity Narratives and the Significance of Religious Difference

Critics of American literature regard captivity narratives as "archetypal texts about the individual/imperial American experience" with some even claiming that the genre has "been part of the American psyche for centuries" (Derounian-Stodola 2009, 47). The first best-selling captivity narrative in the Americas was Puritan Mary Rowlandson's 1682 account of her three-week captivity with the Narragansetts of New England during King Phillip's War, which she titled *The Sovereignty and Goodness of God.* Due in part to the popularity of Mary Rowlandson's narrative in the seventeenth century—it went through four editions in the first year and twenty-three editions by 1828—the literary conventions of the captivity narrative eventually became a trope, or a symbolic short-hand, to represent white racial anxieties and anti-indigenous prejudice on the westward-expanding frontiers of what would eventually become the United States. Over time this trope and its associated negative depictions of Native peoples came to signify the cultural superiority of whites and the perceived rightness of usually white-provoked wars.

Yet when read in conversation with Spanish frontier captivity narratives, these earlier captivity narratives like Rowlandson's signal that portrayals of racial difference and white superiority were not always the primary provenance of the genre. Cabeza de Vaca's *La Relación*, published 150 years earlier, emphasized themes of cultural regeneration and spiritual redemption, as Cabeza de Vaca argues that though the expedition was a failure, his experience and his written account of it can still bring glory and profit to the Crown through the exploitation of the lands and goods of the Americas and the Christian conversion of Native peoples. Although Cabeza de Vaca offers a more nuanced portrayal of indigenous people than subsequent Puritan Indian captivity narratives like Rowlandson's would, he still maintains that the Native peoples of the Americas were in need of European civilization and Christian conver-sion. In spite of his own assimilation into the religion and cultures of sev-eral tribes, Cabeza de Vaca emphasizes his commitment to the Christian conversion of the Indians: "We ordered them to build churches and put crosses in them, which until then they had not done. We also sent for the children of the chiefs to be baptized" (2002, 101). In this sense, as one of the earliest published accounts of the Americas and American Indians, Cabeza de Vaca's Indian captivity narrative participates in the cultural work of the captivity trope by arguing for European cultural superiority. Cabeza de Vaca has to downplay his own assimilation into and acceptance by Native cultures by keeping the Christian/heathen dichotomy securely in place throughout his account in order to justify further Spanish explor-ation of the New World.

While most critics highlight the significance of racial difference in early American captivity narratives, Cabeza de Vaca's *Chronicle* helps us see the significance of religious difference as well. Further, literary critic Rebecca Blevins Faery reminds us that seventeenth-century Puritan colonists such as Rowlandson did not necessarily think of themselves principally as "white," but first and foremost as Englishmen and Christians, privileging a religious identity over—or at least as much as—a racial identity (Faery 1999). The Puritans of New England feared contact with Catholic priests and their indigenous converts more than concerns with a racialized other, as demonstrated in other captivity narratives from the Puritan era (Demos 1994). Indeed, many of Rowlandson's anti-native epithets are religiously, rather than racially, based: "Infidels," "heathens," "hell hounds," and "Pagans" (Rowlandson 1997, 69, 70, 74, 94). Over time, the captivity

42   *Elizabeth Terry-Roisin et al.*

trope would come to be used by white Protestants to communicate fears of a religious and racialized other in other popular nineteenth-century captivity literature such as Barbary captivity narratives, anti-Catholic convent captivity narratives, and especially anti-Mormon polygamy novels.

By the time Mary Rowlandson's Indian captivity narrative had achieved incredible popularity in North America, the Barbary captivity narrative of the Mediterranean world was already well established in Europe. As Paul Baepler reminds us, "Cervantes, himself a captive in Algiers for five years, had dramatized his experience in his play, *El Trato de Argel*" (2004, 228). Indeed, the religious, especially anti-Catholic, fears expressed in Puritan Indian captivity narratives become more transparent when these narratives are read in relation to the seventeenth-century and eighteenth-century Barbary captivity narratives circulating in Europe and the Americas. In the United States, the Barbary captivity account achieved its greatest popularity in the nineteenth century, amid the emerging anti-slavery and abolitionist debates. Most popular was James Riley's 1817 *An Authentic Narrative of the Loss of the American Brig Commerce*: "It came out in at least 28 editions, spawning a sequel and an illustrated children's edition, and is still in print today" (Riley 1817; Baepler 2004, 217).

According to Nabil Matar, "by the end of the seventeenth century the Muslim 'savage' and the Indian 'savage' became completely superimposable in English thought and ideology," and thus there was a great deal of compatibility between North American and Barbary captivity narratives (Matar 1999, 170). Comparisons between Muslim and Native American "others" abound in the Barbary captivity narrative, with Barbary captive Jonathan Cowdery writing in 1806 that "Marriages are reported in Tripoli, by one or two old women, who run through the streets, making a most hideous yelling, and frequently clapping their hands to their mouths, similar to the American Indians in their *pow wows*" (1999, 184). But the Barbary accounts also depict myriad religious animosities, including antagonisms between Islam and Christianity, and even between Protestantism and Catholicism. Riley's and Cowdery's narrative along with the 1820 fictitious account of Eliza Bradley detail the religious struggle to resist the overtures of those "at enmity with our Christian religion" (1999, 267). In some Barbary captivity narratives, this included Catholic priests and monks who were depicted as the traders of Protestant slaves into Islamic slave markets. The Barbary captivity narrative of the Mediterranean world provides insight into "how the terms of the Christian/Islamic conflict were retooled for American colonization" as the captivity narrative evolved on the American frontier (Baepler 2004, 231; Davis 2004).

Captivity narratives about non-Protestant religious minorities were powerful rhetorical tools into the nineteenth century. For example, the nineteenth-century convent captivity narrative can be read as part of a

Moriscos and Mormons   43

sustained tradition of nativist, anti-Catholic rhetoric not far removed from the anti-Indian rhetoric of Puritan and Barbary captivity literature. These salacious narratives describe the experiences of Protestant virgins kidnapped into convents, systematically raped by priests, and then forced by evil nuns to kill their babies. Maria Monk's (1836) *Awful Disclosures of the Hotel Dieu Nunnery of Montreal* was the most popular of these works, appearing in several new editions even after the U.S. Civil War. Reading Monk's narrative in conversation with the popular Protestant minister Lyman Beecher's heavily circulated anti-Catholic sermon "A Plea for the West" reveals that convent captivity stories worked with other Protestant anti-Catholic literature to warn Protestants of the Catholic presence on the new western frontiers (Beecher 1836). The antebellum anti-Catholic captivity narrative simply transferred the religious prejudices and anxieties already communicated in Puritan Indian captivity literatures to a new setting and onto a different, no less threatening, cast of characters.[10]

As Jennie Franchot explains,

> Roman Catholicism figured crucially in this American captivity tradition as a principal and historically resilient captor of the New World Protestant settler. Changing its guise in response to the psycho-social anxieties of successive generations of Protestants, the specter of Roman-ism played captor to each in turn, looming as menacing figure in the New England forests, the Southwest, and the Mississippi Valley region.
>
> (1994, 88)

Despite the historical and geographical differences between Catholic and Protestant empire building, the captivity narrative brings them together, as many more of these narratives were written in the nineteenth century, in the very time that American intellectuals in Boston—including George Ticknor, William H. Prescott, and Washington Irving—were comparing the United States favorably against medieval and early modern Spain (Kagan 1996, 423–446).

Prescott also helped inspire the young men who fought for the United States in the Mexican War. His popular book, the *History of the Conquest of Mexico* (1843), caused some of them to imagine they were "following in the footsteps of Córtes" (Gibson 2019, 210), which was another way in which Spanish history inspired American expansion.

The accumulation of new lands and populations after the 1848 Treaty of Guadalupe Hidalgo revived nativist anxieties about what it meant to be an American as the nation integrated into its body politic peoples embodying a variety of racial, ethnic, national, and religious identities. Along with Mexicans, Mexican-Americans, Spanish Catholics, and indigenous populations, this included the Latter-day Saints in Utah who represented a religious, economic, political, and even racial threat to white

44   *Elizabeth Terry-Roisin et al.*

Protestant cultural authority on the frontiers of the American Southwest. "Mormonism functioned like a screen upon which Americans could project their crises," including the signing of the Treaty of Guadalupe Hidalgo and its aftermath. At this time, mass migration of the Latter-day Saints to Utah made "Mormonism ... less a local annoyance and more a national political issue" (Fluhman 2012, 104, 101).

Throughout the nineteenth century and into the early twentieth century, white Protestants viewed Mormons as both a racial and religious threat to American Christianity and civilization and went to great lengths to deny Mormons the privileges associated with whiteness. As W. Paul Reeve explains, "Being white equaled access to political, social, and economic power: all aspects of citizenship in which outsiders sought to limit or prevent Mormon participation" (2017, 3). From the church's origins in the 1830s, non-Mormons claimed Mormons had devilish horns and cloven hooves, a dehumanizing accusation previously directed against medieval Jews. After the practice of polygamy was officially recognized by the church in 1852, critics used the pseudo-sciences of phrenology and physiognomy to argue that Mormon polygamy led to reproductive demise and the production of a new, degenerate, non-white race. Mormon difference in terms of religious and sexual practice placed them in the "lowest stratum of European or American society," and Mormons were often compared to Native Americans, blacks, and Asians (Reeve 2017, 51). The Protestant white majority in the nineteenth-century United States was "convinced that Mormonism represented a racial—not merely religious—departure from the mainstream, and they spent considerable effort attempting to deny Mormon whiteness" and the political and cultural capital that came with it (Reeve 2017, 4). Anti-Mormon rhetoric in the 1850s engendered the Latter-day Saints into a newly formed ethnic category of "non-white" in order to keep the privileges of whiteness from members of the increasingly popular faith.

A common belief of white Protestants in the nineteenth century, concerned with the nation's millennial destiny, was that the expanding frontiers of the nation needed to be settled not just by white people, but the right kind of white people. "It was Mormonism's flight from the United States and Utah's subsequent status as a federal territory that drew it into larger national conversations about the fate of the West, the spread of civilization, and the national character" (Fluhman 2012, 105). Protestant clergymen were troubled by the ascendancy of Mormonism and were concerned that it would displace the older and more established Protestant sects, especially since "nineteenth-century Protestants instinctively viewed talk of a concretized godly kingdom as a political grab for power" (Fluhman 2012, 84–85). Mormon settlements in the Southwest were viewed as "a menacing empire-in-the-making" and "challeng[ed] the definition of Christianity in the ... nation" (Fluhman 2012, 11). The 1852 establishment of the Mormon doctrine of polygamy threatened Protestant social institutions even outside of Utah, challenging the

Female Life among the Mormons

Along with promoting white racial superiority and attempting to justify white-provoked wars, the captivity narrative was appropriated to condone violence against white religious and ethnic minorities, like the Latter-day Saints of Utah Territory. *Female Life Among the Mormons* by the pseudonymous Maria N. Ward is a fictitious account of Mormon captivity and escape that was published in 1855 and put into several editions, eventually selling 40,000 copies. This sensationalized novel set in Utah Territory was one of at least fifty anti-Mormon polygamy novels published between 1855 and 1903 (Arrington and Haupt 1968, 244). In 1968, historians Leonard J. Arrington and Jon Haupt addressed the novels' relationship to U.S. literary history, reporting that they moved beyond "the usual diatribes of hostile ministers and disenchanted apostates" and included among them "serious works of fiction" by authors who "enjoyed well-deserved reputations for literary excellence" (1968, 243). Many of the novels were written by women and "most of the writers of these novels were the wives or daughters of New England ministers or reformers" (Arrington and Haupt 1968, 245).[11] The American Protestants who wrote, read, and distributed such novels put themselves in the position of the early modern Spanish Catholics who resisted the temptation to convert to Islam.

This salacious novel tells the story of a young woman, Maria Ward herself, duped into a polygamous Mormon marriage and provides her fictitious account of Joseph Smith's and Brigham Young's sexual transgressions with their many wives. Set as an adventure story popular with American readers at the time, the young and naïve Maria leaves her home in upstate New York and begins to converse with a mysterious stranger on a stagecoach. When Maria asks the handsome man if he is a Mormon, he coyly responds, "I am, or I am not" (Ward 1855, 11). Hypnotized by the stranger, she attends a Mormon meeting in a secret room of the house of a woman named Mrs. Bradish. In the middle of the meeting, Joseph Smith arrives to resurrect a young girl from the dead. Soon, an anti-Mormon lynch mob—the Regulators—attack Mrs. Bradish's home, looking for Joseph Smith. Mrs. Bradish fights the mob off by pulling two pistols out of her petticoat and, as the conflict with the Regulators progresses, eventually cross-dresses as a man to bring needed supplies to Joseph Smith and his men, who are hiding out in the nearby woods. In the meantime, Maria marries the mysterious Mr. Ward who, it turns out, is actually an elder in the Mormon church.

Only after her marriage does she learn of the Mormon practice of polygamy and that "women can only be saved by their husbands" (Ward 1855, 49). After the death of Joseph Smith at the hands of the Regulator

46 *Elizabeth Terry-Roisin et al.*

mob, Maria, her husband, and Mrs. Bradish join a group of emigrants to Utah Territory with Brigham Young. Echoing the fears of conversion present within the earlier Spanish narratives, Young is portrayed as a Turkish sultan, as the Orientalist trope of the harem is prevalent in this and other anti-Mormon novels. To be sure, Mormons were often compared to Muslims in early nineteenth-century anti-Mormon rhetoric. Young is often depicted wearing long, loose harem pants and shoes with curvy toes. Since the Protestant women who wrote anti-Mormon novels "had little, if any, first-hand experience with the Latter-day Saints," Arrington and Haupt suggest that the authors drew upon stock stereotypes from other nineteenth-century reform literature to develop "myths and symbols of early anti-Mormon fiction" (1968, 243). These stereotypes included "the image of the drunken, abusive husband," "the white slave procurer," "the seducer," "the cruel, lustful southern slaveholder," and "the lustful Turk" (Arrington and Haupt 1968, 245–248). Christine Talbot explains that in the nineteenth century, "anti-Mormons continued to deploy Orientalism against Mormons to illustrate the difference they saw between Mormons and Americans" (2006, 380). She continues: "the use of Oriental metaphors in anti-Mormonism became ubiquitous, as polygamy quickly became its most central and most useful instrument ... Metaphors of the Orient connected plural marriage to the presumed despotic governments of the Orient" (Talbot 2006, 373–374). Just like how Washington Irving in his *Tour of the Prairies* used his knowledge of Spanish Golden Age literature to understand the American frontier, these authors of captivity narratives drew images and tropes from the Mediterranean world to categorize and criticize the Mormons.

Once the group arrives in Salt Lake City, Ward describes a wide range of polygamous sins—fathers who almost marry daughters; fathers who sell their daughters and then marry another woman the same day; evil young women who scheme to steal older women's husbands; women who kill themselves when they realize their husbands have taken second wives; women and children abandoned and cast aside as the result of polygamy. One family's child is killed by a second wife, and one woman murders herself and her child when she learns that she is the displaced wife. Mrs. Bradish facilitates many of the polygamous marriages that lead to emotional and psychological ruin for unsuspecting women who marry into the Mormon church. In short, as it is depicted, in the system of Mormon polygamy, Mormon women cannot be True Women. Plural wives are portrayed as fallen women who, according to the criteria of the nineteenth-century Cult of Domesticity, were "no wom[e]n at all, but member[s] of some lower order" (Welter 1966, 154). Portraying Mormon women as non-women also placed them outside the category of "white" and diminished their civilizing function. Without true women to civilize them on the frontier, Mormon men are savages—an idea that justified government military campaigns against the Mormons in Utah.

Anti-Indian and anti-Mormon rhetoric were often conflated, since both Native Americans and Mormons were viewed as "unwelcome parasites infesting the American body" on the frontiers (Reeve 2017, 54). Nineteenth-century Mormons felt obligated to bring the gospel to the Indians since they viewed Native Americans as remnants of the lost tribes of Israel. As a result, outsiders were concerned about a "Mormon-Indian conspiracy," an accusation that became more prevalent as Mormons intermarried with the Utah tribes. In the years following the notorious Mountain Meadows massacre—an 1857 Mormon attack on an Arkansas emigrant party on its way to California—accusations circulated of Mormons conspiring with and dressing as Paiutes during the five-day siege. According to historian W. Paul Reeve, these accounts eventually took on a life of their own and were prevalent decades later, indicating that "conflation[s] between Mormons and Indians" occurred wherever and "whenever Mormons or Indians were perceived as a threat" (2017, 100).

Published two years before the Mountain Meadows massacre, *Female Life among the Mormons* portrays Mormons dressing as and conspiring with Indians to rebel against the government. The novel also portrays American Indians as caricatures and sensationalized stereotypes. The novel lies when it claims that Native Americans participate in human sacrifice—an accusation often made against Mormons. The conflation of Mormons and Indians is especially apparent in chapter 40, when a missing woman thought to be captive among the Indians is really a captive in Brigham Young's house—or his "harem," as it is called in the novel, indirectly comparing Young to the Ottoman Sultans of contemporaneous Barbary captivity accounts. When she finally escapes the Mormons, Maria wears Mrs. Bradish's male clothing and "stain[ed] [her] face to look like an Indian" (Ward 1855, 447). In order to leave, Maria has to become exactly what Protestant reform writers accused polygamous Mormon women of becoming: non-white and non-women. Not sure if she can persevere and continue her escape on foot, Maria comes across a horse that had "probably belonged to some soldier or emigrant, who had been slain by the Indians or the Mormons" (Ward 1855, 448). Her mechanism of rescue emphasizes the continued conflation of anti-Mormon and anti-Indian political rhetoric. After she finds the horse, she comes upon an Indian encampment where she finds Ethleen, a native woman who was thought to have been murdered by the Mormons. An American Indian guide thus saves Maria's life and leads her to the "bosom" of friends and white, Protestant civilization.

W. Paul Reeve writes that Mormon removal to the Utah frontier "was evidence that the Mormons has fled civilization and gone native ... In their removal westward, Mormons descended the American racial ladder, away from white and closer to 'red' " (2017, 74). Read as a racial allegory for American Protestant American civilization, this captivity narrative shows Maria leaving the non-white Mormons, being rescued by Native Americans, and restored back to white, Protestant civilization—casting aside her male garb and her darkened skin. Similar to protagonists of earlier captivity narratives, Maria successfully resists the teachings,

48 *Elizabeth Terry-Roisin et al.*

customs, and religion of her captive culture and is redeemed to white, Christian society—with her virtue intact—she resisted and escaped plural marriage. She warns her readers: "The Mormon Church was the center of a secret organization, whose plots and plans were of the blackest description" (Ward 1855, 24). She closes the book with these words:

> I felt a desire to paint a picture of my experiences to the world, that all might know the enormities of the Mormon system, and the crimes and impostures of its leading members, whose baleful influence is paramount in beautiful Utah. If any are thereby warned, my labor will not have been in vain.
>
> (Ward 1855, 449)

Richard Slotkin theorizes the American frontier as a place of "regeneration through violence" or the process "of self-renewal or self-creation through acts of violence" (1973, 556). By conflating the "Mormon problem" and the "Indian problem," white Protestant millennial hopes were revived and perpetuated on the American frontier through individual and government sanction acts of violence. In the novel, the Regulators continually attack the Latter-day Saints in New York and Illinois, which were possible references to the Mormon Wars in Missouri and Illinois. Indeed, as early as 1838, the Governor of Missouri had issued an extermination order against the Mormons. In 1844, Joseph Smith was murdered by a mob in Carthage, Illinois, and in 1857, after the publication of *Female Life among the Mormons*, U.S. President James Buchanan sent an army to Utah. In anti-Mormon polygamy novels, religious and racial prejudice work in tandem to promote frontier "regeneration through violence," a pattern more apparent when they are read in conversation with early modern Spanish narratives. Just like the Spanish sought to Christianize and later expel native Muslim populations from Granada, the American frontier was a place of religious conflict and displacement. Spain's role as a model for American empire building has been unfairly ignored, and as Maria DeGuzmán has claimed, "figures of Spain and Spaniards have occupied, in the process of 'American' identity formation, a position as important as that of Britain and France" (2005, xii–xiii). The American captivity narrative can be understood as part of a long history of Spanish and Mediterranean captivity narratives—not as a genre unique to the young United States.

Conclusion: The Citationary and Capacious Nature of Captivity Literature

On the surface, early modern Spanish Morisco narratives and stories of polygamous wives returning to Protestant domesticity in the United States seem to have nothing in common. Yet even when the trope of captivity sends contradictory and ambiguous messages about religious and racialized others, it is not any less culturally resonant or effective in

Moriscos and Mormons 49

disseminating prejudice. In fact, what Edward Said has described as the "citationary" or self-referential nature of certain sources like captivity narratives is precisely what makes the literature effective in the transmission of ideas about empire and otherness.[12]

Literary scholars' earlier claim that the Indian captivity narrative was the first uniquely American literary genre replicates assumptions of American exceptionalism, since as we see, American authors and audiences simply recycled Old World tropes. Reading Spanish and American frontier captivity narratives as part of a trajectory of religious prejudice reveals that the captivity trope carries within it anxieties of a culture and people scared of losing their special status with God and their dominant place in the world, a fear that extends backward to Old Testament biblical stories of Babylonian captivity and to the literatures of the early modern Mediterranean. Better understanding the ways in which religion and race are intertwined in the American captivity narrative provides new insights into nineteenth-century literary history and reveals that the captivity narrative still resonates with present-day trans-Atlantic religious conflicts and concerns. Current discourse surrounding immigration and the assimilation of minorities with various national origins, religions, and languages in both Spain and the United States indicate the vital need for scholars to understand and *to teach* the trans-Atlantic nuances of the captivity narrative on the Spanish and American frontiers, leading us to what Raúl Coronado calls the "capacious ways of empathizing and thinking of our present" (2013, 495). Indeed, teaching the intersections of racial and religious prejudice is a particularly urgent implication of this work, with the rise of white supremacist nationalism, populism, and government policy in the United States and Europe.

William H. Prescott, like his contemporary Washington Irving, was fascinated by Spanish history. However, unlike Irving, Prescott saw Spain as monarchical, Catholic, and plagued by the Inquisition, while the United States represented democracy, Protestantism, and Progress. This dichotomy, which Richard Kagan (1996) has called "Prescott's Paradigm," made the United States look good at Spain's expense. Yet, it is clear, through the parallels between the expulsions of Cherokees and Moriscos, Washington Irving's view of his fellow travelers as characters from *Don Quixote*, and Maria Ward's description of Mormons as Ottoman Sultans that we have discussed, as well as the genre of captivity narratives which the two contexts shared, that the imperial histories and literatures of the nineteenth-century United States and early modern Spain were more alike than different.

Notes

1 The frontier has long been a subject of study for Spanish medievalists and early modernists, beginning with the work of Burns (1973). For Aragon, see Catlos (2004); for Granada, see Coleman (2003).

50 *Elizabeth Terry-Roisin et al.*

2 Conedera (2015) has recently argued that "Ecclesiastical Knights" is a far better term for the *caballeros* of the military orders than "warrior monks," because calling them warrior monks connects them only with a history of monasticism and does not acknowledge their unique character as consecrated knights.

3 García-Sanjuán (2018) argues that the word "Reconquista" is extremely problematic due to Franco's use of it in his National Catholic ideology.

4 For more on these themes, see Dandelet (2014), Rosenthal (1985), and Beaver (2008).

5 García Luján (2010, 14) also asserts that the poem, *Abenamar, Abenamar*, is about Yusuf IV. According to Juan Torres Fontes, the core of this poem is verifiably from the fifteenth century. However, Gines Perez de Hita, in his *Guerras Civiles de Granada* in the sixteenth century, added several other verses to this poem that relate to the pain of the war (both the war for Granada and the two Morisco revolts) in the countryside and in Granada (Fontes 2006, 174–189).

6 For more on the Moriscos, see Aguilera (2007), Gálan Sánchez (2010), and García-Arenal and Mediano (2010).

7 Some of these Moriscos were believing Christians who were forced to flee their homes (Teuller 2002).

8 See also the classic by Baroja (1957); Antonio Feros (2014, 60–61) has recently argued that the expulsion came not only out of this unique political situation but also out of a long-term ideological debate from the time of Philip II over the place of Moriscos in Spanish society, about whether they would ever truly convert, and whether they would welcome the Turks into Spanish ports; some theologians were against expulsion, including the Bishop of Segorbe, Don Feliciano de Figueroa, Ignacio de las Casas, who himself was a Morisco, and a Jesuit, and Pedro de Valencia, who was an historian, and a chronicler of the Indies and of Castile. Pedro de Valencia wrote against the expulsion in the *Tratado acerca de los Moriscos* (1605), urging Philip III to act as a good shepherd for his people, even for the Moriscos (Magnier 2011, 12, 17).

9 Yet, Jews who had converted to Christianity, judeo-conversos, though under the jurisdiction of the Spanish Inquisition, were never formally expelled.

10 For more on convent captivity narratives, see Fessenden (2000, 451–478) and Pagliarini (1999, 97–128).

11 *Female Life among the Mormons* was one of the first four "pattern setting" anti-Mormon novels published between 1855 and 1856.

12 For more of Said's important work on imperialism and orientalism, see Said (1978; 1994).

Works Cited

Aguilera, Manuel Barrios. 2007. *La convivencia negada: Historia de los moriscos del Reino de Granada*. Granada: Lavela.

Arié, Rachel. 1992. *El Reino Nasrí de Granada, 1232–1492*. Madrid: Editorial Mapfre.

Arrington, Leonard J. and Jon Haupt. 1968. "Intolerable Zion: The Image of Mormonism in Nineteenth-Century American Literature." *Western Humanities Review* 22: 243–260.

Baepler, Paul. 2004. "The Barbary Captivity Narrative in American Culture." *Early American Literature* 39: 217–246.

Moriscos and Mormons 51

Baroja, Julio Caro. 1957. *Los moriscos del Reino de Granada: Ensayo de historia social*. Madrid: Instituto de Estudios Politicos.

Beaver, Adam G. 2008. *A Holy Land for the Catholic Monarchy: Palestine in the Making of Modern Spain, 1469–1598*. Ph.D. Dissertation, Harvard University.

Beecher, Lyman. 1836. *A Plea for the West*, second edition. Cincinnati: Truman & Smith.

Bennett, Charles E. 2001. *Laudonniére and Fort Caroline: History and Documents*. Tuscaloosa: University of Alabama Press.

Boone, M. Elizabeth. 2019. *"The Spanish Element in Our Nationality": Spain and America at the World's Fairs and Centennial Celebrations, 1876–1915*. University Park: Penn State University Press.

Boudinot, Elias. 1983. "Selections from the Cherokee Phoenix, November 12, 1831." *Cherokee Editor: The Writings of Elias Boudinot*, edited by Theda Perdue. Knoxville: University of Tennessee Press.

Bradley, Eliza. 1999. "An Authentic Narrative, 1820." *White Slaves, African Masters: An Anthology of American Barbary Captivity Narratives*, edited by Paul Michael Baepler. Chicago: University of Chicago Press.

Burns, Robert Ignatius. 1973. *Islam under the Crusaders: Colonial Survival in the Thirteenth Century Kingdom of Valencia*. Princeton: Princeton University Press.

Cabeza de Vaca, Alvar Nuñez. 2002. *Chronicle of the Narváez Expedition*, translated by Fanny Bandelier. New York: Penguin Books.

de Las Casas, Bartolomé. 2004. *A Short Account of the Destruction of the Indies*, translated by Nigel Griffin. London: Penguin.

Castro, Américo. 1948. *España en su historia: cristianos, moros y judíos*. Buenos Aires: Editorial Losada.

Catlos, Brian A. 2004. *The Victors and the Vanquished: Christians and Muslims of Catalonia and Aragon, 1050–1300*. Cambridge: Cambridge University Press.

Cervantes Saavedra, Miguel de. 2001. *The Ingenius Hidalgo: Don Quixote de la Mancha*, 1605, translated by John Rutherford. London: Penguin Books.

Coleman, David. 2003. *Creating Christian Granada: Society and Religious Culture in an Old World Frontier City, 1492–1600*. Ithaca: Cornell University Press.

Conedera, Sam Zeno, S. J. 2015. *Ecclesiastical Knights: The Military Orders in Castile, 1150–1330*. New York: Fordham University Press.

Conley, Robert J. 2005. *The Cherokee Nation: A History*. Albuquerque: University of New Mexico Press.

Conrad, Joseph. 1990. *The Heart of Darkness*. New York: Dover Publications.

Coronado, Raúl. 2013. *A World Not to Come: A History of Latino Writing and Print Culture*. Cambridge: Harvard University Press.

Cowdery, Jonathan. 1999. "American Captives in Tripoli, 1806." *White Slaves, African Masters: An Anthology of American Barbary Captivity Narratives*, edited by Paul Michael Baepler. Chicago: University of Chicago Press.

Dandelet, Thomas James. 2014. *The Renaissance of Empire in Early Modern Europe*. Cambridge: Cambridge University Press.

Davis, Robert C. 2004. *Christian Slaves, Muslim Masters: White Slavery in the Mediterranean, the Barbary Coast and Italy, 1500–1800*. New York: Palgrave Macmillan.

DeGuzmán, Maria. 2005. *Spain's Long Shadow: The Black Legend, Off-Whiteness, and Anglo-American Empire*. Minneapolis: University of Minnesota Press.

52 Elizabeth Terry-Roisin et al.

Demos, John. 1994. *Unredeemed Captive: A Family Story from Early America.* New York: Vintage.

Derounian-Stodola, Kathryn Zabella, editor. 1998. *Women's Indian Captivity Narratives.* New York: Penguin.

———. 2009. *The War in Words: Reading the Dakota Conflict through the Captivity Literature.* Lincoln: University of Nebraska Press.

Dodds, Jerrilynn D., María Rosa Menocal, and Abigail Krasner Balbale. 2008. *Arts of Intimacy: Christians, Jews, and Muslims in the Making of Castilian Culture.* New Haven: Yale University Press.

Faery, Rebecca Blevins. 1999. *Cartographies of Desire: Captivity, Race, and Sex in the Shaping of an American Nation.* Norman: University of Oklahoma Press.

Feros, Antonio. 2014. "Rhetorics of the Expulsion." *The Expulsion of the Moriscos from Spain, A Mediterranean Diaspora*, edited by Mercedes García Arenal and Gerard Wiegers. Leiden: Brill.

Fessenden, Tracy. 2000. "The Convent, the Brothel, and the Protestant Woman's Sphere." *Signs* 25: 451–478.

Fluhman, J. Spencer. 2012. *A Peculiar People: Anti-Mormonism and the Making or Religion in Nineteenth-Century America.* Chapel Hill: University of North Carolina Press.

Fontes, Juan Torres. 2006. "La historicidad del Romance *Abenámar, Abenámar.*" *Historia de Andalucía, V: El Reino nazarí y la formación de la nueva Andalucía.* Sevilla: Fundación José Manuel Lara.

Franchot, Jenny. 1994. *Roads to Rome: The Antebellum Protestant Encounter with Catholicism.* Berkeley: University of California Press.

Fuchs, Barbara. 2009. *Exotic Nation: Maurophilia and the Construction of Early Modern Spain.* Philadelphia: University of Pennsylvania Press.

Fuchs, Barbara, Larissa Brewer-García, and Aaron J. Ilika, editors and translators. 2014. *"The Abencerraje" and "Ozmín and Daraja": Two Sixteenth Century Novellas from Spain.* Philadelphia: University of Pennsylvania Press.

Gálan Sánchez, Ángel. 2010. *Una sociedad en transición: Los granadinos de mudéjares a moriscos.* Granada: Universidad de Granada.

Gannon, Michael V. 1983. *The Cross in the Sand: The Early Catholic Church in Florida, 1513–1870.* Gainesville: University of Florida Press.

García-Arenal, Mercedes and Fernando Rodríguez Mediano. 2010. *Un Oriente Español: Los moriscos y el Sacromonte en tiempos de Contrrarreforma.* Madrid: Marcial Pons Historia.

García Luján, José Antonio. 2010. "Genealogía del linaje Granada Venegas desde Yusuf IV, rey de Granada." *Simposio Nobleza y Monarquía: Los linajes nobilarios en el Reino de Granada, siglos XV-XIX, El linaje Granada Venegas Marqueses de Campotéjar*, edited by José Antonio García Luján. Huéscar.

García-Sanjuán, Alejandro. 2018. "Rejecting al-Andalus, Exalting the Reconquista: Historical Memory in Contemporary Spain." *Journal of Medieval Iberian Studies* 10, no. 1: 127–145.

Gibson, Carrie. 2019. *El Norte: The Epic and Forgotten Story of Hispanic North America.* New York: Atlantic Monthly Press.

Irving, Washington. 2004. "A Tour on the Prairies." 1835. *Three Western Narratives.* New York: Library Classics of the United States.

Kagan, Richard L. 1996. "Prescott's Paradigm: American Historical Scholarship and the Decline of Spain." *American Historical Review* 101, no. 2: 423–446.

———. 2019. *The Spanish Craze: America's Fascination with the Hispanic World, 1779–1939*. Lincoln: University of Nebraska Press.

Kolodny, Annette. 1993. "Among the Indians: The Uses of Captivity." *Women's Studies Quarterly* 21: 184–195.

López-Baralt, Luce. 1992. *Islam in Spanish Literature*, translated by Andrew Hurley. Leiden: Brill.

Magnier, Grace. 2011. *Pedro de Valencia and the Catholic Apologists of the Expulsion of the Moriscos: Visions of Christianity and Kingship*. Leiden: Brill.

Matar, Nabil. 1999. *Turks, Moors, and Englishmen in the Age of Discovery*. New York: Columbia University Press.

Monk, Maria. 1836. *Awful Disclosures of the Hotel Dieu Nunnery*. New York: Maria Monk.

Muley, Francisco Nuñez. 2007. *A Memorandum for the President of the Royal Audiencia and Chancery Court of the City and Kingdom of Granada*, edited and translated by Vincent Barletta. Chicago: University of Chicago Press.

O'Callaghan, Joseph F. 2003. *Reconquest and Crusade in Medieval Spain*. Philadelphia: University of Pennsylvania Press.

Pagliarini, Marie Anne. 1999. "The Pure American Woman and the Wicked Catholic Priest: An Analysis of Anti-Catholic Literature in Antebellum America." *Religion and American Culture* 9: 97–128.

Pearce, Roy Harvey. 1947. "The Significances of the Captivity Narrative." *American Literature* 19: 1–20.

Pestana, Carla G. 2010. *Protestant Empire: Religion and the Making of the British Atlantic World*. Philadelphia: University of Pennsylvania Press.

Prada, Antonio Moliner, editor. 2009. *La expulsion de los moriscos*. Barcelona: Nabla Ediciones.

Reeve, W. Paul. 2017. *Religion of a Different Color: Race and the Mormon Struggle for Whiteness*. New York: Oxford University Press.

Riley, James. 1817. *An Authentic Narrative of the Loss of the American Brig "Commerce," Wrecked on the Western Coast of Africa, in the Month of August, 1815, with an Account of the Sufferings of Her Surviving Officers and Crew, Who Were Enslaved by the Wandering Arabs on the Great African Desert, or Zahahrah; and Observations Historical, Geographical, &c. Made During the Travels of the Author, While a Slave to the Arabs, and in the Empire of Morocco*. Hartford: self-published.

Rosenthal, Earl E. 1985. *The Palace of Charles V in Granada*. Princeton: Princeton University Press.

Rowlandson, Mary. 1997. *The Sovereignty and Goodness of God*, 1682, edited by Neal Salisbury. Boston: Bedford.

Said, Edward W. 1978. *Orientalism*. New York: Pantheon.

———. 1994. *Culture and Imperialism*. New York: Vintage.

Sánchez-Albornoz, Claudio. 1956. *España: un enigma histórico*. Buenos Aires, Argentina: Editorial Sudamericana.

Slotkin, Richard. 1973. *Regeneration through Violence: The Mythology of the American Frontier, 1600–1860*. Norman: University of Oklahoma Press.

Strum, Circe. 2002. *Blood Politics: Race, Culture, and Identity in the Cherokee Nation of Oklahoma*. Berkeley: University of California Press.

Talbot, Christine. 2006. "'Turkey Is in Our Midst': Orientalism in Nineteenth-Century Anti-Mormonism." *Journal of Law and Family Studies* 8: 363–388.

54 *Elizabeth Terry-Roisin et al.*

Tanglen, Randi Lynn. 2016. "The Indian Captivity Narrative: A Genre of the Southwest." *Critical Insights: Southwestern Literature*, edited by William Brannon. Ipswich: Salem Press, 65–75.

Terry, Elizabeth Ashcroft. 2015. *The Granada Venegas Family, 1431–1643: Nobility, Renaissance, and Morisco Identity*. Ph.D. Dissertation, University of California.

Teuller, James B. 2002. *Good and Faithful Christians: Moriscos and Catholicism in Early Modern Spain*. New Orleans: University Press of the South.

Turner, Frederick Jackson. 1994. "The Significance of the Frontier in American History," 1893. *The American Frontier: Opposing Viewpoints*, edited by Mary Ellen Jones. San Diego: Greenhaven Press.

Vincent, Bernard. 2014. "The Geography of the Morisco Expulsion: A Quantitative Study." *The Expulsion of the Moriscos from Spain: A Mediterranean Diaspora*, edited by Mercedes García Arenal and Gerard Wiegers. Leiden: Brill.

Ward, Maria. 1855. *Female Life among the Mormons: A Narrative of Many Years' Personal Experience. By the Wife of a Mormon Elder Recently from Utah*. New York: Derby and Jackson.

Welter, Barbara. 1966. "The Cult of True Womanhood, 1820–1860." *American Quarterly* 18, no. 2: 151–174.

Wood, Peter H. 2003. *Strange New Land: Africans in Colonial America*. Oxford: Oxford University Press.

4 The Writings of U.S. Hispanists and the Malleability of the U.S. Empire's Spanish Past[1]

Gregg French

In the early days of August 1898, the Spanish Governor-General of the Philippines, Fermín Jáudenes, found himself in a precarious position. Jáudenes and the Spanish troops who were stationed in Manila were surrounded on land by Filipino insurgent forces. Jáudenes' position was made more problematic by Commodore George Dewey's U.S. Asiatic Squadron, which controlled the entrance to Manila Bay and was preparing to attack the city. For over 300 years, Manila was the epicenter of Spanish colonial rule in the Pacific; however, political instability in the metropole, revolutionary movements in the Philippines, the outbreak of the Spanish–American War, and the U.S. Navy's defeat of Spain's Pacific Squadron during the Battle of Manila Bay left Jáudenes searching for a way to maintain Spain's military honor as the once vast empire crumbled around him. Defying his superiors in Madrid, Jáudenes sent a communication to Dewey in the hopes of amicably resolving the situation and avoiding the perceived embarrassment of the Spanish being forced to surrender the Philippines to their colonial subjects (Dewey 1913, 269–274).

In the lead up to the American attack on Manila, Dewey, Jáudenes, and the future U.S. Military Governor of the Philippines, General Wesley Merritt, established an informal agreement. The three men determined that the Spanish would quickly capitulate once the battle began if U.S. troops blocked the Filipino insurgents from entering the city. The "mock" battle began on the morning of August 13, and within the first few hours of the initial shots being fired by Dewey's Asiatic Squadron, Jáudenes ordered that a white flag be raised over the city. This act welcomed Merritt and his troops into Manila and enabled an interimperial transfer of power to occur in the Philippines ("Dewey and Merritt Force the Unconditional Surrender of Manila" 1898, 3; Faust 1899, 97; Dewey 1913, 72).

In the weeks following the battle, General Merritt and the Eighth Army Corps took control of the city. Merritt began using the palace of the former Spanish Governors-General as his command post, and maintained the Spanish art and décor that was left by the building's previous inhabitants.[2] Due to a lack of coherent instructions from Washington, Merritt ordered that municipal laws and local court proceedings continue as they had under Spanish rule, and he assigned U.S. troops to safeguard

DOI: 10.4324/9781003219460-4

56 Gregg French

the Catholic churches of the city (Merritt 1898; Alger 1899; Faust 1899, 121–122; *Annual Report of the Chief of the Division of Insular Affairs to the Secretary of War for the Year 1901* 1901, 6; Linn 2000, 26–30). Taken collectively, these actions indicate that U.S. military officers were aware that they were building their colonial administration on a foundation that was established by their imperial predecessors.[3]

U.S. military personnel continuously came into contact with remnants of Spain's imperial legacy as they expanded throughout Manila. One of these most noteworthy encounters occurred at the Customs House when U.S. troops discovered pieces of the unassembled Legazpi-Urdaneta Monument. Prior to the Philippine Revolution and the Spanish–American War, funds were collected from the inhabitants of the city to create a statue in honor of the sixteenth-century Spanish "founder" of Manila, Miguel López de Legazpi. It was later decided that the Augustinian friar, Andrés de Urdaneta, would be added to the monument to commemorate his introduction of Roman Catholicism to the region. The monument was created in Spain by the famed sculptor, Agustín Querol, and then shipped to the Philippines. However, Spanish colonial administrators were never able to erect the statue because of their ongoing conflicts with the Filipino insurgents and the United States. The monument was eventually assembled under the supervision of General George W. Davis in 1901 and was positioned just outside of the Intramuros and adjacent to Luneta Park. Three years after the erection of the statue, the former Civil Governor of the Philippines, William Howard Taft, summarized his views on the monument and the reason for its assembly by stating in an address at the University of Notre Dame that

> the whole, as an artistic expression, satisfies the sense of admiration that one feels in reading of the enterprise, courage, and fidelity to duty that distinguished those heroes of Spain who braved the then frightful dangers of the deep to carry Christianity and European civilization into the far-off Orient.
> (*Annual Report of Major General George W. Davis* 1903, 266; *Census of the Philippine Islands* 1905, 31; State Monuments, December 6, 1934; Kramer 2006, 211; Moran 2013, 434–474)

The events that unfolded in the lead up to the Battle of Manila and the subsequent U.S. military occupation of the Philippines can provide scholars with insights into how identities were formed, and power was projected, in a colonial space. However, these types of engagements and events were not isolated to the few years surrounding the Spanish–American War of 1898, nor did they only occur in the Philippines. Since the American Revolutionary War, relationships existed between elite representatives of the United States and Spain (French 2020, 184–196). In the early to middle portion of the nineteenth century, U.S. Hispanists popularized a discourse that celebrated the Columbian legacy and, in turn, developed connections between the United States and the Spanish past. During the decades preceding the Spanish–American War, American writers, event promoters, and politicians from areas of the United States that were once part of the Spanish Empire also celebrated Spanish art and architecture, as well as the country's imperial heritage, in an attempt to exceptionalize the American experience (Kagan 2019, 83–132). The World's Columbian Exposition of 1893 brought this fascination with Spanish history to life, in a visual sense, and further reinforced a trans-Atlantic connection between the United States and the Spanish Empire.

The exposition was held in Chicago, Illinois, to commemorate the 400-year anniversary of the "Spanish explorer" Christopher Columbus' "discovery" of the Americas. By presenting this narrative, exposition organizers at Chicago intended to draw on the Columbian legacy in an attempt to promote a fabricated national narrative that would bond the United States with the perceived superiority of European civilization. Ultimately, these individuals hoped that drawing from this Whig-based historical narrative would reconstruct the nation's collective memory, position the United States as an emerging global power, and legitimize their country's desire to launch an overseas empire (Rydell 1984, 2–4).

The opportunity to acquire this overseas empire presented itself on April 25, 1898, when President William McKinley (1902) declared war on the Spanish Empire. The outbreak of the Spanish–American War led to a resurfacing of anti-Spanish views in many quarters of the United States.[4] Both the conflict and these perceptions have overshadowed a desire that existed in the minds and actions of a group of learned Americans who yearned to draw themselves and their country close to Spain. Furthermore, these influential Americans also hoped to use the Spanish past as the foundation to legitimize their country's imperial actions. As was noted earlier, the events that occurred in the Philippines were not isolated incidents. Not only were these seeds sown in the continental United States during the prewar era, but similar events also took place in Puerto Rico, as well as the far-off outpost of Guam, both of which were previously controlled by the Spanish Empire and were transferred to the United States by the Treaty of Paris at the conclusion of the conflict ("A Treaty of Peace Between the United States and Spain" 1899).

Examined in isolation, the informal relationships that developed between representatives of the U.S. and Spanish empires in the years following the Spanish–American War, as well as the gestures toward Spain's "civilizing mission" throughout America's new imperial possessions, could be seen as a sequence of ad hoc decisions made by U.S. military officers and colonial administrators attempting to make sense of their new surroundings. Although this undeniably influenced the decision-making process, the fact that similar events and practices existed in the American transcontinental empire prior to 1898 and then occurred throughout the country's overseas possessions following the conclusion of the conflict points us to a more complex history and relationship that

58 *Gregg French*

existed within, between, and across the various manifestations of the U.S. Empire.

Previous scholars, such as Richard Kagan, Christopher Schmidt-Nowara, and M. Elizabeth Boone, have explored the American fascination with various aspects of the Spanish past and its relationship to the United States (Schmidt-Nowara 2008; Boone 2019; Kagan 2019). Others, most notably John C. Havard and Iván Jaksić, have analyzed the role that Hispanism played in influencing U.S. literature and American intellectual life (Jaksić 2007; Havard 2018). However, when we explore the actions of the representatives of the U.S. Empire from an intraimperial perspective, questions emerge about both how and why U.S. military officers and colonial administrators chose to appropriate the Spanish legacy to substantiate their imperial actions and selectively draw connections between themselves and their Spanish counterparts in the eyes of their new colonial subjects. This chapter will answer these questions by exploring how agents of the U.S. Empire were influenced by the writings of prominent, nineteenth-century Hispanist scholars, as well as how influential Americans in the periphery of the empire manipulated the Whig-based historical narratives that were promoted by these writers.[5] This perspective will provide scholars with a more nuanced understanding of the relationships that existed between representatives of the two empires, as well as the long-term implications that nineteenth-century transatlantic literary culture had on the creation of the grand narratives associated with the United States and the U.S. Empire.

This chapter will begin by providing the reader with a brief introduction to the works of Washington Irving and William Hickling Prescott, two of the most influential American writers and Hispanist scholars of the early to middle portion of the nineteenth century, as well as how their writings paved America's road to empire by influencing the American historical narrative and views toward Spain and the country's imperial legacy. More specifically, Irving and Prescott developed an American interest in both the Spanish past and influential Spanish figures by tactically portraying Spanish "discoveries" as the expansion of Christianity, entrepreneurship, and civilization; drawing attention to the Spanish military; and strategically normalizing the transfers of power that previously occurred in the Iberian Peninsula and the Americas. This chapter will then shift to the years following the conclusion of the Spanish–American War, as agents of the U.S. Empire moved from the metropole to the periphery of the empire and brought with them their earlier understandings of the trans-Atlantic bonds that existed between the United States and the Spanish past. It was in the periphery of the empire where American representatives manipulated these Whig-based historical narratives, which were popularized by Irving and Prescott. U.S. military officers and colonial administrators engaged with representatives of the Spanish Empire and paid homage to Spain's imperial legacy by strategically substituting the image of Columbus with several other representatives from the Spanish past. While doing this, they still maintained the narrative that Spain discovered the region, brought European civilization with them, and that it was now time for the U.S. Empire to build on the foundation that had been established by their imperial predecessors, as they had in the continental United States. The work will conclude by considering how the creation of these imperial discourses continue to influence the collective memories of the individuals who inhabit these colonial and postcolonial spaces in the twenty-first century.

Irving and Prescott Popularize the Spanish Foundations of the U.S. Imperial Narrative

In the years following the conclusion of the American Revolutionary War, distinguished members of American society were in search of a narrative that would legitimize their country's further colonization of North America and position the United States as a prominent nation on the world stage. These influential Americans perceived Europe as the apex of global civilization and sought a connection with a European power that would substantiate their future imperialistic desires. Their previous bond with Britain was interrupted by the Revolutionary War, so instead, learned Americans began to celebrate the "Spanish" explorer Christopher Columbus in an attempt to establish a linkage between their young republic and Europe. Interestingly, this process of manipulating historical narratives and fabricating connections between fellow imperial powers was not entirely new. Since the seventeenth century, British scholars and statesmen had venerated Columbus, and a belief existed in a segment of British society that their empire required a similar figure to validate their own imperialistic actions (Sale 1990, 328). Building from this tradition, members of the American intelligentsia, such as Philip Freneau, Joel Barlow, and Jeremy Belknap, began to refer to Columbus as a "hero," a "great man," and a "prudent, skillful, and intrepid navigator" (Freneau 1772; Belknap 1794–1798; Barlow 2005). By 1784, King's College was rechristened Columbia College; in 1791, the nation's capital was founded and named the Territory of Columbia; and in the following year, the Tammany Society unveiled a monument in New York City to celebrate their "American Museum" and the 300-year anniversary of Columbus' "discovery" ("Description of the Monument" 1792, 3; Sale 1990, 338–339; Bushman 1992, 54, 81–82). Through these literary works, speeches, name changes, and monuments, the Columbian legacy began to take root.

Despite these commemorations, few outside of the upper rungs of American society knew a great deal about Spain or the country's imperial past prior to the 1820s (Williams 1968, 135, 143). The famed American writer Washington Irving was cognizant of this void, which prompted him to publish a series of romanticized works throughout the 1820s and the 1830s that explored his belief that Spanish history was intrinsically linked to the United States through Columbus' "discoveries"

60   Gregg French

and ultimately could serve as a prototype for the young republic (Gifra-Adroher 2000, 44; Adorno 2002, 51; Kagan 2002b, 22–23). These semi-fictional publications were designed to both educate and entertain readers using a historical narrative. They became so persuasive that Columbus and similar Spanish figures were celebrated throughout the United States and the periphery of their empire for decades to come.

Irving's interest in the Spanish past developed in his youth. As a child, Irving read the series *The World Displayed* and Miguel De Cervantes' *Don Quixote*. Through his engagement with these works, he familiarized himself with not only an image of the Spanish past but also ideas surrounding Spanish honor, the Spanish military, and the voyages of Christopher Columbus. Irving arrived in Spain in 1826. By this time, he was already recognized as an esteemed author throughout the English-speaking world (Jaksić 2007, 7–8). He was invited to visit the country by the U.S. Minister to Spain, Alexander Hill Everett, who believed that Irving would be the ideal candidate to translate Martín Fernández de Navarrete's *Colección de los viajes y descubrimientos, que hicieron por mar los españoles desde fines del siglo XV* (Irving 1979, 168; Tucker 1980, 10–12). In Madrid, Irving explored the literary collections that existed in the city, most notably, the library of the American bibliophile, Obadiah Rich. By April 1826, Irving concluded that a translated version of Navarrete's work would fail to interest American readers. Instead, he decided to write his own work that would draw from Navarrete's research and present readers with a sensationalized image of the "Spanish" explorer, Christopher Columbus (Tucker 1980, 14; Adorno 2002, 63).

A History of the Life and Voyages of Christopher Columbus was published in 1828. The four-volume treatise popularized the belief that a trans-Atlantic bond existed between the United States and Spain, which emerged through Columbus' discoveries. The work made Irving the foremost expert on Spanish history in the English-speaking world, resulting in his induction into the Real Academia de la Historia in Madrid. Building on his success and the American public's interest in romanticized images of the Spanish past, Irving published *Chronicle of the Conquest of Granada* in 1829, *Voyages and Discoveries of the Companions of Columbus* in 1831, and *Tales of Alhambra* in 1832. These works went on to shape American perceptions of the United States, Spain, and the Spanish Empire for the foreseeable future (Williams 1968, 24; Adorno 2002b, 65).

Through these publications, Irving developed the image of Columbus as the father of the United States who was motivated by his entrepreneurial spirit. By positioning Columbus in this way, Irving was attempting to draw connections between the "Spanish" explorer and the commerce-driven United States, which at the time was undergoing the so-called "market revolution" of the early nineteenth century. Irving also went on to praise the support that Queen Isabella provided to Columbus, a narrative that was later picked up by the organizers of the Woman's Building at the World's Columbian Exposition of 1893.[6] Regarding religion, Irving

Whig-based Historical Narratives 61

often reinforced the anti-Catholic beliefs that permeated many segments of American culture, particularly as immigration from Ireland, southern Germany, and Italy increased over the course of the nineteenth century. However, in *Chronicle of the Conquest of Granada*, he celebrated the united Christian victory during the Reconquest of the Iberian Peninsula. This led to some influential Americans associating any form of Christianity with European civilization, illustrated by the comments that were made by William Howard Taft in 1904. This Christian victory also drew readers' attention to the past successes of the Spanish military, another common theme that future Hispanist scholars and representatives of the U.S. Empire continually returned to later in the century. Although Irving was prudent when addressing imperialism and encouraged Americans to learn from Columbus' treatment of Indigenous peoples, these themes were often selectively ignored by his readership (Irving 1831; 1835; 1836; Jaksić 2007, 15–19; Bartosik-Vélez 2014, 85). Irving's works undeniably drew attention to Spain, developed an American fascination with prominent Spanish figures, reinforced connections between Christianity and civilization, and promoted the belief that the Spanish military was a once powerful force. Collectively, these parables became the foundation that future U.S. Hispanists and influential Americans continued to promote in the following decades.

One of these U.S. Hispanists was William Hickling Prescott. Prescott grew up in the Boston area, which was the focal point of both Spanish studies and intellectual life in the early nineteenth-century United States (Wolcott 1925, ix–x). Although Prescott was initially interested in exploring Roman history, his friend and fellow Hispanist scholar, George Ticknor, encouraged him to explore the Spanish past. Ticknor became the first Smith Chair for the study of French and Spanish at Harvard University in 1819.[7] He was convinced that historical connections existed between Spain and the United States, and that these relationships would interest the American public (Williams 1968; Kagan 2002a, 9).

After over ten years of research, Prescott's *History of the Reign of Ferdinand and Isabella* went into circulation in 1838. This publication established Prescott as the first true scholar of Spanish history in the United States (Prescott 1838). In the two-volume work, Prescott commemorated Spain's imperial achievements and the Spanish monarchs who supported Columbus' voyages; later stating in a letter to Nicolaus Heinrich Julius that it would be wonderful to live in a country "whose exertion is in the past, and who may now repose in the retrospect of the great things they have already accomplished" (Prescott 1925b, 72). Prescott also believed that late fifteenth-century Spain and the nineteenth-century United States were on comparable imperial trajectories but that the rise of the Inquisition and Spain's absolute monarchy had thwarted the country's imperial mission. He went on to articulate that it was now the "young and healthy" American republic's time to continue this undertaking (Prescott 1925a, 48; 1925b, 72; Kagan 1998, 327). This

62   *Gregg French*

Whig-based interpretation of the past drew on Irving's works and was later appropriated by representatives of the United States in both the metropole and the periphery of the empire.

In the decade following Prescott's publication of *History of the Reign of Ferdinand and Isabella*, he transferred his attention to Spain's early imperial endeavors in the Americas. In 1843 and 1847, he published *History of the Conquest of Mexico* and *History of the Conquest of Peru*, respectively. The two works chronicled the Spanish conquest of the Indigenous empires of the regions and reinforced beliefs associated with the power, influence, and honor of the Spanish military. It was these perceptions that continued to reemerge and influence the interactions between representatives of the U.S. and Spanish empires both during and after their conflict in the late nineteenth century (Prescott 1843, 653). These venerations of Spain's conquests were also justified by Prescott because he believed that the Spanish brought with them European civilization and Christianity, recurring themes that were later addressed by agents of the U.S. Empire (Prescott 1843, 51–52). Despite the presentation of these tropes, in many ways, Prescott, like Irving before him, believed that imperialism may have made for an entertaining story but had dangerous repercussions (Jaksić 2007, 153). For example, in a letter to Lord Morpeth about the ongoing Mexican–American War (1846–1848), Prescott stated, "See I have been carrying on the Conquest of Peru while the Government has been making the Conquest of Mexico. But mine is the best of the two, since it cost only the shedding of ink instead of blood" (1925c, 634).

Irving's and Prescott's works formulated a discourse in the United States that was based on a fabricated trans-Atlantic imperial linkage between the United States and the Spanish past. The discourse became further cemented into the collective memory of nineteenth-century Americans as they celebrated the Spanish foundation of the United States in the lead up to the War of 1898. This collective memory traveled with U.S. military officers and colonial administrators as they attempted to justify their imperialistic actions to themselves and their colonial subjects in the periphery of their new empire. These publications also glorified the Spanish military and influential figures from the country's past. Furthermore, their writings drew connections between civilization and Christianity. All of these allegories were continuously presented throughout the U.S. Empire in the years following the Spanish–American War of 1898 and will be explained in greater detail in the following two sections of this chapter.

Adapting the Columbian Legacy in the Caribbean Basin

Throughout the nineteenth century, U.S. politicians, military officers, and businessmen were fixated on increasing American influence in the Caribbean Basin, particularly on the island of Cuba. The island

Whig-based Historical Narratives   63

represented one of the last remaining vestiges of the Spanish Empire, and multiple colonial uprisings on the island continued to be viewed by American observers as signs of imperial instability in what many perceived as the United States' emerging sphere of influence (Pérez 2008; Monroe 2011, 13–16). These opinions, as well as those of the general public, who were influenced by members of the jingoistic, yellow press, promoted a belief that the United States should go to war with Spain to liberate the Cuban people (Miller 2011). The explosion in Havana Harbor that led to the destruction of the *U.S.S. Maine* and the release of a letter that was written by the Spanish Ambassador to the United States, which criticized President William McKinley and his administration, gave members of the yellow press plenty of fodder in the months leading up to the American declaration of war. However, much of this attention was fixated on liberating the island of Cuba, rather than attempts by U.S. politicians and diplomats to avoid a conflict. Furthermore, little consideration was initially paid to Spain's other colonial possessions throughout the Caribbean Basin and the Pacific (Notes from the Spanish Legation 1790–1906; "Destruction of the War Ship Maine Was the Work of an Enemy" 1898; Dupuy de Lôme 1898).[8]

Despite the American declaration of war on April 25, 1898, it took an additional three months for General Nelson A. Miles and his troops to land on Puerto Rico (Miles 1898a). When the war began, little was known in the United States about the island or its inhabitants. Although small, disorganized rebellions broke out on Puerto Rico in 1868 and in 1897, many colonial elites were content with the autonomous government that was granted by the Spanish in 1897 (Carr 1984, 8–20; Johnson 1997, 5; Dávile-Cox 1999, 112). This relationship served as a challenging dilemma to U.S. military officers and future colonial administrators, as they attempted to substantiate a colonial regime on the island that they believed was legitimized by the United States' trans-Atlantic connection with the Spanish Empire.

Fighting between U.S. and Spanish troops lasted from July 25 until a cease fire was established on August 12. In the midst of the conflict, General Miles (1898b; 1898c) announced to the inhabitants of Ponce that "It is not our purpose to interfere with any existing laws and customs that are whole and beneficial to your people so long as they conform to the rules of military administration of order and justice." Once the fighting came to an end, Miles remained in constant contact with the Spanish Governor-General of Puerto Rico, Manuel Macías. The U.S. and Spanish militaries divided their occupation of the island, and Macías provided Miles with valuable information regarding the preexisting communication systems on the island and how best to move troops throughout the colony (Brooke 1898; Miles 1898d). This interimperial relationship was akin to those that developed in the Philippines, immediately following the American occupation of Manila. This level of affinity supports the claim that Americans acknowledged Spanish colonial administrators as their

64   *Gregg French*

imperial brethren, a perception that was influenced by the discourse that was previously developed in the United States.

Unlike Cuba, which was destined to become a pseudo-independent nation, it was initially unclear if Puerto Rico was going to be granted its independence, become a state within the American Union, or remain a colonial possession of the U.S. Empire (Congress of the United States 2011, 73–74). The establishment of the Organic Act of 1900 provided the inhabitants of the island with Puerto Rican citizenship and granted them a civil government; however, it also positioned the island as an American colonial possession (Congress of the United States 1900). The decision to make Puerto Rico a colony of the U.S. Empire resulted in American military officers and colonial administrators Americanizing aspects of the island, such as its legal system. These actions received pushback from the island's inhabitants, who began to reminisce about the affinity they had for Spanish rule (Fernandez 1996, 7; Jimenez de Wagenheim 1998, 218–219). In turn, the American colonial government looked to the education system on the island as a way to draw connections between the United States, Spain, and the inhabitants of Puerto Rico. This was initially done by shifting the Columbian legacy from the United States to the periphery of the empire, which would enable both teachers and colonial administrators to indoctrinate young Puerto Ricans, in much the same way that many Americans had been convinced of the national myth that had been started by U.S. Hispanists earlier in the century. American colonial administrators also believed that this process of adapting the Columbian legacy would draw positive imperial connections between the United States and Spain, ultimately justifying the existence of the U.S. Empire to their new colonial subjects.

General Guy Vernon Henry appointed the former U.S. Commissioner of Education, John Eaton Jr., as the superintendent of the education system on the island ("Death of Gen. Eaton" 1906). In Puerto Rico, Eaton and the American Insular Board for Education attempted to borrow from the works of Irving and Prescott by encouraging pedagogical practices that integrated the Columbian legacy into both English language and history lessons (Insular Board of Education 1898–1945; Navarro 2002, 140). Additionally, in 1903, commemorations were encouraged by the Board of Education to honor the 410th anniversary of Columbus' landing on Puerto Rico. However, unlike the events that occurred in Chicago ten years earlier, the Puerto Rican people displayed little interest in the Columbian legacy. This forced American colonial administrators to consider new ways of adapting the Whig-based historical narrative that had been so well tested in the United States (Morris 1995, 23–28).

What Eaton and his fellow colonial administrators initially failed to realize was that many of the inhabitants of Puerto Rico, particularly members of the Federalist Party and those of Spanish descent, were dissatisfied with U.S. colonial rule, and in turn, they began to reminisce about the limited rights offered to them by the Spanish Empire (Cabán 1999, 167–186). While under Spanish rule, many of these individuals gravitated to the image of Columbus, as Americans had throughout the nineteenth century. However, following the American occupation of the island, many Puerto Ricans began to perceive the explorer as a representation of U.S. colonial rule, and in response, they rejected him. Instead, they began to draw themselves closer to the first Spanish Governor of Puerto Rico, Ponce de León. They did this by celebrating the 400-year anniversary of the start of his reign over the island in 1908. Under Spanish rule, León had been perceived by the inhabitants of Puerto Rico as the conqueror of the island; however, the hope was that by venerating him under American rule, Puerto Ricans could celebrate their connection to Spain and present themselves as civilized, Hispanized subjects. This movement became known as hispanoamericanismo and emerged in direct opposition to American incursions into Latin American in the decades following the conclusion of the Spanish–American War of 1898 (Pike 1971; Antonio Barreto 2009, 147–48; Schmidt-Nowara 2009, 231–235; Boone 2019, 121).

The American colonial administration responded by manipulating the Whig-based historical narratives that had been promoted by U.S. Hispanists during the nineteenth century. This was done by replacing Columbus with León but still maintaining the themes associated with Christianity, civilization, and a connection with the Spanish past, which were also the goals of the Puerto Ricans. This was not an entirely new practice that U.S. colonial administrators developed in the Caribbean Basin. In reality, León had previously been celebrated in the United States as the first European to come into contact with the present-day state of Florida. Additionally, U.S. colonial administrators in both Guam and the Philippines supplanted Columbus for a variety of different historical figures, most notably, the "Spanish explorer" Ferdinand Magellan ("The Spanish Discoverers" 1896, 20).

A series of celebrations were held to commemorate the first Spanish governor of Puerto Rico and the establishment of the Roman Catholic Archdiocese of San Juan in 1912 and 1913. These events were highlighted by a Spanish statue of León receiving a new base from the Insular Treasury and being moved to the newly renamed Ponce de León Avenue (Joint Resolution No. 10 1913). American, Spanish, and Puerto Rican dignitaries attended these events, reinforcing a connection between the three peoples. These events illustrate the malleability of the narratives that were created by U.S. Hispanists and then appropriated by representatives of the U.S. Empire, as they attempted to reconstruct the collective memories of the Puerto Rican people. This chapter will now shift to the Pacific, as these Whig-based historical narratives, which were initially rooted in the Atlantic World, were once again adapted to suit local conditions in Guam and the Philippines.

66 *Gregg French*

"Rendering Homage" to the Spanish Past in Guam and the Philippines[9]

Similar to Puerto Rico, few individuals in the United States knew a great deal about Guam or the Philippines at the outset of the Spanish–American War. In search of credible information, Commodore George Dewey was only able to locate an outdated naval report from 1876, and when General Wesley Merritt's aid requested information from the War Department, he received a rather nondescript encyclopedia entry about the Philippine Islands (*Military Notes on the Philippines* 1898). Furthermore, in 1898, the U.S. Army was made up of less than 30,000 soldiers, as well as many aging Civil War Era officers, who were unprepared to wage a multifront war and colonial occupation across the Caribbean Basin and the Pacific. To put this number into perspective, the Spanish had approximately 250,000 troops stationed throughout the Caribbean Basin and the Pacific (Coffman 1986; Linn 2000, 3–5; Clodfelter 2017, 254–256). Undermanned and poorly informed, U.S. military officers and colonial administrators searched for familiarities in the periphery of their new empire. Drawing from their collective memories and the discourses that had been created by U.S. Hispanists, they located these familiarities in their imperial predecessors. However, rather than using the trans-Atlantic Columbian legacy, representatives of the U.S. Empire venerated a variety of different "Spanish" figures in Guam and the Philippines, such as Miguel López de Legazpi; Andrés de Urdaneta; and, most notably, Ferdinand Magellan.

On June 20, 1898, U.S. Navy Captain Henry Glass arrived off the coast of Guam and notified the Spanish Governor, Juan Marina, that the United States and Spain were at war. News from abroad had failed to reach the colonial outpost for several months, and in turn, Marina and his 110 insular troops were unprepared to engage in a battle with the U.S. Navy. Ultimately, Spanish forces surrendered the island to the United States on the following day without a military engagement taking place ("Guam" 1900; Cook 1917, 40–41; "History of First Regiment California"; Rogers 1995, 110).

On December 23, 1898, President William McKinley placed the Department of the Navy in charge of the island of Guam. Until an American naval governor could arrive, the former Spanish treasurer, José Sixto, was left in control of the island. U.S. naval officers later created an advisory committee, which was made up of Guam's local Hispanicized elites (Cook 1917, 42). Captain Richard Leary became the first American naval governor of the island in August 1899. Despite several missteps, including a failure to acknowledge the attachments that the inhabitants of the region had with Spanish customs and practices, he still maintained Spanish municipal laws and the Spanish judicial system on the island (Leary 1897–1915; *Annual Report of the Naval Governor of the Island of Guam* 1906, 23, 37).

Over time, Spanish customs and practices were slowly replaced by those imposed by the U.S. Navy. Nevertheless, these agents of the U.S. Empire continued to search for ways to connect themselves with their imperial predecessors in the region. This was done by preserving many of the Spanish names of areas, buildings, and streets in the capital of Agaña, such as the Plaza de España, Fort Santa Agueda, and the domed cathedral of Dulce Nombre de María (Roberts 1995, 133). American colonial administrators also continued the process of gravitating to influential "Spanish" figures who they perceived as the first individuals to "discover" the region. In the case of Guam, this meant celebrating Ferdinand Magellan. However, they were not alone in this pursuit. Similar to events that occurred in both Puerto Rico and the Philippines, members of the local, Hispanicized elite also hoped to draw connections between themselves and the Spanish past, in an attempt to present themselves as civilized individuals to their new colonial overseers.

In 1925, U.S. Naval Captain Alfred Winsor Brown oversaw the creation of the Guam Teachers' Association (Blauch and Reid 1939, 187–188). The following year, the organization erected a monument to Ferdinand Magellan in the village of Umatac, where it is believed that the "Spanish" explorer landed in 1521. The Magellan Monument became the focal point for Magellan Day celebrations, which became an annual event that was well attended by prominent local businessmen, U.S. naval officers, and representatives from American companies that frequented the region, such as Pan American Airways. One of the most celebrated Magellan Days occurred on March 6, 1940. The U.S. Aide for Civil Administration, Commander S.D. Jupp, oversaw the event, which included a naval maneuver from the Boy Scouts of America, the singing of songs, and the reciting of a story by the local children of the area, which described Magellan's voyage and his "discovery" of Guam (Edgar 1940, 7–8, 16). These events were encouraged by U.S. naval officers in the area and were clearly rooted in a Whig-based historical narrative, which had been inspired by the writings of nineteenth-century U.S. Hispanists.

As was addressed earlier, U.S. military officers encountered many aspects of the Spanish past as they moved throughout Manila. This continued as American troops shifted their focus outside of the city and began to experience armed resistance from Filipino insurgent forces. Fighting began in February 1899 and did not end in the northern portion of the archipelago until July 1902.[10] Throughout the conflict, American troops borrowed from the policies, practices, and knowledge that they were able to acquire from the remaining Spanish military personnel in the region. The U.S. military also rescued Spanish troops, friars, and families that were being held as prisoners by the Filipino insurgent forces (Headquarters Bell's Expeditionary Brigade 1900; Headquarters Schwan's Expeditionary Brigade Report 1900). Similar events occurred in the Southern Philippines, as General John C. Bates attempted to establish colonial rule over the Muslim inhabitants of the island of Mindanao and

68 *Gregg French*

the Sulu Archipelago. Most notably, the first U.S. treaty with the Sultan of Sulu was heavily influenced by the knowledge that Bates acquired from his study of the earlier Spanish agreements with the representatives of the region (Bates 1900; *Treaty with the Sultan of Sulu* 1900, 3–5). Despite the Spanish–American War, the situational relationships that developed between U.S. and Spanish military officers throughout the Caribbean Basin and Pacific speak to a deeper reverence that dates back to Spanish support during the American Revolutionary War, as well as ongoing interest and respect for the Spanish military, which was promoted by the works of Irving and Prescott.

When it came to legitimizing U.S. rule in the Philippines, American colonial administrators continuously drew from the Whig-based historical narratives that were developed by U.S. Hispanists. However, the image of Christopher Columbus was replaced in the Philippines by a variety of different "Spanish" figures. As was noted in the introduction, a statue of Miguel López de Legazpi and Andrés de Urdaneta was erected in 1901. Three years later at the St. Louis World's Fair, a replica of the Anda Monument in Manila, which was built to celebrate the former Spanish Governor-General of the Philippines, Simón de Anda y Salazar, was erected by American organizers as part of the Philippine Exhibit (*Report of the Philippine Exposition Board to the Louisiana Purchase Exposition* 1904). However, much like on the island of Guam, the "discoverer" of the Philippines, Ferdinand Magellan, played the most influential role as American colonial administrators attempted to draw connections between themselves and their imperial predecessors in the region.

Most notably, in the lead up to the 400-year anniversary of Magellan's arrival in the Philippines, the colonial government began preparations for the Manila Carnival. The carnival was an annual event that was designed to celebrate the bonds that existed between the American and Filipino people. From an American perspective, it was also an opportunity to display the evolutionary progress of the Filipinos at the hands of American colonial administrators. Furthermore, for the Christianized Filipinos who helped American colonial administrators organize the event, it was a chance to draw connections between themselves and the civilizational narrative promoted by their colonial overseers (Karrow 1989; Torres 2010).

The Manila Carnival of 1921 was entitled the Carnaval Magallanico and was held on both Wallace Field and in the Luneta Auditorium to celebrate the influence that Spanish, American, and the Filipino people had "upon the formation of Philippine civilization." During the event, an elaborate play involving over 100 actors re-created Magellan's "discovery" of the Philippines and Legazpi's friendship with a sixteenth-century regional monarch in the archipelago, Rajah Soliman. The celebrations also included the playing of the Spanish, American, and Filipino national anthems by the Philippine Constabulary Band; a coronation ball for the Carnival Queen; and an address from the Associate Justice of the Philippine Supreme Court, George A. Malcolm (Philippine Carnival Association 1921). In his speech, which he entitled "Democracy in the Philippines—Magellan to Dewey," Malcolm drew on the Whig-based historical narratives that had been promoted by U.S. Hispanists throughout the nineteenth century and were being reinforced by the celebrations to honor Magellan's "discovery" of the Philippines. Similar to the comments made by William Howard Taft when he reminisced about the erection of the Legazpi-Urdaneta Monument nearly two decades earlier, Malcolm spoke of the "steady advance of civilization," which was promoted by the implementation of "Latin civilization" on the region. He also went on to state that it was vital to "give unstinted credit to the varied and preeminent accomplishments of our friends, the Spanish people, and to render homage to the heroic navigator and discover Ferdinand Magellan" (Malcolm 1921, 312–333). These comments reinforced the narrative that was being promoted by the overseers of the Manila Carnival of 1921 and points to the continuing influence of the works of U.S. Hispanists, nearly 100 years after Irving's publication of *A History of the Life and Voyages of Christopher Columbus.*

Conclusion

As I write this chapter in July 2020, many societies throughout the world appear to be at a crossroads. In the fallout of the ongoing COVID-19 pandemic and the deaths of various people of color at the hands of police officers, social justice groups and their allies have taken to the streets to challenge institutional racism and the state-sponsored representations of imperial nostalgia that dominate their landscapes (Francis 2012, 252–276; Hill et al. 2020). However, these are by no means new movements. In 1992, Indigenous groups in the United States challenged celebrations associated with the 500-year anniversary of Christopher Columbus' "discovery" of the Americas by establishing Indigenous Peoples' Day and holding a variety of protests throughout the country (Arnold 1992). In 2015, the Rhodes Must Fall movement successfully advocated for the removal of a statue of Cecil Rhodes at the University of Cape Town, which protesters believed was a veneration of British imperialism (Hall 2015). While more recently in the United States, over 70 Confederate statues have been taken down from public spaces, since the start of 2017 (Berkowitz and Blanco 2020). Collectively, these movements can provide us with insight into how individuals within a region perceive both their varying and collective histories. They can also inform our understanding of the connections that exist between a region's colonial past and the imperial discourses that have been established over time in an attempt to justify the actions of state officials and their supporters.

Over the past few decades in the United States, there has been a challenge to the power of the Whig-based historical narratives that developed in

70 Gregg French

the country during the nineteenth century and were appropriated to justify the United States' imperial actions. For example, states throughout the American Union are choosing to celebrate Indigenous Peoples' Day, rather than Columbus Day, and statues of the "Spanish" explorer are being removed from public spaces by both protesters and government officials (Ashmelash 2020). More recently, and perhaps in less documented events, statues of Juan de Oñate and Junípero Serra have been removed from public spaces in New Mexico and California, respectively; while in the Melbourne Beach area of Florida, a monument to Ponce de León was vandalized in June 2020 (Burnett 2020; CBSLA Staff 2020; Tribou 2020). It is difficult to determine if these protesters were familiar with the works of nineteenth-century U.S. Hispanists and how the narratives that these writers created were used to legitimize U.S. imperialism, but what we do know is that individuals in the United States are recognizing the country's colonial past and are beginning to ask questions about why these statues were erected in the first place. If they are asking these questions, they soon may come to the realization that the works of Irving and Prescott influenced their construction.

In the United States' existing overseas possessions and the Philippines, there has been a mixed response to the removal of imperial statues, as well as the events that continue to pay homage to the regions' imperial pasts. In the Commonwealth of Puerto Rico, which continues to exist as a colonial territory of the U.S. Empire, peaceful protests by Indigenous and Afro-Caribbean activists occurred in July 2020. These protests were designed to draw attention to the statues of Christopher Columbus and Ponce de León that continue to exist in San Juan, the capital of the island. However, these are not the only remaining statues that commemorate Spain's colonization of the island. For example, most recently, the sculpture entitled *Birth of the New World* was completed in 2016 and stands at a height of 360-feet over the municipality of Arecibo, on the northern coast of the island (Valentin 2020). The protests mentioned earlier, as well as the continued existence of these statues in Puerto Rico, illustrate the undeniably complex relationship between the island's colonial past and its ongoing position as a U.S. territory, an eerily similar predicament that Puerto Ricans were grappling with at the outset of the U.S. occupation of the island in 1898.

Over the past several decades, the inhabitants of Guam have begun to challenge their colonial heritage, as well as the island's ongoing existence as a territorial possession of the U.S. Empire. Magellan Day was renamed Guam History and Chamorro Heritage Day in 1970, and although nearly 100 performers still reenact Magellan's landing on an annual basis, more recent versions of the event conclude with the "Spaniards" setting fire to the huts of the Umatac villagers who provided aid to the explorer and his crew, a significantly different series of events than those of the Magellan Day celebrations that were described earlier (Taruc 2020). Furthermore, a commission has been established by the local government on the island

Whig-based Historical Narratives 71

to decide how the inhabitants of Guam will participate in the 500th anniversary of Magellan's attempt to circumnavigate the globe in 1521. Commission members have stated that it is essential that the people of Guam have a voice in these events and that with this voice they have the opportunity to provide agency to the Chamorro people. Additionally, commission member and former University of Guam professor, Robert Underwood, believes that the celebration will offer a unique opportunity for representatives of the island to form bilateral relationships with national governments, rather than the U.S. government continuing to speak on behalf of their territorial possession (Limtiaco 2019).

The ongoing challenges to the Whig-based narratives that were influenced by the works of U.S. Hispanists and promoted by U.S. colonial administrators in Guam and Puerto Rico stand in somewhat of a contrast to the existence of Spain's imperial legacy in the Philippines. Although the populist President of the Philippines, Rodrigo Duterte, proposed in February 2019 that the country be renamed, in an attempt to cut ties with its Spanish past, it seems that many Filipinos do not support this initiative (Winn 2019). On the contrary, a limited number of individuals have openly objected to the continued existence of the Legazpi-Urdaneta Monument, few have protested in favor of racial justice, and it appears that representatives of the country are working with their counterparts in Portugal and Spain to jointly plan the celebrations associated with the 500th anniversary of Magellan's attempted circumnavigation of the globe and subsequent "discovery" of the Philippines (Ocamp 2020). However, similar to events in Guam, Filipino organizers will be attempting to establish their own agency by also venerating Lapulapu, the leader of the Mactan people who resisted Spanish colonial rule (Yambo 2020).

It is difficult to predict what will ultimately happen to the numerous monuments of Spanish imperial figures that dot the landscape of the United States, Puerto Rico, Guam, and the Philippines, as well as how the commemorations associated with Magellan's 500th anniversary will be received in 2021. Looking forward even further, it is equally challenging to forecast how the U.S. Empire will change over the forthcoming decades, and what that will mean for Puerto Rico and Guam. What we do know is that the imperial relationships that existed, and continue to endure, in these regions, were undeniably influenced by the writings of U.S. Hispanists, whose Whig-based historical narratives established the trans-Atlantic foundation of the U.S. Empire for many U.S. military officers and colonial administrators at the turn of the twentieth century.

Notes

1 Portions of this chapter were influenced by my dissertation, *The Foundations of Empire Building: Spain's Legacy and the American Imperial Identity.*
2 This was a common practice for American military personnel in the Philippines. For more information: Worcester (1898).

72   Gregg French

3 For more information: Kramer (2011, 125–144); Schumacher (2004, 59–76).
4 Anti-Spanish views in the United States were often associated with the Black Legend narrative. For more information: Juderías (2007); DeGuzmán (2005).
5 For more information on Whig history: Howe (1979).
6 For more information: Handy (1893, 140); *Official Guide to the World's Columbus Exposition* (1893, 109).
7 The Smith Chair for the study of French and Spanish was established in 1815, but Ticknor did not commence with his responsibilities until 1819.
8 These politicians and diplomats included President William McKinley; the U.S. Minister to Spain, Stewart L. Woodford; and the Assistant Secretary of State, William R. Day.
9 See Malcolm (1921).
10 Fighting continued between U.S. troops and the Muslim inhabitants of the Southern Philippines until 1913.

Works Cited

Adorno, Rolena. 2002. "Washington Irving's Romantic Hispanism and Its Columbian Legacies." *Spain in America: The Origins of Hispanism in the United States*. edited by Richard L. Kagan. Urbana: University of Illinois Press, 49–105.

Alger, Russell A. Letter to Elwell Stephen Otis. April 15, 1899. National Archives and Records Administration (NARA), Record Group (RG) 350, Stack Area 150, Entry 5—General Classified Files, 1898–1945, Box 88.

Annual Report of the Chief of the Division of Insular Affairs to the Secretary of War for the Year 1901. 1901. Washington, D.C.: Government Printing Office.

Annual Report of Major General George W. Davis, United States Army Commanding Division of the Philippines from October 1, 1902 to July 26, 1903. 1903. Manila, Philippine Islands: Headquarters, Division of the Philippines.

Annual Report of the Naval Governor of the Island of Guam for the Fiscal Year Ending June 30, 1905. 1906. Washington, D.C.: Government Printing Office.

Arnold, Michael S. 1992. "Protesters Stop Mock Landing of Columbus." *Los Angeles Times*, October 12, 1992.

Ashmelash, Leah. 2020. "Statues of Christopher Columbus Are Being Dismounted Across the Country." *CNN News*, June 11, 2020.

Barreto, Amilcar Antonio. 2009. "Enlightened Tolerance or Cultural Capitulation? Contesting Notions of American Identity." *Colonial Crucible: Empire in the Making of the Modern American State*. edited by Alfred W. McCoy and Francisco A. Scarano. Madison: University of Wisconsin Press, 145–150.

Barlow, Joel. 2005. *Visions of Columbus: The Columbiad*. Ann Arbor: Scholarly Publishing Office, University Library, University of Michigan.

Bartosik-Vélez, Elise. 2014. *The Legacy of Christopher Columbus in the Americas: New Nations and a Transatlantic Discourse of Empire*. Nashville: Vanderbilt University Press.

Bates, J. C. 1900. Report, Headquarters First Division, Eight Army Corps, March 8, NARA, RG 395, Department of Pacific and 8th Army Corps, Reports of Operations, April 1899–April 1900, Box 2.

Whig-based Historical Narratives 73

Belknap, Jeremy. 1794–1798. *American Biography: An Historical Account of Those Persons Who Have Been Distinguished in America.* Boston: Isaiah Thomas and Ebenezer T. Andrews. Faust's Statue, No. 45, Newbury Street.

Berkowitze, Bonnie and Adrian Blanco. 2020. "Confederate Monuments Are Falling, but Hundreds Still Stand. Here's Where." *The Washington Post,* July 2, 2020.

Blauch, Lloyd B. and Charles F. Reid. 1939. *Public Education in the Territories and Outlying Possessions—Staff Study Number 16.* Washington, D.C.: United States Government Printing Office.

Boone, M. Elizabeth. 2019. *The Spanish Element of Our Nationality: Spain and America at the World's Fair and Centennial Celebrations, 1876–1915.* University Park: Pennsylvania State University Press.

Brooke, John R. 1898. Letter to Major General Miles, Guayama, Puerto Rico. August 29, 1898. NARA, RG 108, Entry 121, Box 1, File: 127—Headquarters of the Army in the Field, May 28–July 7, 1898.

Burnett, John. 2020. "Statues of Conquistador Juan de Oñate Come Down as New Mexico Wrestles with History." *National Public Radio,* July 13, 2020.

Bushman, Claudia L. 1992. *America Discovers Columbus: How an Italian Explorer Became an American Hero.* Hanover, New Hampshire: University Press of New England.

Cabán, Pedro A. 1999. *Constructing a Colonial People: Puerto Rico and the United States, 1898–1932.* Boulder: Westview Press.

Carr, Raymond. 1984. *Puerto Rico: A Colonial Experiment.* New York: New York University Press.

CBSLA Staff. 2020. "Ventura Removes Controversial Junipero Serra Statue Following Protest." *CBS News Los Angeles,* July 23, 2020.

Census of the Philippine Islands: Taken Under the Direction of the Philippine Commission in 1903—Volume I. 1905. Washington, D.C.: United States Bureau of the Census.

Clodfelter, Michael. 2017. *Warfare and Armed Conflicts: A Statistical Encyclopedia of Casualty and Other Figures, 1492–2015—Fourth Edition.* Jefferson: McFarland.

Coffman, Edward M. 1986. *The Old Army: A Portrait of the American Army in Peacetime, 1784–1898.* New York: Oxford University Press.

Congress of the United States. 2011. "The Teller Amendment." *Latin America and the United States: A Documentary History.* 2nd edition. edited by Robert H. Holden and Eric Zolov. New York: Oxford University Press, 73–74.

Congress of the United States. 1900. "An Act Temporarily to Provide Revenues and a Civil Government for Porto Rico, and Other Purposes." April 12, 1900. https://scholarscollaborative.org/PuertoRico/items/show/103

Cook, M.G. 1917. *The Island of Guam.* Washington, D.C.: Government Printing Office.

Dávile-Cox, Emma. 1999. "Puerto Rico in the Hispanic-Cuban-American War: Re-assessing 'the Picnic.'" *The Crisis of 1898: Colonial Redistribution and Nationalist Mobilization.* edited by Angel Smith and Emma Dávile-Cox. New York: St. Martin's Press Incorporated, 96–127.

"Death of Gen. Eaton: Was Formerly U.S. Commissioner of Education." 1906. *The Evening Star,* February 9, 1906, p. 20.

DeGuzmán, Maria. 2005. *Spain's Long Shadow: The Black Legend, Off-Whiteness, and Anglo-American Empire.* Minneapolis: University of Minnesota Press.

74 *Gregg French*

"Description of the Monument." 1792. *The Baltimore Evening Post*, October 25, 1792, p. 3.

"Destruction of the War Ship Maine Was the Work of an Enemy." 1898. *New York Journal*, February 17, 1898, p. 1.

"Dewey and Merritt Force the Unconditional Surrender of Manila." 1898. *The San Francisco Call*, August 16, 1898, p. 3.

Dewey, George. 1913. *Autobiography of George Dewey: Admiral of the Navy*. New York: Charles Scribner's Sons.

Dupuy de Lôme, Enrique. 1898. "Facsimile of Letter Written by the Spanish Minister." February 9, 1898.

Edgar, Harold B. 1940. *The Guam Recorder*. April, 1940.

Faust, Karl Irving Faust. 1899. *Campaigning in the Philippines*. San Francisco: The Hicks-Judd Company Publishers.

Fernandez, Ronald. 1996. *The Disenchanted Island: Puerto Rico and the United States in the Twentieth Century*. Westport: Praeger Publishers.

Francis, Margot. 2012. "The Imaginary Indian: Unpacking the Romance of Domination." *Power and Everyday Practices*. edited by Deborah Brock, Rebecca Raby, and Mark P. Thomas. Toronto, Ontario: Nelson Education Limited, 252–276.

Freneau, Philip Morin. 1772. *The Rising Glory of America*. Philadelphia: Printed by Joseph Crukshank for R. Aitkin.

French, Gregg. 2017. *The Foundations of Empire Building: Spain's Legacy and the American Imperial Identity*. PhD Dissertation, University of Western Ontario.

————. 2020. "Spain and the Birth of the American Republic: Establishing Lasting Bonds of Kinship in the Revolutionary Era." *Spain and the American Revolution: New Approaches and Perspectives*. edited by Gabriel Paquette and Gonzalo M. Quintero Saravia. New York: Routledge, 184–196.

Gifra-Adroher, Pere. 2000. *Between History and Romance: Travel Writing on Spain in the Early Nineteenth-Century United States*. Mississauga: Associated University Presses Incorporated.

"Guam." 1900. NARA, RG 80, General Correspondence, February 12, 1900, 1897–1915, Box 384.

Hall, Martin. 2015. "The Symbolic Statue Dividing a South African University." *BBC News*, March 25, 2015.

Handy, Moses P. 1893. *The Official Directory of the World's Columbian Exposition: A Reference Book*. Chicago: W.B. Conkey Company.

Havard, John C. 2018. *Hispanicism and Early US Literature: Spain, Mexico, Cuba, and the Origins of U.S. National Identity*. Tuscaloosa: University of Alabama Press.

Headquarters Bell's Expeditionary Brigade, First Division, Eight Army Corps. 1900. NARA, RG 395, Department of Pacific and 8th Army Corps, Reports of Operations, April 1899–April 1900, March 3, 1900, Box 2.

Headquarters Schwan's Expeditionary Brigade Report. 1900. NARA, RG 395, Department of Pacific and 8th Army Corps, Reports of Operations, April 1899–April 1900, February 8, 1900, Box 1.

Hill, Evan et al. 2020. "How George Floyd Was Killed in Policy Custody." *The New York Times*, August 13, 2020.

"History of First Regiment California: Volunteer Infantry." United States Army Heritage and Education Center, Spanish-American War Veterans Survey Collection, Alfred R. Dole Collection—Box 1, Folder 2.

Whig-based Historical Narratives 75

Howe, Daniel Walker. 1979. *The Political Culture of the American Whigs.* Chicago: University of Chicago Press.

Insular Board of Education. "Teaching Bulletin, Number Two." NARA, RG 350, Stack Area 150, Entry 5—General Classified Files, 1898–1945, Box 78.

Irving, Washington. 1979. "Letter to Alexander H. Everett, January 31, 1826." *Washington Irving: Letters—Volume II, 1823–1838.* edited by Ralph M. Aderman, Herbert L. Kleinfield, and Jenifer S. Banks. Boston: Twayne Publishers.

———. 1828. *A History of the Life and Voyages of Christopher Columbus.* London: John Murray.

———. 1831. *Voyages and Discoveries of the Companions of Columbus.* Philadelphia: Carey and Lea.

———. 1835. *Tales of the Alhambra.* London: Richard Bentley.

———. 1836. *Legends of the Conquest of Spain.* London: John Murray.

Jaksić, Iván. 2007. *The Hispanic World and American Intellectual Life, 1820–1880.* New York: Palgrave Macmillan.

Jimenez de Wagenheim, Olga. 1998. *Puerto Rico: An Interpretive History from Pre-Columbian Times to 1900.* Princeton: Markus Wiener Publishers.

Juderías, Julián. 2007. *La Leyenda Negra: Estudios Acerca del Concepto de España en el Extranjero.* Madrid: Ediciones Altas.

Johnson, Roberta Ann. 1997. *Puerto Rico: Commonwealth or Colony?* New Haven: Yale University Press.

Joint Resolution No. 10. 1913. NARA, RG 350, Stack Area 150, Entry 5—General Classified Files, 1898–1945, March 13, 1913, Box 954.

Kagan, Richard L. 1998. "Prescott's Paradigm: American Historical Scholarship and the Decline of Spain." *Imagined Histories: American Historians Interpret the Past.* edited by Anthony Molho and Gordon S. Wood. Princeton: Princeton University Press, 324–348.

Kagan, Richard L. 2002a. "Introduction." *Spain in America: The Origins of Hispanism in the United States.* edited by Richard L. Kagan. Urbana: University of Illinois Press, 1–19.

———. 2002b. "From Noah to Moses: The Genesis of Historical Scholarship on Spain in the United States." *Spain in America: The Origins of Hispanism in the United States.* edited by Richard L. Kagan. Urbana: University of Illinois Press, 21–48.

———. 2019. *The Spanish Craze: America's Fascination with the Hispanic World, 1776–1939.* Lincoln, Nebraska: University of Nebraska Press.

Karrow, Stanley. 1989. *In Our Image: America's Empire in the Philippines.* New York: Random House.

Kramer, Paul A. 2006. *The Blood of Government: Race, Empire, the United States, and the Philippines.* Chapel Hill: University of North Carolina Press.

Kramer, Paul A. 2011. "Historias Transimperiales: Raíces Españolas del Estado Colonial Estadounidense en Filipinas." *Filipnas, Un País Entre Dos Imperios.* edited by María Dolores Elizalde and Josep M. Delgado. Barcelona, Spain: Edicions Bellaterra, 125–144.

Leary, Richard P. 1897–1915. "Proclamation to the Inhabitants of Guam." NARA, RG 80, General Correspondence, 1897–1915, Box 384.

Limtiaco, Steve. 2019. "Guam to Have Voice in 500th Anniversary of Magellan Voyage." *Pacific Daily News*, July 5, 2019.

Linn, Brian McAllister. 2000. *The Philippine War, 1899–1902.* Lawrence: University of Kansas Press.

76 Gregg French

Malcolm, George A. 1921. "Democracy in the Philippines—Magellan to Dewey." Bentley Historical Library—University of Michigan, George A. Malcolm Papers, 1896–1965, Box 10, Bound Volume: *Occasional Addresses and Articles—Volume II*, 312–333.

McKinley, William. "Declaration of War (1898)." 1902. *A Compilation of the Messages and Papers of the President.* edited by James D. Richardson. Washington, D.C.: Library of Congress.

Merritt, Wesley. 1898. "General Merritt's Proclamation of Occupation of Manila," Headquarters, Department of the Pacific, August 14, 1898.

Miles, Nelson A. 1898a. Letter to the Secretary of War, Pto. Guanica, Puerto Rico, July 25, 1898, United States Army Heritage and Education Center, Nelson A. Miles Papers, Spanish-American War—1898, Box 5, Folder: Puerto Rico Campaign, May–September 1898.

———. 1898b. Letter to Captain Francis J. Higginson, En Route to Puerto Rico, July 22, 1898, United States Army Heritage and Education Center, Nelson A. Miles Papers, Spanish-American War—1898, Box 5, Folder: Puerto Rico Campaign, May–September 1898;

———. 1898c. "Proclamation. Headquarters of the Army of the United States," Ponce, Puerto Rico, July 28, 1898, United States Army Heritage and Education Center, Nelson A. Miles Papers, Spanish-American War—1898, Box 5, Folder: Puerto Rico Campaign, May–September 1898.

———. 1898d. Letter to Captain General Macias, Port Ponce, Puerto Rico, September 1, 1898, NARA, RG 108, Entry 118, Box 1, File: 37—Letters Sent, Headquarters of the Army in the Field, July 7–September 7, 1898.

Military Notes on the Philippines. 1898. Washington, D.C.: Government Printing Office.

Miller, Bonnie. 2011. *From Liberation to Conquest: The Visual and Popular Cultures of the Spanish-American War of 1898.* Amherst: University of Massachusetts Press.

Monroe, James 2011. "The Monroe Doctrine." *Latin America and the United States: A Documentary History.* 2nd edition. edited by Robert H. Holden and Eric Zolov. New York: Oxford University Press, 13–15.

Moran, Katherine D. 2013. "Catholicism and the Making of the U.S. Pacific." *The Journal of the Gilded Age and Progressive Era* 12, no. 4: 434–474.

Morris, Nancy. 1995. *Puerto Rico: Culture, Politics, and Identity.* Westport: Praeger Publishers.

Navarro, José-Manuel. 2002. *Creating Tropical Yankees: Social Science Textbooks and U.S. Ideological Control in Puerto Rico, 1898–1908.* New York: Routledge.

Notes from the Spanish Legation in the U.S. to the Department of State. 1790–1906. NARA, RG 59, www.archives.gov/historical-docs/todays-doc/index.html?dod-date=209

Ocampo, Ambeth R. 2020. "Erasing, Understanding History." *Inquirer.Net*, June 24, 2020.

Official Guide to the World's Columbian Exposition. 1893. Chicago: The Columbian Guide Company.

Pérez, Louis A. 2008. *Cuba in the American Imagination: Metaphor and the Imperial Ethos.* Chapel Hill: University of North Carolina Press.

Philippine Carnival Association: Magallanes Carnival and Exposition. 1921. *Official Program: Magallanes Carnival and Exposition—January 29th to February 6th, 1921.* Special Collections Library—University of Michigan.

Whig-based Historical Narratives   77

Pike, Fredrick B. 1971. *Hispanismo, 1898–1936: Spanish Conservatives and Liberals and their Relations with Spanish America*. South Bend: University of Notre Dame Press.

Prescott, William Hickling. 1838. *History of the Reign of Ferdinand and Isabella*. New York: A.L. Burt Publishers.

Prescott, William H. 1843. *History of the Conquest of Mexico and History of the Conquest of Peru*. New York: Modern Library.

———. 1925a. Letter to Arthur Middleton, January 10, 1839. *The Correspondence of William Hickling Prescott, 1833–1847*. edited by Roger Wolcott. Boston: Houghton Mifflin Company, 47–48.

———. 1925b. Letter to Nicolaus Heinrich Julius, May 20, 1839. *The Correspondence of William Hickling Prescott, 1833–1847*. edited by Roger Wolcott. Boston: Houghton Mifflin Company, 70–72.

———. 1925c. Letter to Lord Morpeth, April 30, 1847. *The Correspondence of William Hickling Prescott, 1833–1847*. edited by Roger Wolcott. Boston: Houghton Mifflin Company, 634.

Report of the Philippine Exposition Board to the Louisiana Purchase Exposition. 1904. St. Louis: Greeley Printery of St. Louis.

Rogers, Robert F. 1995. *Destiny's Landfall: A History of Guam*. Honolulu: University of Hawaii Press.

Rydell, Robert W. 1984. *All the World's a Fair: Visions of Empire at American International Expositions, 1876–1916*. Chicago and London: University of Chicago Press.

Sale, Kirkpatrick. 1990. *The Conquest of Paradise: Christopher Columbus and the Columbian Legacy*. New York: Alfred A. Knopf.

Schmidt-Nowara, Christopher. 2008. "Spanish Origins of the American Empire: Hispanism, History, and Commemoration, 1898–1915." *International History Review* 30, no. 1: 32–51.

———. 2009. "From Columbus to Ponce de León: Puerto Rican Commemorations between Empires, 1893–1908." *Colonial Crucible: Empire in the Making of the Modern American State*. edited by Alfred W. McCoy and Francisco A. Scarano. Madison: University of Wisconsin Press, 230–237.

Schumacher, Frank. 2004. "Creating Imperial Urban Spaces: Baguio and the American Empire in the Philippines, 1898–1920." *Taking up Space: New Approaches to American History*. edited by Anke Ortlepp and Christoph Ribbat. Trier, Germany: Wissenschaftlicher Verlag Trier, 59–76.

"The Spanish Discoverers." 1896. *The Bay View Magazine* 4, no. 1: 19–21.

State Monuments. 1934. NARA, RG 350, Stack Area 150, Entry 5—General Classified Files, 1898–1945, December 6, 1934, Box 1267.

"A Treaty of Peace Between the United States and Spain." 1899. U.S. Congress, 55th Congress, 3rd session, Senate Doc. No. 62, Part 1. Washington, D.C.: Government Printing Office.

Taruc, Norman M. 2020. "Umatac Holds Annual Reenactment of Magellan's Landing." *The Guam Daily Post*, March 4, 2020.

Torres, Cristina Evangelista. 2010. *The Americanization of Manila, 1898–1921*. Quezon City, Manila, Philippines: University of the Philippines Press.

Treaty with the Sultan of Sulu. 1900. Senate Document 136, 56th Congress, 1st Session. Washington, D.C.: Government Printing Office.

Tribou, Richard. 2020. "Ponce de Leon Statue in Brevard County Vandalized." *Orlando Sentinel*, June 24, 2020.

78 Gregg French

Tucker, Norman P. 1980. *Americans in Spain: Patriots, Expatriates, and the Early American Hispanists, 1780–1850*. Boston: Boston Athenaeum.

Valentine, Brittany. 2020. "Puerto Rican Activists Fight to Remove Columbus from the Island." *Al Día*, July 27, 2020.

Williams, Stanley T. 1968. *The Spanish Background of American Literature*. Hamden: Archon Books.

Winn, Patrick. 2019. "Duterte's Wild Proposal: Changing the Name of the Philippines." *The World*, February 18, 2019.

Wolcott, Roger. 1925. "Introduction." *The Correspondence of William Hickling Prescott, 1833–1847*. edited by Roger Wolcott. Boston: Houghton Mifflin, ix–xxxi.

Worcester, D. C. Letter, August 23, 1898. Special Collections Library—University of Michigan, WPC Papers, Volume 17, pp. 1–39.

Yambo, Jaime J. 2020. "Anti-racism Protests Go Beyond Borders." *The Manila Times*, July 25, 2020.

5 Sketches of Spain

The Traveling Fictions of Frances Calderón de la Barca's *The Attaché in Madrid*

Nicholas Spengler

In September 1853, the Scottish-born writer Frances Calderón de la Barca (1804–1882) took up residence in Madrid after more than two decades in North America, where she had lived variously in Boston, New York, Mexico City, and Washington, D.C. She had traveled to Spain with her youngest sister, Lydia, and with her husband, Ángel, who had been recalled from his long-standing appointment as Spain's ambassador to the United States (from 1835 to 1839, and again from 1844 to 1853) in order to serve as Minister of State within Spain's newly formed Moderate government. This was not her first visit to Madrid, and she was well accustomed to the social expectations placed on the wives of men of state. Nevertheless, in a November 3 letter to her friend William Hickling Prescott, the Boston-based historian and Hispanist, Calderón describes the thrill of escape and anonymity in a foreign city:

> You can have no idea what a *dramatic* place this is—no day passes without some event occurring, curious or interesting. Indeed the every day life is strange and varied. Even the streets are a constant source of amusement. As I go to mass every morning in a mantilla with my veil down, so that I am not much known, I have an opportunity of seeing the people in a way which I cannot do when my hours of carriage and etiquette begin. […] The whole is so animated, and the people look so busy and so happy, and the sky is so bright and blue, that it is a pleasure to walk along the streets.
>
> (qtd. Fisher and Fisher 2016, 289)

Calderón's partaking in the strangeness and variety of everyday life of Madrid depends, somewhat paradoxically, on her ability to blend in with that life, for which the veil of her mantilla serves as both practical accoutrement and emblem. Her indistinguishability from the other "ladies with mantillas going to church like myself" gives her license to walk the streets and to get to know the city without being "much known" herself—a license that ends as soon as she steps back into Madrid's social and political elite as Madame Calderón de la Barca, dealing with the "troublesome" business of arranging places for guests, "from the august

DOI: 10.4324/9781003219460-5

80   Nicholas Spengler

Duke down to the lowest clerk" (qtd. Fisher and Fisher 2016, 289). This passage illustrates the tension between the privileged access and notoriety that Calderón enjoyed as the wife of a Spanish diplomat and politician, on one hand, and the pleasure she takes in veiled observation, knowing without being known, on the other hand. This tension, moreover, shapes her work as a travel writer: the interest and liveliness of Calderón's writing comes not only from her first-hand experience and knowledge of political events and social situations in the places she resides but also from the arch and incisive observations she makes from behind the textual veils through which she narrates her travels.

Indeed, the publication of Calderón's first and most famous travelogue, *Life in Mexico* (1843), had depended both on her notoriety and on her anonymity. Presented as a series of letters written, as the subtitle has it, "during a residence of two years in that country," where Ángel had been temporarily reposted (1839–1841), *Life in Mexico* was published under the lightly disguised name of "Madame C——de la B——."[1] This was a practical consideration, given her husband's position as Spain's first ambassador to Mexico. As Prescott wrote to Charles Dickens, on whom he had prevailed to find a British publisher for the book,

> [t]he name of the fair author is sheltered under her initials, it being thought by her *caro sposo* contrary to diplomatic etiquette, etc., for the name of the ambassador's wife to be flaring on the front of a work which shows up the court and country of her residence.
>
> (qtd. Fisher and Fisher 2016, 239)

And yet this nominal gesture of discretion only increased the intrigue and appeal of her book, inviting the reader at once to see through this rather transparent textual veil and to infer that the insights the work contained were sufficiently revealing to warrant such a gesture. If her name did not flare on the front of this work, it certainly teased. Prescott, in a preface to *Life in Mexico* that was instrumental both to its semblance of concealment and to its widespread success in the U.S. market, described the work as

> the result of observations made during a two years' residence in Mexico, by a lady, whose position there made her intimately acquainted with its society, and opened to her the best sources of information in regard to whatever could interest an enlightened foreigner.
>
> (1843, n.p.)

For all this tact, Calderón makes her identity clear when she identifies her husband as "the first minister from Spain" (1843, 48). Indeed, she was readily identified as the author by readers in the United States, where her book was celebrated, and in Mexico, where its reception was less

Sketches of Spain 81

enthusiastic.[2] If we see the author purchasing "an indispensable man-tilla" (Calderón 1843, 13) in Havana en route to Mexico and donning one on Catholic holidays and during her investigative visits to religious institutions, her critical distance as an "enlightened foreigner" never collapses into the degree of anonymity she describes a decade later as one of the "ladies with mantillas going to church" in her letter to Prescott from Madrid.

That greater anonymity she experienced in the Spanish capital was integral, as this chapter will argue, to the writing and publication of Calderón's second and lesser-known travelogue, *The Attaché in Madrid; or, Sketches of the Court of Isabella II* (1856), in which her textual disguise is more substantial and her facility for getting lost in the crowd more pronounced. Two important factors separate this work from *Life in Mexico*. First, Calderón, who had been baptized into the Scottish Presbyterian Church, had converted to Catholicism at Washington's Holy Trinity Church in 1847. Her conversion surely helped Ángel's position as a Spanish diplomat and politician, but as her biographers Howard and Marion Hall Fisher observe, she was "a wholehearted and deeply committed convert, despite her many deprecatory comments about Catholic priests and practices in *Life in Mexico*" (Fisher and Fisher 2016, 273). Thus, when she donned a mantilla in Madrid, she did so not as a foreigner respecting local customs but as a committed Catholic going to mass, and this relative insider status is reflected in the more intimate and admiring portrait of Catholic life in *The Attaché in Madrid*. Second, and most strikingly, Calderón adopts in *Attaché* the narrative persona of a young German nobleman and Hispanophile whose family connections allow him to secure a diplomatic post in the Spanish capital, hobnobbing with Madrid's social and political elite, including Madame Calderón de la Barca herself. As Beth Bauer notes in the only article dedicated to this overlooked text, the choice of the German attaché as pseudonymous narrative persona provided "more effective camouflage" (2011, 49) for her new work, protecting Ángel's reputation and also shielding Calderón herself from accusations of unladylike comportment in choosing to write critically and insightfully about the rarefied circles in which she moved. Beyond these practical considerations, the fictional attaché grants Calderón distance from her own life—she moves as a char-acter at the margins of the text—and license to experiment with literary forms, themes, and genres not typically available to female travel writers. As Bauer writes, "the creation of a male narrative persona represents a more sustained venture away from the biographical and into fiction and masquerade" (2011, 50). Bauer argues that Calderón uses her attaché not only to achieve "heightened anonymity and sanctioned access to 'male-only' arenas" (2011, 50) but also to challenge "the theme of Spanish degeneration" (2011, 53) in U.S. travel writing on Spain, with its "menu of *topoi* that sustained US exceptionalism and expansionist designs on former Spanish colonies near its borders" (2011, 52). In this

82 *Nicholas Spengler*

way, *The Attaché in Madrid* undermines the exceptionalist and imperialist discourses in which her *Life in Mexico* was entangled, the latter published in the same year as Prescott's *The History of the Conquest of Mexico* (1843) and on the eve of the annexation of Texas (1845) and the Mexican–American War (1846–1848).[3] Indeed, Calderón's *Attaché* subtly unsettles what Richard Kagan has called "Prescott's paradigm," according to which "America was the future—republican, enterprising, rational; while Spain—monarchical, indolent, fanatic—represented the past" (1996, 430). Bauer identifies as a key intertext the travelogue of U.S. diplomat John Esaias Warren, *Vagamundo, or an Attaché in Spain* (1851), reading Calderón's *Attaché* as a riposte to Warren's "orientalism" and "rhetorical domination of the Spanish other" (2011, 56). Calderón's young German romantic, likewise captivated by Spain's otherness but more sympathetic to its religious and cultural institutions, provides a strategic guise through which she can both parody U.S. travel writing about Spain and offer alternative perspectives.

In this chapter, I build on Bauer's reading of *The Attaché in Madrid* as both playing on and resisting the "othering" discourses of U.S. travel writing on Spain, though I approach the traveling fictions of Calderón's attaché from a different intertextual angle. Taking a cue from the subtitle, "Sketches of the Court of Isabella II," as well as the use of an invented narrative persona, I place Calderón's work in the "sketch" tradition of narrative fiction established by one of the earliest and most famous of U.S. Hispanophile writers, Washington Irving. As Jeffrey Rubin-Dorsky writes, Irving had inaugurated this genre with the publication of *The Sketch Book of Geoffrey Crayon, Gent.* (1819–1820), "transform[ing] the popular travel sketch into a form uniquely his own" (1986–1987, 226). The widespread touristic practice of painting or sketching picturesque scenes encountered in Europe had given rise to the "travel sketch" as a "a brief piece of writing that sought to present mainly the author's dominant impressions of his travels, including his responses to the mandatory sights"; as opposed to a comprehensive survey, the "sketch" suggested "an unfinished production, the working-out of an idea rather than the idea itself" (Rubin-Dorsky 1986–1987, 230). In his reinvention of the travel sketch through the persona of Geoffrey Crayon, Irving at once appropriates a popular form for his fictional compendium of travelers' tales and legends, granting an affably improvised quality to a work of high literary polish. Irving also subtly ironizes his own position as storyteller, as Crayon's romantic flights of fancy are bathetically deflated by the more mundane elements of his cross-cultural encounters. Beyond *The Sketch Book*, Crayon returns as the "author" not only of *Bracebridge Hill* (1822) and *Tales of a Traveller* (1824) but also of *Tales of the Alhambra* (1832), which he describes as "a few 'Arabesque' sketches from the life, and tales founded on popular traditions" (Irving 1832, vi). "Arabesque" here refers both to the subject of the sketches—Granada's Moorish palace with its ornamental motifs—and to the style of those

Sketches of Spain 83

sketches, interweaving scenes and set pieces from Crayon's first-hand experience with tales of the legendary past. It also suggests the elaborate textual screen through which Irving writes. After traveling to Spain in 1826 and carrying out the research that would contribute to his *History of the Life and Voyages of Christopher Columbus* (1828) and *Chronicle of the Conquest of Granada* (1829), Irving spent his final months in Spain in the spring of 1829 living in the Alhambra. (He would later return as U.S. Minister to Spain, from 1842 to 1846, and it was in this capacity that Calderón met him during her first visit to Madrid, in 1843.[4]) In his Alhambra sketches, Irving reconstructs and reimagines his time there, using Crayon mainly to champion, but also to gently mock, his own romantic and antiquarian impulses as a U.S. traveler in Spain. As Pere Gifra-Adroher writes, "by posing as an amateur ethnographer-folklorist, [Irving] valorizes and historicizes his narration of the Other in a way that permits him to escape a direct confrontation with the here-and-now" (2000, 123). Crayon's Alhambra is a romantic mystification. And yet, like the most astute and wryly self-aware of those travelers, Crayon (and Irving, by extension) hints at the partiality of his perspective, mediated as it is not only by the prejudices, desires, and expectations of the individual traveler but also by the literary-textual traditions that have shaped those prejudices, desires, and expectations. As Crayon puts it, "[t]he Alhambra has been so often and so minutely described by travellers, that a mere sketch will, probably, be sufficient for the reader to refresh his recollection" (Irving 1832, 49). In Crayon's Spanish "sketches," the idea being "worked out" is both Spain itself and, more subtly, the accumulated discourse of romantic writing about Spain.[5]

Irving's fictional sketchbooks, I propose, provide a literary model and genre for Calderón's sketches of Spain in *The Attaché in Madrid*, even as Calderón resists Irving's romantic mystifications of Spanish life and culture. Like Geoffrey Crayon, the German attaché is at once a pseudonymous disguise, a narrative persona, and a kind of authorial surrogate. Moreover, he shares Crayon's fascination with Spain's legends and traditions, which color his perspective long before he sets foot in the country. The first chapter, dated "Madrid, September 1853" (the month of Calderón's own arrival), begins with our attaché describing his delight at waking up for the first time in the capital of "romantic, chivalrous Spain," "the land of my day-dreams" since childhood: "Land of cloaked Caballeros; of Señoras, with dark eyes gleaming from beneath black mantillas; of serenades and adventures, of love and song" (Calderón 1856, 1). His Hispanophilia is at once cultured and sentimental. He invites us to picture him lying in his boat on one of Germany's "cold blue lakes" (Calderón 1856, 1), "covered with my cloak, wrapped in the adventures of Gil Blas, puzzling over the delightful Don Quixote, or mystifying myself" with the plays of Pedro Calderón de la Barca (Calderón 1856, 2). (When he learns that Ángel Calderón de la Barca has been recalled from Washington to serve as Minister of State, he remarks, "I liked his name

84 *Nicholas Spengler*

[...] which recalled my northern reveries to my mind, and my favorite passages of *La Vida es sueño*" [Calderón 1856, 12].) But he also tells us that his Italian mother had rocked his cradle "to the sound of Neapolitan ballads"—an analogue to the Spanish ballads that Irving and others document in their travelogues—and that his father had "represented his sovereign, not many years ago, at the Court of Madrid" (Calderón 1856, 2). "In short," he declares, "Spain was my vocation; and there is no struggling against manifest destiny" (Calderón 1856, 2). The curious incidence of this phrase associated with U.S. expansionism—coined by John L. O'Sullivan in 1845, in an article advocating the annexation of Texas and predicting the incorporation of Mexican California—seems out of character for our young German attaché. For the author of *Life in Mexico*, however, this allusion signals the debt of U.S. travel writing on Spain (and of the expansionist project it supported) to German Romantic Hispanists such as August Schlegel, who translated the plays of Pedro Calderón de la Barca, and Johann Nikolaus Böhl von Faber, who lived in Cádiz and befriended Irving during the latter's time in Spain. As Rolena Adorno writes, "Böhl devoted himself to the recovery of medieval oral traditions of Castilian balladry (the *Romancero*) and sixteenth- and seventeenth-century Spanish drama," and his friendship allowed Irving "to confirm his romantic views about Spanish themes" (2002, 58). Calderón's attaché provides a Crayon-like persona through which she interrogates those romantic views, effectively amplifying Irving's affable self-ironizing into a more pointed critique: not only of the mystifications of U.S. travel writing on Spain but also the implication of this writing in nationalist narratives of a "manifest destiny" that depended on the decadence of Spain and its American empire.

By briefly sketching Calderón's use of the sketch form as an intertextual engagement and riposte, this chapter aims to recover *The Attaché in Madrid* from the margins of scholarship on nineteenth-century literary relations and mediations between Spain and the United States, relocating it at the center of those narrative mediations. I do not want to suggest that Calderón's *Attaché* responds directly or solely to Irving's *Tales of the Alhambra* but rather that it engages with the sketch tradition that Irving reinvented as a hybrid genre combining travel writing and narrative fiction. The widespread emulation and diffusion of this tradition—in Henry Wadsworth Longfellow's *Outre-Mer* (1833); in Herman Melville's "sketches" of the Galápagos Islands, "The Encantadas, or Enchanted Isles" (1854); and even to a degree in Warren's *Vagamundo* (though that text employs no narrative guise), to name just a few examples—indicates the popularity of the sketch within the broader discourse of U.S. writing on Spain and on Spain's American empire. What is distinctive about Calderón's appropriation of this male-dominated genre in *The Attaché in Madrid* is her use of the sketch tradition to achieve a critical distance—not only from her narrative persona but also from "Madame Calderón de la Barca"—that far exceeds the lightly worn guise

Sketches of Spain   85

of Irving's Geoffrey Crayon. As we will see, Calderón's sketchbook both describes and performs her facility for blending in with the crowd—and also for carrying out her own vanishing act, in the climactic description of Madrid's 1854 revolution that expelled the Moderate government and forced the Calderóns and other political families to flee, departing Madrid under cover of night just as she departs the pages of her text under the cover of her fictional attaché.

In some ways, *The Attaché in Madrid* can be read as a continuation of the arch and incisive travelogue style that Calderón develops in *Life in Mexico*. As Bauer notes, both are examples of epistolary travel writing, and as such they share an intimate register reflective of the upper-class tastes and sensibilities of their author and of the social-diplomatic circles in which she moved. As Prescott writes in his preface, *Life in Mexico* "consists of letters written to the members of her own family, and *really*, not intended originally—however incredible the assertion—for publication" (1843, n.p.). Calderón de la Barca herself repeats, or imitates, this gesture in the "translator's" preface to *The Attaché in Madrid*, claiming that "[t]he work, if we may judge from its general aspect and structure, was not at first intended for publication"; it is, rather, "a series of rapid, but sincere and earnest notes, made by a young German diplomate in the whirl of fashion" (Calderón 1856, v), ostensibly for the edification and amusement of his family. And yet *Attaché* is not divided into "letters" like *Life in Mexico* but rather into "chapters," and while the basis for these chapters is Calderón's letter-writing to family and to friends such as Prescott, the "notes" of her fictional attaché do not take the form of letters per se. They bear an implicit relation to the (unseen) letters the young German reportedly sends to his family, but despite the prefatory disclaiming of an intent to publish, we have a narrator who directly addresses an imaginary reader:

> Behold me, then, taking a hurried leave of my family, and receiving injunctions from each individual to write by every courier. My father desired me to give him an account of the state of political affairs; my mother—a strict and pious Catholic—of the state of religion, of the churches, and charitable institutions; my sisters, of the court, the balls, and especially the dress and manners of the Spanish ladies; my younger brothers, of the clubs, the sport, the horses, the bull-fights, &c.; in short, I was to write a kind of modern history of Spain.
>
> (Calderón 1856, 2–3)

Calderón thus establishes not only the epistolary conceit that will justify the attaché's investigations into different aspects of life and society in Madrid but also the narrative tone and posture that defines the travel sketch: an affable and confiding address not to the diegetic circle of family and friends but rather to the reader who peruses these "rapid, but sincere and earnest notes."

86 *Nicholas Spengler*

This tone continues in the attaché's description of his travels: "To Madrid I came via France. Every one knows the journey" (Calderón 1856, 3). Like Irving's Crayon, the attaché registers the ink that has already been spilled in travel writing on Spain. Everyone knows the journey not (or not only) because they have personally experienced it—though tourism to Spain was on the rise—but because they have read about it. In Longfellow's description of "The Journey into Spain" in *Outre-Mer*, for example, he remarks the "desolate tract of country" that first greets the traveler from France, "cheered only by the tinkle of a mule-bell, or the song of a muleteer" (1835, 193). Readers of *Tales of the Alhambra* will recall Crayon's depiction of the Spanish muleteer, who travels in "united numbers" with "weapons at hand, slung to their saddles" to defend them "against petty bands of marauders," and who draws from "an inexhaustible stock of songs and ballads, with which to beguile his incessant wayfaring" (Irving 1832, 9). In *Vagamundo*, Warren describes his own "striking" "transition from France to Spain":

> We were in the very Spain of Don Quixote and Gil Blas, and a life of rare adventure opened in perspective before our eager vision. Mules, mantillas, and balconies, confusedly rushed through our minds, and filled our fancy with a strange variety of ridiculous conceits and incongruous images. We were waxing heroic, and were quite ready for anything in the shape of an adventure (whether to fight banditti or make love to charming senhoritas,) when our diligence suddenly stopped at the town of Irun, for the purpose of a custom-house examination—that most abominable of all "bores" to the poetical traveller. Our romantic ideas took flight in an instant.
>
> (Calderón 1856, 18–19)

Calderón's attaché similarly struggles to reconcile his fanciful conceits and poetical expectations of Spain with the more prosaic experience of this well-trod journey into Spain: "I came with the English courier, not the shadow of an adventure on the way" (1856, 3). The efficiency of this conveyance is a disappointment, though it provides the frame for several comic set pieces contrasting the Hispanophilia of the eager attaché with the xenophobic disdain of his English traveling companion. He is allowed "ten minutes to run into the cathedral at Burgos, where I would gladly have lingered for hours" (Calderón 1856, 4). He admires what his companion dismissively refers to as "dirty peasant women," among whom the attaché remarks "several worthy of figuring on the canvas of Murillo": "from the moment of entering Spain, I could not but remark that we scarcely passed one object which would not have afforded a good subject for the pencil" (Calderón 1856, 4). The attaché's verbal sketch thus compensates for, and wryly alludes to, the limitations of modern travel in rushing travelers from place to place without sufficient time for

Sketches of Spain 87

rumination, let alone setting up an easel. The attaché is more generously indulged when

> [t]he lucky derangement of a wheel gave me half an hour to enter a *fonda*, and with my head full of the *ventas* of the immortal Cervantes, I was surprised to find a number of diligence travellers seated before an excellent breakfast.
>
> (Calderón 1856, 4)

The attaché enjoys his breakfast and quickly "sketch[es] the head of the handsomest" of two "girls in waiting," and then he and his abstemious companion are on the road again, reaching Madrid by evening (Calderón 1856, 4). Gone is the Spain of Geoffrey Crayon, who proclaims "what a country is Spain for a traveller, where the most miserable inn is as full of adventure as an enchanted castle, and every meal is in itself an achievement!" (Irving 1832, 15–16). The difference between Irving's Spain and Calderón's is only partly attributable to the improved transportation, hospitality, and security for mid-century travelers to Spain.[6] More significant is Irving's commitment to maintaining the enchantments of Spain, abstracting the country from its social and political realities to present a fixed series of types and tropes, while Calderón is committed to a vision of Spain that, notwithstanding its assertion of an essential and unique national character—"the noble, chivalrous character which seems to belong by right to the true Spaniard" (Calderón 1856, 29)—portrays everyday life and politics in Madrid in all their richness and complexity.

This remains the case even, or especially, in those episodes in which the young attaché, like Crayon, indulges in romantic flights of fancy, as in the chapters relating the birth, death, and burial of the Infanta or princess, Queen Isabella's second child. Through her attaché, Calderón sardonically describes the "lugubrious silence [that] reigned throughout Madrid" upon the birth of the princess. Given the excitement at the prospect of a male heir, "[t]he poor little Ynfanta does not see the light under happy auspices": "Sorrow, anger, or consternation appears upon the generality of countenances. It is evidently regarded as another ministerial blunder" (Calderón 1856, 169). The princess soon catches cold, likely from being displayed in an unheated chamber, and in the entry for January 8, 1854, the attaché notes, "The Ynfanta died yesterday. Went to the weekly *tertulia* at the house of Madame Calderon de la Barca; very pleasant, rather crowded; but, on account of the Ynfanta's death, no music as there usually is" (Calderón 1856, 171). Calderón's insertion of herself into the text at this juncture indicates her own respectful observation of the royal death amidst her obligatory hosting duties, in contrast to the callous silence of the opposition press and the comment of the attaché's "chief," the German ambassador, "Fortunate now that it was not a prince!" (Calderón 1856, 171). The attaché's own posture in the

88 *Nicholas Spengler*

following chapter, describing the *Infanta*'s burial at the Escorial Palace, is somewhat lacking in due respect, as he is thrilled to visit "this wonderful monument of the stern Catholic monarch [Phillip II], into whose domains we thus entered in the darkness of the night, to deliver up, as it were, to his guardianship an innocent little descendant of his race" (Calderón 1856, 180): "All my day-dreams of old Spain were realized, or rather surpassed" (Calderón 1856, 174). The burial becomes an occasion for the exercise of the attaché's romantic imagination:

> it seemed as if all the winds of heaven were unchained that night, their hoarse voices howling round the massive building, blowing through the vaults, extinguishing the great torches, and moaning in tones that sounded like the wailing of infernal spirits, or of souls in agony.
>
> (Calderón 1856, 181)

But the substance of the attaché's gothic conceits underscores rather than mystifies the reality of the Infanta's death and the literal and figurative coldness with which she was received:

> The iron doors were closed, and the little princess was left to moulder into dust amongst her royal ancestors. The absurd fancy that she must suffer from the coldness and gloom to which she was abandoned haunted me for hours afterwards.
>
> (Calderón 1856, 185)

Indeed, the attaché dreams that "[t]he little Ynfanta, with her waxen face, sat up in her coffin and bowed to [her ancestors] as they formed a circle round her" (Calderón 1856, 187). The Escorial episode contains echoes of Crayon's description of "the Author's Chamber" among the "romantic halls of the Alhambra" (Irving 1832, 99). Crayon is likewise subject to "a perversion of fancy" (Irving 1832, 120) when he decides to take up residence in the half-ruined apartment of a long-dead queen, and he hears "[l]ow moans" and "indistinct ejaculations" (Irving 1832, 121). These "shadows and fancies" disperse by the light of day, and the moans are explained as "the ravings of a poor maniac" who lives in the palace complex. But if this episode serves to reinforce Irving's representation of the Alhambra (and Spain more generally) as a romantic "refuge from the forces of reform and change" (Gifra-Adroher 2000, 124), Calderón's gothic sketch draws attention both to the sadness beneath the pomp and ceremony of the Infanta's birth and burial and to the social and political attitudes and tensions that shaped Madrid during this tumultuous period leading up to the 1854 revolution.

A more lighthearted gothic pastiche follows in Chapter 24, which begins with the heading gloss: "*Masked Ball—An Adventure—A Mysterious Beauty—May have been a Ghost*" (Calderón 1856, 201). The attaché describes the "adventure" that ensues when he meets a "masked

Sketches of Spain 89

figure" at this Carnival ball who is "dressed in mourning, even her mask fringed with black lace" (Calderón 1856, 201–202). She leads the attaché outside, where he worries that she will catch cold, to which she responds, "I am colder than the night" (Calderón 1856, 203). He "feel[s] a kind of absurd, vague uneasiness" as if he "was following the footsteps of a phantom, a kind of Lurelei"; he follows her through the city's "least frequented streets" and into "the old church of San José," where she tells him, "Tell no one. I was buried there this morning. Adieu," and vanishes (Calderón 1856, 203–204). As Bauer writes, this gothic "set piece" provides an example of "the would-be seducer-rescuer duped by his own desires" (2011, 57), satirizing Warren's *Vagamundo* and other male-authored texts that present the tantalizing beauty of exotic female "others" as vehicles for imperial desire. But the masked ball and the mysterious beauty also suggest figures for Calderón's own masquerade in *The Attaché in Madrid*, both as the veiled author of the text and as a character within it. The young German attaché moves through the city's public and private spaces with more freedom—or a different kind of freedom, at least—than Calderón enjoyed. At a "soirée dansante" at the French embassy earlier in the narrative, for example, we find that "Madame Calderon de la Barca" is in attendance, along with the wives of other politicians and noblemen, but the attaché remarks that "as most of my time was spent in the waltzing circle, in which none of these ladies joined, I had no opportunity of seeing them very near" (Calderón 1856, 51). This distance does not register a lack of mobility on Calderón's part so much as it measures the relative licenses and limitations of different "circles" within the same soirée; the attaché dances with the daughters of the elite, but the rarefied world of Madrid's Madames and Marquesas remains beyond his ken. The attaché later comes into closer proximity with Calderón at the *tertulias* she hosts, but she consistently stands at the edges of his consciousness, at the margins of his circle.

An integral part of this distance is Calderón's ability not only to mix but also to blend in with Madrid's society—and, crucially, with the city's Catholic institutions—achieving an insider status that the attaché himself cannot achieve. His mother's Catholicism does grant him a measure of that status, and his narrative notably departs from the anti-Catholic (or at least exoticizing) attitude conveyed in most U.S. and British travel writing on Spain—thus the disclaimer in the "translator's" preface that "[w]ith many of the views entertained by the author of these sketches, most American readers will not agree" (Calderón 1856, v). He describes the prejudices of an Irish Protestant friend, M—, who has lived in Madrid for many years. On All Souls' Day, that "occasion when all the sympathies and sorrows of the human heart are called into action" (Calderón 1856, 109), M— dismisses the prayers offered up for the dead as the product of "superstition," "habit," and "hypocrisy," but he cannot help being affected by this "sublime and touching spectacle," and the attaché remarks that he "took his leave with a very forced smile, and the air of

90   *Nicholas Spengler*

one who would gladly get rid of his own thoughts" (Calderón 1856, 111). The attaché describes many such spectacles with admiration. On a visit to the Carmelite church of Santa Teresa in Madrid, the attaché remarks its "quiet, venerable aspect":

> Nothing can have a more devotional effect than the kneeling figures on the floors of the church, the complete absence of all distinction in dress or place; the women enveloped in their mantillas, rich and poor together. How infinitely I prefer this to the cushioned pews of the London churches [...] Here, at least, is true republicanism; equality in the worship of God.
>
> (Calderón 1856, 77)

There are direct echoes here of Calderón's earlier comparison in *Life in Mexico* of "the appearance of a fashionable London chapel with that of a Mexican church, on the occasion of a solemn fête":

> The one, light, airy, and gay, with its velvet-lined pews [...], the ladies a little sleepy after last night's opera, but dressed in the most elegant morning toilet [...] and exchanging a few fashionable nothings at the door [...]—the other, solemn, stately, and gloomy, and showing no distinction of rank. The floor covered with kneeling figures—some enveloped in the reboso, others in the mantilla, and all alike devout, at least in outward seeming.
>
> (Calderón 1856, 240)

The difference in *Attaché* is that Calderón herself may be counted among those kneeling women, and the Catholic convert is less circumspect about the appearance of devotion now that she has experienced it for herself. Later, in a passage describing the Holy Thursday ceremonies during Easter, the attaché notes the women taking contributions at different churches, including "the Countess de Montijo," the "Marquesa de V—," and "Mme. Calderon de la Barca, accompanied by her sister" (Calderón 1856, 242). Calderón significantly pictures herself here performing a function for the Church like any Spanish noblewoman. It is at these moments when Calderón's textual disguise, and her integration into Madrid's society and ceremonies, is most complete. If, as the attaché observes in the same chapter, "few Englishwomen wear a mantilla gracefully, [just as] few Spanish women look at their ease in a bonnet," we may be allowed to imagine here that Calderón manages to wear her own "black lace mantilla" with elegance (Calderón 1856, 237).

There are other moments when the narrative guise is allowed to slip to reflect the text's place as a piece of travel writing prepared for a U.S. American readership. The attaché devotes a chapter to the arrival of the new U.S. Minister to Spain, Pierre Soulé, "a red-hot democrat, whose late speeches in his own country, in favor of the annexation of Cuba, have

Sketches of Spain 91

naturally excited a vast amount of prejudice against him, in this," and he notes that Ángel Calderón de la Barca's appointment as Minister of State serves as "a kind of counterbalance" given the latter's familiarity with the United States and with the strident exceptionalism and expansionism of many of its politicians (Calderón 1856, 72–73); Ángel had, after all, been Spain's ambassador in Washington during the Mexican–American War. A more flattering, if unexpected, reference to U.S. democracy and republicanism comes in the climactic description of the Vicalvarada, the revolution that swept the streets of Madrid and other Spanish cities in the summer of 1854 and which terminated in a coup that expelled the Moderate government (including Ángel Calderón de la Barca). This revolution prompts an unlikely reflection from our young German attaché, horrified by the "spirit of sedition [that] has spread throughout the country":

> Would the chiefs of the revolution have paused in their career, could they have foreseen these results? Perhaps not; for it is only a Washington, one guided by no personal motives, who with a cool head, an unbiassed judgment and an honest heart, can weigh and calculate with solemn earnestness the good or evil likely to accrue from a step which scarcely any amount of evil can render justifiable.
>
> (Calderón 1856, 368)

This meditation, on the final page of the narrative, mirrors the perspective of many U.S. travel writers and political observers regarding Spain (and Spanish America, for that matter) as a land ruined by factionalism and anarchic violence, whose power-hungry leaders lack the integrity and cool calculation of a Washington. Indeed, this is the kind of argument advanced by "red-hot democrats" like Soulé who presented the prospective U.S. annexation of Cuba as an act of liberation rather than conquest, ending Spain's tyranny over the island and welcoming Cuba into the democratic family of the United States.

Just a few pages previous, however, our attaché has presented us with another U.S.–Spanish analogy that complicates this exceptionalism. The revolution has prompted an exodus among Madrid's political and social elite, and the attaché reports "tak[ing] leave of the family of the minister of state" at midnight, marking Calderón's departure from Madrid and from the narrative.[7] This parting is immediately followed by a striking allusion to one of Washington Irving's most famous tales:

> Madrid has completely changed its aspect, and without having the miraculous seven years of slumber of Rip Van Winkle, it would suffice that one should have fallen asleep seven weeks ago, and awakened this 1st of September, to find an entire alteration in men and things.
>
> (Calderón 1856, 363)

92 *Nicholas Spengler*

For the attaché, this passing reference to Irving's romantic tale of revolutionary transformation, published in *The Sketch Book*, registers the suddenness of the change he experiences in Madrid. But this reference also shows how Calderón's intertextual positioning of her book works to unsettle the conceits of U.S. writing about Spain. Rip descends from his long sleep in the Catskill mountains to find his Hudson River village both transformed and strangely familiar, the "rubicund portrait of His Majesty George the Third" (Irving 1820, 63) on the sign at the village inn now "singularly metamorphosed" into a portrait of "General Washington"; he recognizes the "ruby face of King George," but a blue coat has been swapped for the red, a sword for the scepter, and a cocked hat for the crown (Irving 1820, 78). Irving's arch treatment of revolution as the swapping of one George for another, and one set of symbols for another, is echoed in Calderón's transatlantic analogy, hinting at the public signs and spectacles of power that endure despite revolutionary transformations. Indeed, the attaché describes the careful political choreography required both to mobilize and to placate an unruly populace. The two rebel generals and erstwhile enemies, the renegade Moderate Leopoldo O'Donnell and the Progressive Baldomero Espartero, appear before the crowds "locked in a fast embrace, typifying the fusion of the Moderado and Progresista party": "How cordial was the embrace, let those judge who know their antecedents. But the people comprehend only what they see, and patriots and Nationals rent the air with one simultaneous shout in honor of O'Donnell, Espartero, and Liberty" (Calderón 1856, 340–341). Calderón's allusion to "Rip Van Winkle" thus signals that she understands Spain neither as romantic refuge nor as tyrannical empire but rather as a nation as susceptible to political and social upheavals as any other, not excepting the United States.

Calderón had spent enough time in the political and social circles of Washington, D.C., Mexico City, and Madrid to know that governments and personages everywhere fall in and out of favor. Her husband's career on both sides of the Atlantic was tied to the fortunes of the Moderate Party, and her own career as a travel writer can be seen as an attempt to weather those periods of uncertainty when Ángel was out of work; it is no accident that both *Life of Mexico* and *The Attaché in Madrid* were written and published during the periods of Progressive rule that bookended Spain's so-called *década moderada* (1844–1854).[8] But this contingency also informs Calderón's distinctive style and approach as a travel writer who constantly qualifies and reframes her narrative perspectives. In *Life in Mexico*, we can find her describing a monastery at sunset as resembling "a vision, or a half-remembered sketch, or a memory of romance" (Calderón 1843, 74), before remarking with some deflation on a routine social gathering: "There is no romance here. Men and women are the same everywhere, whether enveloped in the graceful mantilla, or wearing *Herbault's last*, whether wrapped in Spanish cloak, or Mexican sarape, or Scottish plaid" (Calderón 1843, 75). Likewise,

Sketches of Spain 93

Calderón's *Attaché* at once expresses the uniqueness of Spain's culture and institutions and conveys this antiromantic sense of underlying sameness; as the German attaché remarks upon declining to enter the zoo on a visit to Madrid's Retiro park, "wild beasts, like civilized men, are the same all the world over" (Calderón 1856, 41). Calderón thus adapts the alternately romantic and bathetic gestures of the fictional travel sketch to her own narrative devices, using the genre to portray the Spain of Isabella II in its political and social intrigues as well as the more mundane dramas and pleasures of everyday life in Madrid.

Notes

1 Calderón follows the model of female epistolary travel writing established by another diplomat's wife, Lady Mary Wortley Montagu, whose *Letters of the Right Honourable Lady M—y W—y M—e* were published posthumously in 1762. Moreover, Calderón's later remarks on the anonymity afforded by the veil of her mantilla in Madrid echo Montagu's famous observation of the relative freedom of Istanbul's veiled women: "This perpetual masquerade gives them entire liberty of following their inclinations without danger of discovery" (1781, 95).

2 See Fisher and Fisher (2016, 241–242) for an account of the Mexican reception of *Life in Mexico*. Much of the controversy centered on Calderón's criticisms of Mexican customs and fashions, as well as her unflattering portrayals of certain men of state, such as Antonio López de Santa Anna, who returned to the presidency in a coup in 1841.

3 See Kaplan and Gervassi-Navarro (2005) for a discussion of the position of *Life in Mexico* within U.S. and Spanish imperial discourses.

4 In a letter to his niece dated December 20, 1843, Irving writes: "We have here, also, Mr. Calderon, formerly Minister to the United States, and his wife. The latter recently wrote a very lively work on a residence in Mexico" (1883, III.33).

5 Despite (or perhaps because of) his tendency toward romantic mystification, Irving was keenly aware of the gap between travel writing and the actual experience of travel. In a November 15, 1842, letter, the then-ambassador wrote to his sister from Madrid:

> My present home is enlivened by the return of the young travellers [his attachés] from their tour in Andalusia, which has been a very satisfactory one, excepting that they have not been robbed, at which they appear rather disappointed, an adventure with robbers being looked upon as essential to the interest and romance of a tour in Spain.
>
> (Irving 1883, III.1)

6 The English travel writer and Hispanophile Richard Ford notes these material improvements in his immensely popular *Handbook for Travellers in Spain* (1845), published in the United States as *The Spaniards and their Country* (1848), but he notes that "the dangers and difficulties that are there supposed to beset the traveller" have long been exaggerated. He wryly remarks that those

94   *Nicholas Spengler*

who wish to make a picture or chapter, in short, to get up an adventure for the home-market, may manage by a great exhibition of imprudence, chattering, and a holding out luring baits, to gratify their hankering, although it would save some time, trouble, and expense to try the experiment much nearer home.

(Ford 1848, 40)

7   This entry in the text is dated August 28, 1854, marking the date of Calderón's departure for France, and it is followed by two brief concluding entries, dated October 1 and October 15. With her (biographical) self now removed from the narrative, Calderón tactfully arranges in these final entries for the departure of her attaché in order to accompany his ailing supervisor, the German ambassador, to take a restorative trip to the baths at Aix-en-Provence. Ángel and Frances Calderón de la Barca would return to Madrid in 1856, at the end of the *bienio progresista* (the "Progressive Biennium") that followed the Vicalvarada.

8   Calderón's first visit to Spain (September 1843 to April 1844) had, in fact, immediately followed Espartero's ouster as Regent of Spain (1840–1843), and so she witnessed both the beginning and the end of the *década moderada*. With Espartero's rise, Ángel had lost his posting to Mexico in 1841, but he returned to Washington, D.C., in 1844 as Spanish Minister to the U.S. under the new Moderate government (Fisher and Fisher 2016, 247–264). The U.S. Minister to Spain at this time was none other than Washington Irving, who had seen a romantic hero in Espartero and lamented his ouster. In a letter to his sister, Catherine, dated September 2, 1842, Irving writes:

"The future career of this gallant soldier, Espartero, whose merits and services have placed him at the head of the Government, and the future fortunes of these isolated little princesses, the Queen and her sister, have an uncertainty hanging about them worthy of the fifth act of a melodrama.

(Irving 1883, II.260)

Works Cited

Adorno, Rolena. 2002. "Washington Irving's Romantic Hispanism and· Its Columbian Legacies." *Spain in America: The Origins of Hispanism in the United States*, edited by Richard L Kagan. Urbana: University of Illinois Press.

Bauer, Beth. 2011. "Crossing Over: Gender and Empire in Fanny Calderón de la Barca's 'The Attaché in Madrid.'" *Hispanic Review* 79, no. 1: 43–65.

Calderón de la Barca, Frances. 1843. *Life in Mexico, During a Residence of Two Years in That Country*. Boston: Little, Brown and Company.

———. 1856. *The Attaché in Madrid; or, Sketches of the Court of Isabella II*. New York: D. Appleton and Company.

Fisher, Marion Hall, and Howard T. Fisher. 2016. *Frances Calderón de la Barca née Frances Erskine Inglis: A Biography of the Author of* Life in Mexico *and* The Attaché in Madrid, edited by Alan Hall Fisher. Bloomington: Xlibris.

Ford, Richard. 1848. *The Spaniards and Their Country*. New York: George P. Putnam.

Gifra-Adroher, Pere. 2000. *Between History and Romance: Travel Writing on Spain in the Early Nineteenth-Century United States*. Madison: Fairleigh Dickinson University Press.

Irving, Pierre M. 1883. *The Life and Letters of Washington Irving*, 3 vols. New York: G.P. Putnam's Sons.

Irving, Washington. 1820. *The Sketch Book of Geoffrey Crayon, Gent*, vol. 1. London: John Murray.

———. 1832. *Tales of the Alhambra, by Geoffrey Crayon*, vol. 1. London: Henry Colburn and Richard Bentley.

Kagan, Richard L. 1996. "Prescott's Paradigm: American Historical Scholarship and the Decline of Spain." *The American Historical Review* 101, no. 2: 423–446.

Kaplan, Amy, and Nina Gervassi-Navarro. 2005. "Between Empires: Frances Calderón de la Barca's *Life in Mexico*." *Symbiosis* 9, no. 1: 3–25.

Longfellow, Henry Wadsworth. 1835. *Outre-Mer; a Pilgrimage Beyond the Sea*, vol. 1. New York: Harper & Brothers.

Montagu, Lady Mary Wortley. 1781. *Letters of the Right Honourable Lady M—y W—y M—e*. Edinburgh: Alexander Donaldson.

Prescott, William Hickling. 1843. "Preface." *Life in Mexico, During a Residence of Two Years in That Country*, by Frances Calderón de la Barca. Boston: Little, Brown and Company.

Rubin-Dorsky, Jeffrey. 1986–1987. "Washington Irving and the Genesis of the Fictional Sketch." *Early American Literature* 21, no. 3: 226–247.

Warren, John Esaias. 1851. *Vagamundo; or the Attaché in Spain*. New York: Scribner.

6 "Benito Cereno," Spaniards, and Creoles

John C. Havard

This chapter investigates Herman Melville's choice in "Benito Cereno" (1855) to reposition the historical Benito Cerreño, who was Spanish, as a Chilean creole. I argue that Melville did so to emphasize, against Delano's pretensions to moral differentiation from Cereno, that the two captains shared "creole" status as men of power engaged in New World economic processes of racialized labor exploitation.

Differences between Melville's Novella and Its Historical Prototypes

Melville's repositioning of Cereno as Chilean has gone unacknowledged by scholars, surprisingly so given the recent tendency of critics to analyze "Benito Cereno" in light of transnational and hemispheric processes of commerce and racial violence (e.g., Emery 1984; Sundquist 1993, 135–221; DeGuzmán 2005, 47–67). In his 1986 study *A Reader's Guide to the Short Stories of Herman Melville*, Lea Bertani Vozar Newman (1986, 98–100) enumerated the differences between the historical Amasa Delano's description of his experiences aboard the Spanish trader *Tryal* and Melville's fictionalization of those events. Scholars have frequently referred to such differences in their analyses of Melville's tale. However, Newman does not identify the difference I will explore here. The historical Delano refers to Cerreño simply as "the Spanish captain" (1994, 249). However, Melville, while indeed frequently referring to Cereno as "the Spaniard," specifies twice that Cereno is Chilean. The first reference comes early in the narrative, as Delano muses on Cereno's strangely "precise" attire, which is inconsistent with the dress of others on board as well as the more general state of affairs on the *San Dominick*:

> However unsuitable for the time and place, at least in the blunt-thinking American's eyes, and however strangely surviving in the midst of all his afflictions, the toilette of Don Benito might not, in fashion at least, have gone beyond the style of the day among South Americans of his class. Though on the present voyage sailing from Buenos Ayres, he had avowed himself a native and resident of

DOI: 10.4324/9781003219460-6

"Benito Cereno," Spaniards, and Creoles   97

Chili, whose inhabitants had not so generally adopted the plain coat and once plebeian pantaloons; but, with a becoming modification, adhered to their provincial costume, picturesque as any in the world. Still, relatively to the pale history of the voyage, and his own pale face, there seemed something so incongruous in the Spaniard's apparel, as almost to suggest the image of an invalid courtier tottering about London streets in the time of the plague.

(Melville 1987, 57–58)

Here, the narrator highlights Cereno's claim to being a "native and resident" of Chile, and Delano explains away Cereno's odd dress by reasoning that it is typical of the trappings of the nation's creole gentry. The second reference comes at the end of the deposition, in which Cereno avers that

he is twenty-nine years of age, and broken in body and mind; that when finally dismissed by the court, he shall not return home to Chili, but betake himself to the monastery on Mount Agonia without; and signed with his honor, and crossed himself, and, for the time, departed as he came, in his litter, with the monk Infelez, to the Hospital de Sacerdotes.

(Melville 1987, 114)

Here, Cereno again claims Chilean birth, this time while stating his intention to reside at a Peruvian monastery after surviving the *San Dominick* revolt. No references to Chilean birth appear in Delano's source text.

It stands to reason they would not: Melville's choice to position Cereno as Chilean is all the more striking because the historical prototype was, in fact, Spanish. Moreover, the historical Cerreño was not only Spanish but a Spaniard who would have been disliked by Juan Martínez de Rozas, the creole Chilean advocate and future revolutionary who took part in presiding over the legal proceedings to determine Delano's compensation for providing supplies to the *Tryal* and quelling the slave revolt. As Greg Grandin elaborates in *The Empire of Necessity*, the historical Cerreño was Andalusian. He was from Calañas, Spain, an agricultural town outside Seville, and he had emigrated to Peru to enter the shipping industry (2014, 175–176). In the aftermath of the *Tryal* revolt, the historical Delano and Cerreño were unable to come to terms over Delano's compensation. Mediating their dispute in Concepción, Chile, was Martínez de Rozas, an enlightened creole. Martínez de Rozas would later figure prominently in Chile's revolution against Spain and is now considered a Chilean founding father. As might be expected of someone who constructed creole national consciousness in Chile, Martínez de Rozas was resentful of peninsular merchant shipmen, who monopolized maritime trade on South America's Pacific coast and charged creole merchants and planters exorbitant fees. His resentment toward peninsular Spaniards colored his attitude toward Cerreño (Grandin 2014, 232).

98 John C. Havard

Why would Melville reposition Cereno as Chilean despite the fact that the character's prototype was not only Spanish but, in fact, disliked by a leading Chilean creole precisely due to his Spanish ancestry? To be sure, Melville was likely unaware of the information unearthed by Grandin's research into the aftermath of the *Tryal* affair; his knowledge of the historical Benito Cerreño was presumably limited to Delano's narrative. In fact, the historical Delano himself, despite his prolonged interactions with Cerreño, Martínez de Rozas, and other South American merchants, lawyers, and royal officials, would not have been completely aware of some of the political dynamics Grandin describes. All the same, Delano's source text indeed describes Cerreño as a Spaniard, with no reference to Chilean origins. Melville's repositioning must be taken as intentional and thus warrants greater reflection than it has yet received.

I argue that Melville repositioned Cereno as Chilean to emphasize that Delano and Cereno share status as creole participants in a racialized system of labor and commerce, a shared status Delano is at pains to deny because he wishes to morally differentiate himself as a liberal U.S. American from what he perceives to be the illiberal creole Cereno. While this emphasis on their shared investments could be made without repositioning Cereno, that repositioning makes it clearer.

Similarities between the Historical Delano and Cerreño

That the emphasis could have been made, though with less clarity, without the repositioning is evident from the fact that despite their differences in continent of origin, the historical Delano and Cerreño had much in common. Both engaged in maritime commerce as part of frustrated bids for upward mobility. Delano went to sea at a young age, but his voyages were unprofitable (Grandin 2014, 78). By the time he took part in the *Tryal* affair, he had turned to sealing (Grandin 2014, 90). This enterprise, too, proved abortive. Sealing was a brutally exploitative practice that, soon after its inception in the eighteenth century, rapidly depleted the stock of seals in the South American islands where it was practiced. Delano frequently found his sealing grounds empty. His voyage prior to encountering the *Tryal* had been disastrous, including not only commercial failures but also unrest among his crew. His motivation for helping the *Tryal* was to recoup his losses through remuneration for his assistance. So powerful was this desire that to claim what he argued Cerreño promised for his services, which the Spanish captain disputed, Delano spent months in Chile and Peru appealing to the colonial government.

Cerreño's connection to New England shipping was more than one of mere resemblance to Delano. As Grandin elaborates, the *Tryal*'s origins were as a New England sealer whose captain had gotten involved in smuggling on the South American Pacific coast. The ship was purchased by a group of New England Quakers in 1801, who told the sailors they hired that they intended it for a sealing voyage. However, it had been

"Benito Cereno," Spaniards, and Creoles 99

outfitted with secret holds that would be used to smuggle contraband and to evade Spanish tariffs. In 1802, the ship was seized by Spanish authorities in Chile with $2000 of illegal luxury goods in its hold. It was purchased from the authorities by a merchant who then sold it to Cerreño, who in turn outfitted it as a merchant vessel that would transport goods between Chile and Peru. Cerreño was not a slaver by trade, but he sometimes transported slaves, as in the case of the voyage that was the basis for Melville's tale (Grandin 2014, 160–165). The *Tryal*'s history poignantly captures the intricate connections between the New England sealing industry, the South American commerce in trade goods, and the South American slave trade—as well as the similar roles played by New England and Spanish shipmen in those trades.

Indeed, both Delano and Cerreño resorted to shipping as an effort to stake out a better place for themselves in the social order. Their contexts and origins differed. Cerreño was born into a gentry family that had fallen on hard times due to the decline in agricultural prices in Spain in the late 1700s. Delano's native New England lacked Spain's social stratifications, and his origins were more modest. Cerreño emigrated to Peru in the early 1800s intending to recoup his fortunes in the South American shipping industry, which grew in tandem with the trade in slaves. He primarily transported goods and freight along the Pacific coast between Chile and Peru. His business was not primarily as a slavetrader, but he sometimes engaged himself to transport slaves when the opportunity presented itself (Grandin 2014, 175–176). As such, both staked their bids for upward mobility on exploitative practices that were characteristic of the exploding maritime trade of the day, sealing in Delano's case, and slaveholding in Cerreño's. Although Cerreño had established an aristocratic life for himself by the time of his death (Grandin 2014, 253), both experienced frequent setbacks in these attempts: Delano's sealing efforts were often mired in frustration, and Cerreño fell prey to a successful slave revolt.

Delano's Self-Differentiation from Cereno

Melville would have been unaware of some of this context, his knowledge of Cerreño being based on the limited information found in Delano's narrative. However, he was surely aware of the interconnections between U.S. and Spanish-American commerce, the similarities between the players, and South American social structures based on his experience in whaling and knowledge of maritime commerce (e.g., Lazo 2017). In Melville's retelling of the *Tryal* affair, the fictional Delano is at great pains to deny these similarities and to differentiate himself from Cereno. Delano thinks of himself as a genial, optimistic yet stern, effective leader. His self-perceptions of benevolent optimism are indicated in the story's opening, in which the narrator describes him as "a person of a singularly undistrustful good nature, not liable, except on extraordinary and

100 John C. Havard

repeated incentives, and hardly then, to indulge in personal alarms, any way involving the imputation of malign evil in man" (Melville 1987, 47). Those self-perceptions often also emerge in his romantic racialist interpretations of the master–slave relationship, particularly that which he observes in Cereno and Babo, in which he observes a kind, generous master and a faithful slave. For instance, in one passage, Melville writes,

> As master and man stood before him, the black upholding the white, Captain Delano could not but bethink him of the beauty of that relationship which could present such a spectacle of fidelity on the one hand and confidence on the other.
>
> (1987, 57)

In attesting to his view of slavery as a benevolent institution that brings out the best in master and slave, the passage illustrates Delano's upbeat attitude and tendency to wrest positive interpretations from violent, problematic circumstances. This tendency recurs throughout the narrative as Delano struggles to determine whether Cereno's report of a disastrous voyage is true or if the Spaniard is a pirate plotting his murder. For instance, after one such mental debate, Delano decides that Cereno has simply struggled with his voyage, has lost command of his crew and indeed his own mental well-being, and needs Delano to assume his captaincy and lead the *San Dominick* back to a Chilean port. As Melville writes,

> Such were the American's thoughts. They were tranquilizing. There was a difference between the idea of Don Benito's darkly preordaining Captain Delano's fate, and Captain Delano's lightly arranging Don Benito's. Nevertheless, it was not without something of relief that the good seaman presently perceived his whale-boat in the distance. Its absence had been prolonged by unexpected detention at the sealer's side, as well as its returning trip lengthened by the continual recession of the goal.
>
> (1987, 70)

The passage illustrates his tendency to choose the "tranquilizing," genial option when presented with such choices.

Despite this tendency toward geniality, Delano is also a stern disciplinarian who values the effective management necessary for a captaincy. When he boards the *San Dominick*, Melville emphasizes Delano's perceptions of disorder and mismanagement. While pondering the *San Dominick's* state, he ruminates on how "long-continued suffering seemed to have brought out the less good-natured qualities of the negroes, besides, at the same time, impairing the Spaniard's authority over them" (Melville 1987, 51); he moreover ponders "the noisy indocility of the blacks in general, as well as what seemed the sullen inefficiency of the whites" (Melville 1987,

"Benito Cereno," Spaniards, and Creoles   101

52). This focus leads him to ascribe some of the *San Dominick*'s struggles to Cereno's management. For instance, he wonders whether "this hapless man is one of those paper captains I've known, who by policy wink at what by power they cannot put down? I know no sadder sight than a commander who has little of command but the name" (Melville 1987, 59). Moreover, he at times presumes to offer Cereno advice on the subject of management. For instance, after he and Cereno observe a black boy hit a white one on the head with a knife, with no discipline from the whites, Delano exclaims, "Had such a thing happened on board the *Bachelor's Delight*, instant punishment would have followed" (Melville 1987, 59). Delano continues by explaining

> that you would find it advantageous to keep all your blacks employed, especially the younger ones, no matter at what useless task, and no matter what happens to the ship. Why, even with my little band, I find such a course indispensable. I once kept a crew on my quarter-deck thrumming mats for my cabin, when, for three days, I had given up my ship—mats, men, and all—for a speedy loss, owing to the violence of a gale, in which we could do nothing but helplessly drive before it.
>
> (Melville 1987, 59–60)

Such passages illustrate Delano's tendency to extend his explanation of the *San Dominick*'s struggles past Cereno's narrative of a disastrous voyage that has been fatal to much of the crew and into the arena of analysis of failed management, and his willingness to assume the authority to advise Cereno on such matters.

Despite these perceptions, Delano seeks Cereno's recognition of their shared status as captains, a desire that is frequently frustrated. Upon boarding the *San Dominick*, Delano quickly becomes preoccupied with what he perceives as Cereno's "unfriendly indifference towards himself," the "sour and gloomy disdain, which he seemed at no pains to disguise" (Melville 1987, 52–53). Delano feels a general sense of unease on the ship, and "[a]t bottom it was Don Benito's reserve which displeased him" (Melville 1987, 53). This frustration is increased at times when Cereno fails to comport himself in ways that Delano believes befit a captain, for instance, when he refuses to dismiss Babo when business needs to be discussed. Delano "could hardly avoid some little tinge of irritation" at Cereno's apparent decision, and he takes further offense at Cereno's "indifference and apathy" during the discussion (Melville 1987, 91–92). Subsequently to this frustration of his expectations regarding the propriety of fellow captains discussing business in confidence, Delano is further exasperated when Cereno refuses to join him for a drink on board Delano's *Bachelor's Delight*, at which "Captain Delano's pride began to be roused. Himself became reserved" (Melville 1987, 95). The passage's odd syntax suggests the extent of his frustration; Delano has at this point

102 *John C. Havard*

become so piqued that he has lost control of his own gentility (Van Wyck 2015, 431).

Considering the centrality of this social drama to the tale, scholars have read "Benito Cereno" as a novel of manners that probes Delano's understanding of etiquette between ships' captains, as well as his responses when those expectations are not met (e.g., Van Wyck). As Rodrigo Lazo explains, Delano, somewhat familiar with South American social structures, becomes obsessed with whether Cereno is a true "don" or in fact a low-born "cholo" in some way impersonating a man above his station (Lazo 2017, 122). This obsession, as Dana Nelson contends, serves to stage a drama of white managerial identity. Delano seeks recognition of himself as a white man of the managerial class. When Cereno fails to adhere to captainly etiquette by acknowledging this cherished self-perception, by, for instance, refusing to treat financial discussions as a matter only for captain's ears, Delano is extremely frustrated and entertains the idea that Cereno is not truly of his class and may not be capable of maintaining his captaincy (Nelson 1998, 2, 16). His preoccupation with etiquette and what it signifies for his self-understanding is so strong that he does not recognize that Cereno's failures in acknowledging their shared status owe not to Cereno being an imposter but rather to a slave revolt. For instance, he feels compelled to ascribe Cereno's decision to "querulousness"—a comment upon Cereno's comportment—rather than seeing the pattern of Cereno's refusal to speak to him without Babo present, which is evidence of the revolt. This failure reveals the inadequacy of his mode of interpreting what he sees on the *San Dominick* via the protocols of the novel of manners: Until he learns of the revolt in the tale's conclusion, Delano believes that he can interpret the *San Dominick*'s shipboard culture and the behaviors of its captain in terms of genteel codes of conduct, a belief that fails him (Van Wyck 2015, 423).

Delano's fixation on these relationships over and above the slave revolt that is happening right below the surface of his perceptions demonstrates the centrality of his relationship with Cereno to his self-understanding. Delano's self-image as a genial, yet stern commander is inextricable from his perception of Cereno as nothing of the sort. Whereas Delano is genial and open-hearted, Cereno responds to his offers of assistance with "grave and ceremonious acknowledgements, his national formality dusked by the saturnine mood of ill health" (Melville 1987, 51). Whereas Delano is optimistic, he perceives in Cereno a "sour and gloomy disdain" (Melville 1987, 53) and a pessimism bred of his disastrous experiences. Moreover, whereas Delano takes pride in his efficient management, he believes that Cereno is incompetent, not just because his disastrous voyage has undermined his capacities but also because he has not been trained to the craft properly. For instance, Melville (1987, 58) writes that Delano, while observing Cereno's "small, yellow hands," then "inferred that the young captain had not got into command at the hawsehole, but the cabin-window; and if so, why wonder at incompetence, in youth, sickness, and

"Benito Cereno," Spaniards, and Creoles   103

gentility united?". Here, Delano ascribes Cereno's ineptitude to an aristocratic apprenticeship to his command.

Delano's reference to Cereno "small, yellow hands" suggests the role race plays in his self-differentiation from Cereno. Delano identifies as an Anglo-American of the managerial class in distinction to the black slaves and Spanish captain. By contrasting himself to the slaves on board the *San Dominick*, Delano gains a sense of himself as a man with agency and the capacity for freedom. He describes the slaves using animalistic metaphors. For instance, he compares a woman to a deer: "His attention had been drawn to a slumbering negress, partly disclosed through the lace-work of some rigging, lying, with youthful limbs carelessly disposed, under the lee of the bulwarks, like a doe in the shade of a woodland rock" (Melville 1987, 73). In another passage, he analogizes Atufal to a bull, thinking curious "the tyranny in Don Benito's treatment of Atufal, the black; as if a child should lead a bull of the Nile by the ring in his nose" (Melville 1987, 78). Finally, he reacts to them as others do to Newfoundland dogs: "like most men of a good, blithe heart, Captain Delano took to negroes, not philanthropically, but genially, just as other men to Newfoundland dogs" (Melville 1987, 84). As these thoughts suggest, he views Africans as subhuman, a point he explicitly expresses when he muses to himself,

> But if the whites had dark secrets concerning Don Benito, could then Don Benito be any way in complicity with the blacks? But they were too stupid. Besides, who ever heard of a white so far a renegade as to apostasize from his very species almost, by leaguing in against it with negroes?
>
> (Melville 1987, 75)

As Toni Morrison (1993, 5, 17) argues, these racist metaphors have a reflexive function: by labeling Africans as animals, Delano imagines cherished self-perceptions of himself as a man with a "good, blithe heart" who is capable of doing what animals cannot, namely, exercise agency.

These thoughts demonstrate the central role race plays in Delano's worldview and sense of himself. As the phenotypical reference to "yellow hands" suggests, race also plays a role in Delano's views regarding Cereno. Delano participates in what Maria DeGuzmán describes as the U.S. American construction of an "off-white" Spanish racial category (2005, xxiv–xxvii; see also Nelson 1993, 122). This construction, which Richard Kagan refers to as "Prescott's hypothesis" for its role in William Hickling Prescott's historiography (1996; 2019, 34–35) and which elsewhere I have described as an Anglo-American "Hispanicism" similar to Orientalism in its reflexive role in the construction of U.S. national identity, construed Spanish-speaking peoples as inclined toward inefficient, despotic styles of leadership in contrast to Anglo-Americans thought to be adept in more productive, liberal-democratic styles (Havard 2018, esp. 1–34). In this sense, his racial construction of Cereno plays a different

104 *John C. Havard*

role in Delano's self-construction than does his attitude toward Africans. Delano racializes Cereno as a despotic, inefficient captain not to confirm his humanity and agency, generally, but more specifically to construct his capacity for managerial leadership. After concluding that Cereno is not a pirate plotting Delano's doom but is rather "not fit to be entrusted with the ship" and that he would need to divest him of his command (Melville 1987, 69). Delano is gratified to think, "There was a difference between the idea of Don Benito's darkly pre-ordaining Captain Delano's fate, and Captain Delano's lightly arranging Don Benito's" (Melville 1987, 70). Although Delano has decided here that Cereno is not, in fact, a pirate, the passage illustrates his tendency to contrast himself and his style of leadership with that of Cereno: as a Spaniard with racially determined proclivities toward despotic styles of command, Cereno is likely to "darkly preordain" the fate of others, whereas Delano's own style of leadership, consistent with his sense of himself as an Anglo-American who is a benevolent but stern commander, is more inclined to "lightly arrange" in his leadership—to do so "lightly," but to arrange when needed regardless.

Melville is at pains to demonstrate that these efforts at self-differentiation are mistaken. Delano's distinction, after all, between his "lightly arranging" Cereno's fate and Cereno's "darkly preordaining" his own is strained, an effort to use labels to distinguish between what he views as, at core, possibilities for one captain to establish mastery over the other. Melville puts a fine point on their shared status in the narrative's conclusion. Delano ruminates over the course of the tale on the possibility that Cereno might be a pirate plotting to murder him and commandeer his ship, and in the climax, when Cereno flees from the mutinied slaves by jumping over the San Dominick's bulwarks into Delano's boat, the uncomprehending Delano responds, "this plotting pirate means murder!" (Melville 1987, 98). Yet as he plans the countermutiny, Delano appoints his chief mate to lead the attack; the narrator describes the mate as "an athletic and resolute man, who had been a privateer's-man, and, as his enemies whispered, a pirate" (Melville 1987, 101). The passage gives the lie to Delano's pretensions to superiority over Cereno on the basis of a more lawful, benevolent engagement in maritime trade, indeed hearkening back to the historical context of the *Tryal*'s history as a confiscated vessel captained not by a Spanish pirate but by a New England smuggler.

More to the point, Delano makes gestures toward racial benevolence in his response to Babo, for instance, exclaiming to Cereno that "I envy you such a friend; slave I cannot call him" (Melville 1987, 57), and he finds fault with what he views as Cereno's cruelty as a slave owner, thinking after Babo cuts himself during the cuddy shaving scene that Cereno has exercised his "Spanish spite against this poor friend of his" and that "This slavery breeds ugly passions in man" (Melville 1987, 88). The passage suggests Delano's association between Spaniards as a people racially inclined toward despotism and his New England posturing as an enemy of slavery. Yet it is Delano who in the end leads a brutal counterrevolt to

"Benito Cereno," Spaniards, and Creoles   105

retake the *San Dominick*, showing no sympathy with the Africans when it is revealed that they have acted to secure their freedom. Unlike in the case of his historical prototype, the fictional Delano's primary motivation in doing so is not financial. It is racial. As Lawrie Balfour explains, Delano's geniality is not neutral: "the generosity and openness so characteristic of the American character were inseparable from an insatiable demand for gratitude," and Delano's "easy friendship could and would at any moment give way to cruelty". His initial perceptions of Babo as a loyal slave having been frustrated, he responds violently in order to restore what he views as the rational order of white over black. As such, the distinctions Delano makes between himself and Cereno are false: both are committed to racial subjection.

Melville gives the lie to Delano's self-differentiation not only to emphasize U.S. American racism but also to challenge the imperial national identity construction Delano represents. As several scholars have observed, Melville's representation of Delano's assumption of the authority to command the *San Dominick* due to what he perceives as Cereno's despotic, inept style of management mirrors the imperialist discourse that argued that the United States was warranted in interfering with Spanish-American state sovereignties due to those nations' perceived governmental instability and failure to capitalize upon their natural and economic resources (e.g., Emery 1984; Havard 2014, 137–138). These discourses were elaborated in, among other venues, the pages of *Putnam's Monthly*, the periodical that originally published the novella. While Sarah Robbins has demonstrated that Melville's *Putnam's* fiction, which also includes "Bartleby, the Scrivener" and *Israel Potter*, was aesthetically consistent with *Putnam's* preference for ironic commentary on the era's sociopolitical issues, Melville's attitude vis-à-vis *Putnam's* commentary imperialism is more complex. *Putnam's* discussion of the Spanish-speaking world is generally consistent with the antebellum Anglo-American tendency to view Hispanophone peoples as inefficient and illiberal and their nations as, consequently, likely beneficiaries of U.S. imperialism. This rationale, *Putnam's* readers might have perceived, was called into question by Melville's dismantling of Captain Delano's pretensions to moral superiority to his Chilean counterpart.

Melville's Repositioning of Cerreño as a Chilean Creole

Melville's repositioning of the Andalusian Cerreño as a Chilean creole supports this interpretation of the tale. The repositioning provides further evidence favoring the claims of scholars who have read it not only as a commentary on U.S. debates over slavery but also as one on slavery's transatlantic and hemispheric contexts, as well as those who interpret it as a critique of U.S. imperialism in the Spanish-speaking world. To be sure, Melville could have made the point without this repositioning. Although Anglo-Americans of the era recognized some differences between the

106 *John C. Havard*

peoples of Spanish-speaking nations, such as the influence of racial inter-mixture and indigenous or African cultures in some American nations, they also tended to view all Hispanophone peoples according to the same constellation of stereotypes (Kagan 2019, 18–19). By questioning Amasa Delano's self-differentiation from an Andalusian, therefore, Melville could have highlighted the shared role of Anglo-Americans and Spanish-speaking peoples in violent processes of racialized labor exploitation and, thus, the incoherence of U.S. rationales for benevolent imperialism in Spanish America. But by positioning Cerreño as Chilean, Melville puts a finer emphasis on the point. His Delano and Cereno share not an invest-ment in trade in black bodies but, also, origins in New World nations that defined themselves by revolt against Old World imperial powers' oppressive policies.

As such, the significance of the repositioning can be seen by reading it in the context of the hemispheric discourse of creolism. Ralph Bauer and José Antonio Mazzotti argue that creolism had a Janus-faced character. Historically, creole consciousness emerged as an insurgent discourse, by which subjects in New World settler colonies elaborated their dis-tinctive cultures and interests in contrast to those of England and Spain during times of imperial consolidation. For instance, Bauer and Antonio Mazzotti (2009, 31) point out that Cotton Mather's celebratory biog-raphies of New England's most important sixteenth-century personages occurred in the context of England's centralization of colonial governance in the early eighteenth century. "[I]n both Spanish and British America," they continue,

> a creole consciousness emerged largely in reaction to what colonials perceived to be unfair metropolitan biases and policies: the result of a combination of factors, such as a European ethnocentrism that equated cultural difference with cultural degeneracy, the inevit-able Baroque disenchantment of the European utopianism that had underwritten much of the cultural energy of Renaissance expan-sionism, and the deliberate exploitation of this disenchantment for the geopolitical purpose of imperial consolidation. Finally, the colo-nial ambiguity of creoles originated with the ill-defined nature of an unprecedented imperial project.
> (Bauer and Antonio Mazzotti 2009, 31–32)

In an eighteenth-century context in which the European metropoles constructed prejudicial attitudes toward their settler colonies in order to support the consolidation of imperial power, creoles struck back by elab-orating a vision of their own cultural and social advantages.

While in this sense an oppositional discourse, American creoles triangulated this opposition to Europe by also defining themselves against the African, Native American, and mixed-race populations in the Americas. For instance, Bauer and Antonio Mazzotti explain that

"Benito Cereno," Spaniards, and Creoles   107

In colonial Spanish America, for example, where the particular colonial exchanges between Spanish, native American, and African culture had produced a regionally highly variable mosaic of cultural and racial *mestizaje* (racial mixture), the category *criollo* was used to distinguish American-born peoples of European descent not only from Peninsular Spaniards, Africans, and Indians but also (and often primarily) from those of mixed ancestry (mainly mestizos) in an elaborate system of *castas* (castes) in which the criollos insisted on their pure Spanish ancestry.

(2009, 34)

Indeed, as it emerged in the eighteenth century and reached its apex during the U.S. and Spanish-American revolutions, creolism occurred concurrently with the emergence of the discourse of racial essentialism. This concurrence, for instance, is captured poignantly in Thomas Jefferson's *Notes on the State of Virginia*, in which the author of the Declaration of Independence defends against European condescension toward the New World while also elaborating a theory of essential African inferiority in Query XIV (1999, 137–155). Arguing against the environmental determinism fashionable at the time, Jefferson and other creoles developed theories of racial essentialism to explain why some New World inhabitants built advanced cultures while others, so Jefferson believed, did not (Bauer 2009, 457). This discourse would not be fully articulated and theorized until the nineteenth century, but its origins can be observed in the writings of creoles such as Jefferson who, on the one hand, defined their cultures and interests in distinction to those of the imperial metropole but also with those of the African and native peoples they exploited and displaced. Creolism was, in this sense, a discourse of whiteness.[1]

As Grandin and an increasing number of scholars observe, U.S. and Spanish-American appeals to liberty are inextricable from the practice of slavery in these nations. This was true in a double sense, both in that slaveholders understood their liberty in distinction to the bondage of their slaves, and in that the processes of trade and commerce that American peoples wished to liberalize from the control of European colonial powers were underwritten by slave labor (Grandin 2014, e.g., 8, 27–28). Melville's point in rewriting Cerreño as Chilean is that Anglo-Americans and Chileans, despite the pretensions of U.S. American exceptionalists, both had stakes in this process and were thus similarly hypocritical in identifying with liberty.

This conclusion is further supported by an additional difference between Melville's tale and Delano's source text. As said, both the historical Delano and Cerreño resorted to shipping to improve their social standing, only to experience frustrations; Cerreño barely overcame a slave revolt on the *Tryal*, while Delano struggled to make the money he hoped for in the sealing industry because his sealing grounds had been overharvested. However, Melville deemphasizes Delano's struggles in his

108 *John C. Havard*

retelling. His narrative opens by highlighting the success of the fictional Delano's voyage: "In the year 1799, Captain Amasa Delano, of Duxbury, in Massachusetts, commanding a large sealer and general trader, lay at anchor, with a valuable cargo, in the harbor of St. Maria" (Melville 1987, 46). This deemphasis is repeated during Cereno's attempts to determine Delano's crew's ability to withstand an attack from the mutinied slaves:

> "Señor, may I ask how long you have lain at this isle?"
> "Oh, but a day or two, Don Benito."
> "And from what port are you last?"
> "Canton."
> "And there, Señor, you exchanged your sealskins for teas and silks, I think you said?"
> "Yes, Silks, mostly."
> "And the balance you took in specie, perhaps?"
>
> (Melville 1987, 65)

The conversation is suggestive of Delano's prosperous voyage indicated in the opening lines. Finally, Melville reduces Cereno's promise of remuneration to the part of a motivational speech given to the sailors who retake the *San Dominick* (Melville 1987, 101), delivered after Delano has already decided to retake the ship out of a desire not for compensation but to quell the rebellion. The source text concludes with Delano's narration of the legal recourses he took to gain compensation from Cereno (Delano 1994, 255–257). This emphasis on these proceedings suggests the historical Delano's desire to be remunerated was not an afterthought; he desperately sought to recoup his disastrous losses. Melville's retelling does not make that emphasis, consistent with his portrayal of Delano as a more prosperous sealer.

Why did Melville reposition Delano as prosperous? One possibility is that Melville seeks to emphasize that the wealth generated by the liberalization of trade in the wake of the American revolutions is underwritten by racism and the practice of slaveholding. By portraying Delano as a prosperous captain who nevertheless takes it upon himself to lead a counterrevolt against the *San Dominick* rebels despite not needing to do so to recoup losses, Melville emphasizes the inextricability between success and belief in the superiority of white over black in the world of trans-oceanic commerce in which Delano and Cereno operate. This illustration is crucial to Melville's ironic gloss upon Delano's efforts in national identity construction. As we have seen, over the course of the tale, Delano regularly self-differentiates his magnanimity to slaves from what he views as Cereno's violent, despotic form of mastery. Yet despite his veneer of geniality, Melville's Delano is sufficiently committed to the racial order to put his men's lives at risk, without the need of financial gain, in order to maintain that order once he perceives the truth of the rebels' achievement. Maintenance of that order is shared between Delano

"Benito Cereno," Spaniards, and Creoles 109

and Cereno as representatives of creole identity in the United States and Chile, and Melville's tale illustrates both the violence necessary to that maintenance and gives the lie to the stories Anglo-Americans tell themselves to deny that violence.

Note

1 This interpretation of creolism is often positioned against that proposed by Benedict Anderson in his classic *Imagined Communities*. Anderson (1983, 47–66) argued that the creole nationalisms that spurred the Anglo- and Spanish-American revolutions could be explained by two factors. First of all, Anderson emphasizes the cramped administrative circuits of creole administrators, who administered American colonies but were barred from peninsular posts open to non-creoles. These circuits fostered identification between fellow provincial functionaries rather than between the functionaries and peninsular leadership. Second of all, Anderson points to local print culture, which focused on provincial matters and thus forged readers' identification with their fellow creoles and undermined identification with the metropole. While scholars have continued to find compelling Anderson's concept of national community as an imagined construct, the tendency in recent years has been to focus on the importance of race in this construct, rather than administrative circuits and print culture.

Works Cited

Anderson, Benedict. 1983. *Imagined Communities: Reflections on the Origin and Spread of Nationalism*. Rev. ed. London: Verso, 1991.

Balfour, Lawrie. 2013. "What Babo Saw: 'Benito Cereno' and 'the World We Live In.'" *A Political Companion to Herman Melville*, edited by Jason Frank. Lexington: University of Kentucky Press, 259–280.

Bauer, Ralph. 2009. "The 'Rebellious Muse': Time, Space, and Race in the Revolutionary Epic." *Creole Subjects in the Colonial Americas: Empires, Texts, and Identities*, edited by Ralph Bauer and José Antonio Mazzotti. Chapel Hill: University of North Carolina Press, 442–464.

Bauer, Ralph and José Antonio Mazzotti. 2009. "Introduction." *Creole Subjects in the Colonial Americas: Empires, Texts, and Identities*, edited by Ralph Bauer and José Antonio Mazzotti. Chapel Hill: University of North Carolina Press, 1–57.

DeGuzmán, María. 2005. *Spain's Long Shadow: The Black Legend, Off-Whiteness, and Anglo-American Empire*. Minneapolis: University of Minnesota Press.

Delano, Amasa. 1994. *Delano's Voyages of Commerce and Discovery: Amasa Delano in China, the Pacific Islands, Australia, and South America, 1789–1807, 1817*, edited by Eleanor Roosevelt Seagraves. Stockbridge: Berkshire House Publishers.

Emery, Allan Moore. 1984. "'Benito Cereno' and Manifest Destiny." *Nineteenth-Century Literature* 39, no. 1: 48–68.

Grandin, Greg. 2014. *Empire of Necessity: Slavery, Freedom, and Deception in the New World*. New York: Picador.

110 *John C. Havard*

Havard, John C. 2014. "Ironizing Identity: Cosmopolitanism and Herman Melville's 'Benito Cereno' as Critique of Hispanicist Exceptionalism." *Literature Interpretation Theory* 25: 128–150.

———. 2018. *Hispanicism and Early US Literature: Spain, Mexico, Cuba, and the Origins of US National Identity*. Tuscaloosa: University of Alabama Press.

Jefferson, Thomas. 1999. *Notes on the State of Virginia*, 1785, edited by Frank Shuffelton. New York: Penguin.

Kagan, Richard. 1996. "Prescott's Paradigm: American Historical Writing and the Decline of Spain." *American Historical Review* 101: 423–446.

———. 2019. *The Spanish Craze: America's Fascination with the Hispanic World, 1779–1939*. Lincoln: University of Nebraska Press.

Lazo, Rodrigo. 2017. "Dons and Cholos." *Herman Melville in Context*, edited by Kevin J. Hayes. Cambridge: Cambridge University Press, 116–125.

Melville, Herman. 1987. "Benito Cereno." *The Piazza Tales and Other Prose Pieces 1839–1860*, 1855, edited by Harrison Hayford, Alma A. MacDougall, and G. Thomas Tanselle. Evanston: Northwestern UP and the Newberry Library, 47–117.

Morrison, Toni. 1993. *Playing in the Dark: Whiteness and the Literary Imagination*. New York: Vintage.

Nelson, Dana D. 1993. *The Word in Black and White: Reading Race in American Literature 1638–1867*. Oxford: Oxford University Press.

———. 1998. *National Manhood: Capitalist Citizenship and the Imagined Fraternity of White Men*. Durham: Duke University Press.

Newman, Lea Bertani Vozar. 1986. *A Reader's Guide to the Short Stories of Herman Melville*. Boston: G.K. Hall.

Sundquist, Eric J. 1993. *To Wake the Nations: Race in the Making of American Literature*. Cambridge: Harvard University Press.

Van Wyck, James M. 2015. "*Benito Cereno* and the Impossibility of Civility." *The New England Quarterly* 88, no. 3: 422–448.

7 Inspiration or Coincidence? Guadalupe Gutierrez and María Berta Quintero y Escudero's *Espinas y rosas* as Discursive Doubles

Vanessa Ovalle Perez

No hay duda que el título de la novelita es muy adecuado. Espinas para la autora, y rosas, nos suponemos, parecerán los labios y mejillas de la misma.[1]

[There is no doubt that the title of the little novel is very appropriate. Thorns for the author, and roses, we suppose, resemble her lips and cheeks.]

(*Las Dos Repúblicas* 1877, 2)

Is it any wonder that Guadalupe Gutierrez was met with thorns? In 1877, the Mexican immigrant author attempted to gain a foothold in the male-dominated world of Spanish-language literature in California. She succeeded in serializing her novel *Espinas y rosas* in San Francisco's Spanish-language newspaper *La Sociedad*, but not without obstacles. The reprinted text from *Las Dos Repúblicas* quoted above was included in a series of editorials in *La Crónica* of Los Angeles and detailed Gutierrez's many trials with *La Sociedad*'s publication of her work. It contained numerous typographical errors which rendered certain parts of the story unreadable,[2] and, to make matters worse, a subheading in small print in early installments of the novel apparently read "este folletin no sirve" ["this serial is no good"][3] (*Las Dos Repúblicas* 1877, 2). But even sympathetic editorials about Gutierrez's book were often patronizing and laden with condescension. The fact that her lips and cheeks are compared to the roses of her novel's title serves as just one example of the objectification she faced as a nineteenth-century Latina[4] author. The most destructive thorn was perhaps the editorial choice to not clearly attribute the novel's authorship to Gutierrez at all. In the October 27, 1877, issue of *La Sociedad*, the only one I have recovered thus far which includes an installment of the novel, the title *Espinas y rosas* is clearly indicated but not the author's name.

Without having read *La Crónica*'s editorials criticizing *La Sociedad*'s publication of *Espinas y rosas*, it would be easy for contemporary

DOI: 10.4324/9781003219460-7

112 Vanessa Ovalle Perez

researchers to pass over *Espinas y rosas* without realizing its uniqueness or importance. Since Latina novelists were seldom given opportunities to publish, Gutierrez's novel is incredibly rare in the Spanish-language presses of the nineteenth century, especially in California. Just a few minutes' drive from my home on the east side of Los Angeles, the East Los Angeles Chicano Resource Center holds a microfilm containing this particular issue of *La Sociedad*, most of whose print run seems not to have survived. The fact that I was able to find just one issue of the novel to confirm its existence was a cause for celebration but also for grief at not being able to read *Espinas y rosas* in its entirety. It set in motion a search for more issues containing installments of the novel, which led me on an unexpected path to the Biblioteca Nacional de España, where I encountered an early twentieth-century Spanish novel titled *Espinas y rosas*, written by another female author, María Berta Quintero y Escudero.

Reading the surviving pages of Gutierrez's serialized novel together with Quintero's *Espinas y rosas*, I noted intriguing coincidences between the characters and plotlines of the two novels. In addition to sharing the same title, both books include a protagonist with a sister named "Clotilde." Although Quintero's book is set in Asturias, a Mexican mentor figure is central to the plot and has the same first name as Gutierrez, "Guadalupe." The two novels are written in Spanish primarily, but Quintero often mixes Asturian words into the dialogue, and Gutierrez uses English in a similar fashion. Both novels are *bildungsromane* that follow the personal dramas of young adults taken under the wings of their more cultured, refined, and wealthy uncles. The protagonists are exposed to new acquaintances and social circles through these mentor figures.

Spanish-language newspapers circulated across oceans and national boundaries, and so, it is possible that Quintero came across Gutierrez's novel through issues of *La Sociedad* or reprints of the novel in some other newspaper. It is also possible that a predecessor of *Espinas y rosas* existed that Quintero and Gutierrez both drew inspiration from. I cannot prove that the similarities noted between the novels are anything more than coincidence, and significant differences exist between the approaches of Gutierrez and Quintero. *La Crónica*'s editorials about Gutierrez's book accurately describe her *Espinas y rosas* as a *roman à clef*, in which the characters corresponded to social acquaintances the author had made on a recent trip to Los Angeles. This caused quite a stir among the author's reading public, which in part explains why there was so much reporting on the book. Quintero was a prolific children's writer who targeted an adolescent readership, so it is unlikely that her main audience would have been other adults in her social circle. Additionally, Quintero's *Espinas y rosas* was more overtly instructive, containing strong moral lessons intended to influence her young audience.

Alas, observing these coincidences, similarities, and differences between the texts offers little in terms of arriving at any conclusive historical truth, when it comes to discerning whether Quintero imitated, drew inspiration from, or was in conversation with Gutierrez's novel. By considering these two works jointly, this chapter opens the possibility of finding a discursive connection between these women novelists and their writings. In doing so, I follow the lead of scholars of Latinx literary history, such as Rodrigo Lazo who emphasizes a focus on "not only texts but also on people not only writers but reading publics, even if people are read through texts" (2020, 229). The *Espinas y rosas* novels are a vehicle for reading in this people-centered way. I seek to render visible transnational literary points of contact, shared values, and aesthetic choices that manifest through the genre of the *bildungsroman* without losing sight of the women writers at the core of this study and their reading publics. Gutierrez, as a Latina, and Quintero, as Spanish, were bound up in a colonial history that was not alike but interrelated. Their shared Spanish language is a testament to this, as are many more subtle legacies of colonialism. Andrea Fernández-García, who writes about contemporary Latina *bildungsromane* from a decolonial perspective, has observed that although Latina identities are fluid and heterogeneous, discourses inherited from Spain through coloniality, such as marianismo and machismo, are frequently negotiated in the process of Latina self-realization (2020, 14–15). Building on Fernández-García and others, this chapter will trace how culturally informed sexist discourses crop up in the intensely gendered coming-of-age narratives of both *Espinas y rosas* novels. Furthermore, observing similarities as well as key differences aids in better understanding the complex entanglements of Mexican-American and Spanish women writers. In both Quintero's and Gutierrez's *Espinas y rosas*, important female characters are introduced into the typically all-male mentee and mentor *bildungsroman* dynamic, the protagonists' notebooks and textbooks become symbolic tokens signifying growth and self-direction, and education and character are insistently valued over the pursuit of wealth.

¿Conocidas? Guadalupe Gutierrez and María Berta Quintero y Escudero

In writing the character of Guadalupe into her version of *Espinas y rosas*, Quintero, from her vantage point as a Spaniard, created a portrait of an imagined upper-class *Mexicana*. It is tempting to imagine what Guadalupe Gutierrez might have thought of this fictional Guadalupe. Would she have laughed? Would she have found aspects of the character reductive or exoticizing? Would she have related to certain elements? When it comes to piecing together a biography of Gutierrez, I long to depict her in a way that does justice to her lived reality and have spent quite a bit of time and energy to find only traces of the life Gutierrez left behind. Mentions of Guadalupe Gutierrez in California's Spanish-language newspapers, census records, city directory entries, and of course her own writings merely hint at the woman she might have been.

114 *Vanessa Ovalle Perez*

When Gutierrez was mentioned in the society columns of California's Spanish-language newspapers, her name often was linked with that of her younger sister, the poet Carlota Gutierrez.[5] Many times the editor of *La Crónica*, Pastor de Célis, referred to them together as "las Señoritas Gutierrez," particularly during the festive time around Cinco de Mayo of 1877, when the Gutierrez sisters paid a visit to Los Angeles in the company of Pío Pico, the last Mexican governor of Alta California before it was colonized by the United States. Pico was considered an important leader in California's Mexican-American community. De Célis (1877) writes enthusiastically about Pico's arrival: "El Sr. Pico, á quien es característica la más amable galantería acompaña á las Stas. Gutierrez, distinguidas jóvenes que forman parte esencial de la escogida sociedad mejicana de la metropoli de California" ["Señor Pico, in whom the kindest gallantry is characteristic, accompanies the Señoritas Gutierrez, distinguished young women who are an essential part of the most select Mexican society of California's metropolis"]. The metropolis mentioned is San Francisco, where Gutierrez and her sister resided at the time.

Though *Espinas y rosas* is the only writing Gutierrez is known to have published,[6] she made her mark in other ways as well, particularly speaking at Mexican-American cultural events in Los Angeles and San Francisco. During Gutierrez's visit to Los Angeles in 1877, she and her sister Carlota gave *brindis*, or toasts, at a birthday celebration in honor of their traveling companion, former governor Pico. In an editorial that criticized reporting of the event in *La Sociedad*, for not crediting the Gutierrez sisters for their *brindis*,[7] De Célis (1877) writes of "la admiracion que nos causaron las Stas. Gutierrez con sus discursos" ["the admiration that the Señoritas Gutierrez aroused in us with their speeches"]. He goes on to describe how, upon their departure from Los Angeles, the sisters were accompanied to the Santa Monica train station by a number of new friends made during their short stay, emphasizing that they would not soon be forgotten. He is likely sincere in his effusive, though at times patronizing, editorials. In fact, an article from May 19, 1877, reports that the date of a dance at Los Angeles' Union Hall was moved forward so that the Gutierrez sisters could attend before their departure. It would have taken more than the affection of one newspaper editor to have the date of an event like this one changed at the drop of a hat.

Pico's birthday was not the first time the Gutierrez sisters spoke in public at celebrations of Mexican people and their culture. Reporting in *La Crónica* by a correspondent known only as "Consuelo" describes a Mexican Independence Day celebration in San Francisco, at which Carlota Gutierrez read an original poem and "una alocucion por la Sta. Guadalupe Gutierrez fué bien pronunciada y bien recibida" ["an address by Señorita Guadalupe Gutierrez was well delivered and well received"] (*La Crónica*, September 23, 1876). Although "Consuelo" does not report exactly what Gutierrez had to say, the fact that she spoke at such an important event in the Mexican-American community shows the

Espinas y rosas 115

reputation she had built for herself. These instances when Gutierrez is mentioned in the Spanish-language press emphasize a visibility she had sought actively, alongside her sister.

There is more to Gutierrez than what California's Spanish-speaking public knew from the newspapers. The 1870 U.S. Census gives more details of her family life and background. María de Guadalupe Gutierrez, listed under the name "Marie," was eighteen years old at the time of the census and had attended school within the past year. Along with the fourteen-year-old Carlota, she lived in the household of a forty-four-year-old woman named Rosa Gutierrez, probably her mother or a close family member. The value of Rosa's personal property was $400, which supported herself and at least four children. In addition to the Gutierrez sisters, twelve-year-old Frank and ten-year-old Willie are also listed in the census. Rosa Cuevas, a twenty-four-year-old seamstress, also lived in the Gutierrez home and was accompanied by a seven-year-old girl. All the members of the household were born in Mexico, and there were no adult men present. Many political exiles fled Mexico in the 1860s and sought refuge in the United States from the Second French Intervention, either temporarily or permanently. The unrest in Mexico might have contributed to the absence of a patriarchal figure, since turmoil caused by war often separates the normative family unit. Of course, there might be any number of reasons why this was a household headed by women.

From 1868 through 1880, the *San Francisco Directory*'s listings of members of the Gutierrez family lend insight into the sisters' employment. In 1868, when Guadalupe Gutierrez was around sixteen years old, she was listed as a "domestic," as was Rosario Gutierrez (probably the "Rosa" of the 1870 census record). This description meant that both Gutierrez and the head of her household were working women doing chores in the homes of others. Five years later, in 1873, Guadalupe Gutierrez was listed under a new profession: Spanish teacher. Until records for the Gutierrez family disappear from the *San Francisco Directory* in 1880, she continued to be listed as a Spanish teacher. According to the directories, Carlota began her working life at about the age of eighteen, as a telegraph operator and then followed in her sister's footsteps as a Spanish teacher from 1870 through 1880. Carlota appeared to be especially savvy in terms of marketing her services, regularly taking out classified advertisements in the *San Francisco Chronicle* offering "Spanish lessons" from 1879 through 1880. The portrait of the Gutierrez sisters painted by the directory records and Carlota's advertisements is very different from that of the creative writing, society news, and editorials appearing in *La Crónica* and *La Sociedad*. The English-language sources portray the lives of working women, whereas the Spanish-language press depicts the Gutierrez sisters as socialites, travelers, orators, and talented writers. Reading these sources together brings into focus a fuller picture of the Gutierrez sisters: these were cosmopolitan, multifaceted, multicultural, upwardly mobile, working women.

116 *Vanessa Ovalle Perez*

Quintero's life and journey as a writer are of great interest and lend context to her work. She has been studied extensively in the context of Spanish children's literature by Francisca Sánchez Pinilla, who has recovered and analyzed many of the stories Quintero published in early-twentieth-century periodicals. This includes fifty-two stories published in *El Imparcial* of Madrid and editorials in Catholic periodicals like *La Lectura Dominical* (Sánchez Pinilla 2015, 125). Quintero also published at least thirteen books, both collections of stories and novels: *La castellana de Rose Blanche*; *El collar de gotas de sangre*; *La lucecita rosada*; *Los dos huérfanitos*; *Veladas del hogar: cuentos morales*; *La lección de la Muñeca: boceto cómico en un acto*; *Dos hijos*; *Vida popular de Gema Galgani, la gran Santa del siglo XX*; *En pos de la dicha*; *Las obras de misericordia*; *La esclavita mártir*; and, of course, *Espinas y rosas*. Not only was Quintero a prolific writer, but she began publishing at an astonishingly young age. By the time she was nine years old, she had already published her first story "¡Castigo del cielo!" in the November 30, 1904, issue of Tortosa's *Correo Ibérico*, signing her name "Berta Quintero." She probably had the encouragement of her father, Ramón Quintero y Martínez, a lawyer, journalist, and director of the newspaper *Las Regiones*. The fact that her father was well connected in the press was probably an advantage, not only in terms of gaining attention for her writings but also in providing her with reading material from far and wide.

Based on the content of her writing, it appears that from a young age Quintero was exposed to stories detailing the lives, cultures, and values of diverse people. In a review of her first published book, *Veladas del hogar: cuentos morales*, which came out when Quintero was thirteen years old, she is hailed as a "verdadera niña prodigio" ["true girl prodigy"], and the reviewer mentions her having contributed to Astorga's *El Faro Astorgano* (Sánchez Pinilla 2015, 114). Quintero was going far beyond publishing in her local paper; she was reaching readers across Spain, in newspapers and through her book. As her stories were advertised as the writings of a child prodigy, it is possible that editors were actively seeking them for publication. This might account for how, at such a young age, she was being published so widely across Spain, from Tortosa to Astorga. As an adult, Quintero lived up to the lofty expectations ascribed to her as a child, and she enjoyed a long, productive career publishing stories and novels geared toward youthful and adolescent audiences.

When the Spanish Civil War broke out in 1936, Quintero was about forty-one, still writing, and active in the press. In October of that year, she was detained for three months in a women's prison in Madrid, for "crimes against the regime." She was judged by the Juzgados y Tribunales Populares and accused of being a far-right radical, for having associated with the newspapers *El siglo futuro* and *La Nación o La Mañana*. She was also charged with sheltering a very dangerous member of the Falange in her home: her nephew Eloy Guerra Ballespín. During her trial, Quintero denied any ideological sympathies with far-right newspapers and stated that she only saw herself as a writer of children's stories. In the end, she was sentenced to three months in prison and the loss of her political rights for three years (Sánchez Pinilla 2015, 125).

Plotting the *Sobrina/o* Coming-of-Age

Both Gutierrez's and Quintero's *Espinas y rosas* center on coming-of-age narratives and thus can be read as *bildungsromane*. In the Western literary tradition of the eighteenth and nineteenth centuries, the *bildungsroman* is most often associated with male novelists writing of male experiences, particularly in German- and English-language contexts. Olga Bezhanova has opened up the possibility of reading the *bildungsroman* through Spanish female subjectivity. Even when it comes to conservative or traditionalist female authors, she sees the genre as creating plotlines in which, at times, women can focus on their own development rather than their status in relation to others. She writes that the *bildungsroman* is "a shared territory where female writers and readers can discuss different scenarios of development, voice their concerns about the problematic aspects of growing up female, and participate in a joint endeavor of resolving the issues facing them" (Bezhanova 2014, 5). Quintero is a female author whose novel focuses on the development of a young boy, Angel. Although the main character is male, the role of the boy's mentor, an important archetypal role of the *bildungsroman*, is given to his aunt Guadalupe, who notably takes over the mentor role after the failure of her husband. In this way, a central female character becomes an authority figure in her own right, counseling the boy and supporting him in the struggles he faces. According to Priscilla Clark, who has studied the role of mentors in European literary contexts, in many *bildungsromane*, the

> mentor's instructions determine the education [of the main character] and, hence, define the novel. Why Mentor? Because Mentor is the authoritative educator par excellence, a figure that implies a certain type of education even as it implies a particular society which sanctions that education.
>
> (1984, 200)

From what can be gleaned from the single surviving installment of Gutierrez's novel, the genders of these mentees and mentors are reversed. Two sisters, Clotilde and Leonor, are the protagonists, and their uncle, Don Próspero, serves as a mentor figure. Reading these two versions of *Espinas y rosas* together can complete a picture of the mentorship relationship in the *bildungsroman*, and the many gendered and culturally specific aspects that such a relationship can entail in Spanish and Latinx society.

In Quintero's novel, the elements of *bildungsroman* are easily discernable. The novel's protagonist, Angel, lives with his parents, sister,

118   *Vanessa Ovalle Perez*

and adopted brother in a farmhouse in Asturias, a remote region in northwestern Spain which has its own dialect and customs. Though the family has few means, they are happy, devout Catholics, and loving toward one another. One day a letter arrives from Angel's uncle Joaquín, who plans to return to Asturias after living in the Americas for over twenty years. After much anticipation and several delays, Joaquín arrives in a shiny new car, accompanied by his charming Mexican wife, Guadalupe. Joaquín and his wife adore the children, especially since they were never able to have their own, and Angel becomes more worldly under the tutelage of his uncle. Eventually Joaquín offers to fund Angel's education in the city, and his parents gladly accept. Angel is an excellent student, so when his father becomes sick and dies suddenly, Joaquín encourages Angel to go to seminary and become a priest. Becoming a priest would allow Angel to return to Asturias, support his family, and keep his widowed mother company, and so, although Angel is hesitant, he accepts his uncle's advice. Eventually, Angel comes to the realization that he does not have the spiritual calling to be a priest and confides in Guadalupe. She encourages him to leave the seminary, and he does. Angel's choice infuriates Joaquín, causing him to disown his nephew. Angel struggles on his own, going to Madrid and taking up odd jobs until finally landing an apprenticeship with a professor at a teachers college. Joaquín falls gravely ill and converses with a priest who harbors regrets about having been forced into the religious life. Joaquín has a change of heart and forgives Angel. Following an emotional reconciliation, Angel returns to Asturias, marries his childhood sweetheart, starts a teachers college, and has children of his own. The novel concludes with Guadalupe rocking and singing a Mexican lullaby to Angel's baby daughter.

In the plot of Quintero's book, Angel's original mentor, Joaquín, ends up contributing to the many obstacles and struggles that Angel is forced to overcome. Guadalupe emerges as a true mentor to Angel, helping him get on his feet until he is able to achieve self-reliance. The fact that only one installment of Gutierrez's novel has been found greatly limits full understanding of the plot, including the role of the mentor figure, Don Próspero. Judging from this surviving installment, the book centers around two female protagonists, Leonor and Clotilde, who are staying in the home of their uncle, Don Próspero, in Los Angeles and receiving his mentorship. The installment begins with playful banter between the young ladies and their uncle, who takes them on a carriage ride to lift Leonor's spirits after she has lost her notebook. Upon returning, they find calling cards have been left by two socially prominent older ladies, Señora J... de C... and Señora C... de M.... Don Próspero speaks of these women with esteem, explaining why they are respected in the community. Leonor and Clotilde are eager to meet them. Later that evening, the sisters receive a visit from four young gentlemen, including one Anglo-American, Mr. Plumb. The narrator is quick to point out Mr. Plumb's flaws, especially his arrogance; classist sense of superiority; and, worst of all, his superficial penchant for literature. Fortunately, Mr. Plumb departs early, leaving Leonor, Clotilde, and the remaining three Latino callers to enjoy conversation and laughter, along with some singing and piano playing. The installment concludes with the young gentlemen leaving and Don Próspero reentering the scene, requesting that his nieces indulge him in a little conversation before going to bed.

In these pages of the novel, Gutierrez's narrative breaks from the traditional *bildungsroman* in two important ways: the main characters are young women, and the story seems to focus on both of them fairly evenly. In the coming-of-age tale, there usually is one protagonist, and the plot follows his journey into manhood. As more scholarship has emerged on the topic, however, more attention has been paid to novels with young female protagonists, examining the gendered aspects of the genre's plotlines. Soňa Šnircová, who studies the *bildungsroman* heroine in British texts, outlines the elements of the genre when it comes to female protagonists:

> the heroine's involvement in heterosexual romance, her acceptance of the authority of a male mentor and her acceptance of the identification with her mother's position appear, finally, as the factors that may induce the successful development of the heroine's mature selfhood.
> (2017, 68)

Even from the limited portion of Gutierrez's *Espinas y rosas* available for study, to some degree the narrative suggests all the elements outlined by Šnircová. Leonor and Clotilde have accepted the authority of a male mentor, their uncle Don Próspero, and at least one of the gentleman callers who visit them seems likely to emerge as a romantic interest. Although Leonor and Clotilde's mother is not mentioned in this excerpt, Señora J... de C... and Señora C... de M... are perhaps being set up as surrogate mothers. That Don Próspero speaks so effusively about the matrons' good character, and that visitors Plutarco and Rodolfo promise to bring their mothers—the very same Señora J... de C... and Señora C... de M...—on their next visit support this possibility.

The way these women are referred to, with ellipses after the first letters of their names, signals to the reader that they are reading a *roman à clef*. The fact that Leonor shares a first initial with the author's own nickname, Lupita, and Clotilde with her sister's name, Carlota, only emphasizes this. The intermingling of the *bildungsroman* and *roman à clef* catches the reader between fiction and reality, the text and the world of nineteenth-century California Latinx society. The reader can be lulled into a sense of familiarity when caught up in the predictable plotlines and conventions of the *bildungsroman*, bringing the intrigue and social implications of the *roman à clef* into sharp relief. The mingling of the genres brings together complimentary sensibilities, having the overall effect of making the reader all the more invested in the coming of age of the author herself—her

120　*Vanessa Ovalle Perez*

journey in terms of trials, frustrations, mentors, romances, etc. Gutierrez does not simply stop at drawing the readers into herself through the *roman à clef* but demands that they invest in her development, in the successful achievement of her ambitions.

This alchemy is manifested subtly in the banter between Don Próspero and his nieces at the beginning of the installment. He teases his niece Leonor for having "faltado en una promesa" ["failed in a promise"], and Clotilde jokingly chimes in that "Leonor merece que usted la riña severamente" ["Leonor deserves that you scold her severely"]. Leonor, puzzled, asks her uncle what he means by this, and he responds:

> —Procuraré esplicarme. Ayer, al llegar aquí, me prometieron ustedes que estarían siempre contentas; tú estás ahora enojada, ó como quieras llamarlo, y aquí tiene usted, señorita, que ha faltado á su promesa.
>
> —Pero, querido tio … esto es otra cosa, porque sin mis apuntes del camino se trastorna ….
>
> —No hay pero que valga! que cuaderno ní que Don Jaime! hágame usted favor de mandar poner una calesa para llevar á estas muchachas á pasear; porque si no, vamos á armar camorra esta *diplomática* y yo.

> ["I'll try to explain myself. Yesterday, upon arriving here, you both promised me that you would always be happy. Now you are upset, or whatever you want to call it. And so here you are, miss, who has failed in her promise."
>
> "But dear uncle … this is a different thing, because without my travel diary, it gets confused …."
>
> "There is no 'but' that suffices! Not the notebook or Don Jaime! Do me the favor of having a calèche made ready to take these girls out for an airing; because if not, we are going to get into a quarrel, this *lady diplomat* and I."]

(Gutierrez 1877, 1)

Don Próspero, true to the connotations of his fictional moniker, cannot be content unless his nieces are happy and prosperous. The short exchange shows that living with their uncle and achieving this contentedness is something that Leonor and Clotilde had longed for—or at least, they had made a promise to always be happy in the care of their uncle.

Yet for Leonor, her travel diary, or notebook, is something that she simply cannot be happy without. Later in the text, it is revealed that Don Jaime—apparently an assistant or servant to Don Próspero—has been tasked with finding the lost notebook. He mentions that it was left on the steamer Leonor and Clotilde took to Los Angeles. Though the contents of the diary are not clear, Leonor feels adrift without this outlet for writing down and remembering her thoughts, feelings, and perhaps even creative ideas. Yolanda Doub has examined the crucial, interconnected roles

Espinas y rosas 121

of travel and writing in the Spanish American *bildungsromane,* stating that "traveling has given these heroes a richness in experiences and the knowledge to find their centers; their connection with society is ultimately through writing, and their journeys afford them 'something to talk about,' as Aldous Huxley reminds us" (2010, 89). Based on her anxiety at losing her notebook, Leonor must have jotted down some ideas during her travel to Los Angeles that she valued. In the metaphysical journey of coming of age, writing her thoughts was a means of processing all that she was learning about the world around her and her own development. A parallel between Leonor and the author herself can be drawn as well: as a novelist writing a *roman à clef* based on her own travel experiences in Los Angeles, Gutierrez's own notebook would have likely been incredibly precious to her. Losing it would have felt like losing her own limb. Worse yet, it could have been a liability, exposing private thoughts and opinions that she might have preferred to remain private or, at the very least, coyly concealed under pseudonyms.

Having this plotline focused on the lost notebook draws attention to the importance of writing to the novelist herself and Gutierrez's ambition to be recognized for her literary talents. Furthermore, Don Próspero's comment about Leonor being a *"diplomática"* [*"lady diplomat"*] might be a way of teasing the protagonist about social aspirations she had in the Mexican-American community. Considering that Gutierrez spoke publicly at Mexican Independence Day and other patriotic celebrations, she likely was intent on fashioning herself as a cultural representative in her local community in San Francisco, and perhaps, to a lesser extent, in Los Angeles as well. Don Próspero, playing his *bildungsroman* role of mentor, draws his niece's attention away from her notebook and pokes fun at what he sees as illusions of grandeur, demanding that she come down to earth and be present alongside him and Clotilde.

In this way, the notebook and inward self-fashioning, discovery, and empowerment that it represents compete with Don Próspero's sense of authority. Michael Bell, who considers the *bildungsroman* a means of understanding the limits of the teachable, writes of the "encircling of the pupil" by the mentor and how this can seem benign but actually be imprisoning. Despite the best efforts of the mentor,

> the circle, however vicious in structure or intent, is never entirely closed. The pupil is a centre of otherness and open to many other influences. Hence the historical emphasis has been on the opposite anxiety: that the instruction will escape the authority of the instructor.
> (Bell 2007, 3)

Leonor's notebook represents a radical element of influence outside of Don Próspero's control. Her ideas, written on the page, are private and unsupervised and thus have the potential to guide her toward a coming of age of her own making, outside of her uncle's value system and

122   *Vanessa Ovalle Perez*

expectations. Don Próspero's teasing of his nieces can be read as a subtle defense mechanism to cope with his anxiety over competing authorities of influence. While the notebook is the physical manifestation of that outside authority, it can be understood as a stand-in for Leonor herself. It represents her conscious mind. As a woman novelist, Gutierrez positions the writer's tool—notebook—as also holding the possibility for social self-making, for coming of age.

Don Próspero is not the only mentor uncle vying for influence. In Quintero's *Espinas y rosas*, Joaquín seeks to control his nephew's future by pushing him into the seminary. Even before the death of Angel's father, Joaquín had been acting as a father figure, guiding his nephew and financing his education at a school in the city. Shortly after the funeral, Joaquín takes his patriarchal role a step further by prescribing a vocation for Angel, insisting that by becoming a priest, the boy will always be able to provide for his widowed mother, both financially and emotionally. Wanting to please his uncle, Angel eventually accepts:

> Angelín, siempre dócil y sumiso, aceptó, ignorando en su inexperiencia lo que sabía pero olvidara Joaquín: que el Sacerdocio no es una profesión como otra cualquiera, sino que es un ministerio sagrado y que para cumplir dignamente sus deberes sublimes, espinosos tantas veces, necesítase haber escuchado en el fondo del alma el llamamiento divino.
>
> Guadalupe hizo algunas observaciones a su esposo y habló a solas con Angelín, pero era éste tan niño que, a pesar de su talento, no supo comprenderla.
>
> Y, muy a disgusto de su tía, ingresó Angel en el Seminario.

> [Angelín,[8] always docile and submissive, accepted, in his inexperience not knowing what Joaquín had known but forgotten: that the Priesthood is not a profession like any other, but rather that it is a sacred ministry, and to be worthy of fulfilling its sublime, often thorny, duties, it is necessary to have heard the divine calling in the depths of one's soul.
>
> Guadalupe made some observations to her husband and spoke alone with Angelín, but he was so young that, despite his intelligence, he did not understand her.
>
> And, much to his aunt's displeasure, Angel entered the Seminary.]
> (Quintero *ca.* 1920, 20)

In the vacuum left by his father's death, Joaquín steps into the role of fatherly mentor but immediately fails. By pushing the boy into the priesthood when he is not called to it, the uncle disrespects the divinity of the profession. It is Guadalupe who steps in, from this point on, as a true mentor to Angel, though her tactics are not like those of the normative male *bildungsroman* mentor. Guadalupe's character functions more like

Leonor's diary. Listening to Angel and exchanging letters with him, she acts as a gentle guide who helps the boy realize his own identity, values, and future profession.

Although it cannot be said with certainty that Quintero read Gutierrez's *Espinas y rosas* or was inspired by the book directly, it is still interesting to consider similarities between Guadalupe, the fictional mentor to Angel, and Guadalupe Gutierrez the author of *Espinas y rosas*. They are both immigrant women born in Mexico, with the same first name and nickname, "Lupe." While Gutierrez served as an unofficial ambassador of Mexican culture in San Francisco and Los Angeles, Guadalupe did so in the fictional realm of Quintero's novel. The character Guadalupe met and married Joaquín while he was making his fortune as a businessman in the Americas. Her foreignness and Mexican identity are emphasized throughout the book, most notably in the last two sentences of the novel. In this closing scene, Guadalupe cradles Angel's sleeping baby daughter in her arms, as Joaquín gushes about how happy Guadalupe makes him and how she is an angel, a saint. "—Calla, tontín, —dijo a su esposo con dulzura mirándole con amor, —vas a despertarla. Y tornó a cantar muy bajito, con su voz dulcísima la suave *nana* del país lejano y tan querido" ["'Hush, you fool,' she said sweetly to her husband, looking at him with love. 'You're going to wake her.' And she returned to softly singing, in her incredibly sweet voice, the gentle *lullaby* of a country far away and so beloved"] (Quintero *ca.* 1920, 180). Though the words of the lullaby are not cited, there is a sense of longing and nostalgia for Mexico at the novel's conclusion. Aside from frequent mentions of the Virgin of Guadalupe, however, the character Guadalupe gives almost no specific details about her life in Mexico. She is so consumed by Angel's coming-of-age drama, that she has only traces of a backstory. Despite this, the reader is left with a tender moment of connection between Guadalupe and Angel's baby. It suggests that the child will grow up with the influence of at least three interconnected, but distinct, cultures: Mexican, Asturian, and Spanish. In a way, this multicultural blending will help undermine any homogenizing encircling of the baby girl.

The fact that Quintero would choose to end the novel with Guadalupe telling Joaquín to hush, cradling their family's symbolic next generation in her arms, solidifies her role as the true *bildungsroman* mentor and, to some degree, a secondary hero of the story. It is no coincidence that this next generation is female, like both Guadalupe and the author herself. According to the analysis of Bell, who draws on Goethe's "anxiety of influence," mentor figures in a *bildungsroman* "stand not just between the author and the character but between the author and the reader. Mentor and author, in their parallel attempts to form the same human being, throw an analytic light on each other" (2007, 4). Although it would be beautiful to think of Gutierrez factoring into this relationality of influence, throwing analytic light on both Quintero and the novel's mentor character Guadalupe, this constellation is still not clearly visible. What

124 *Vanessa Ovalle Perez*

can be seen is Quintero's role in shaping the values of her intended youth readership in the way Guadalupe also seeks to guide future generations.

Unlike her husband, who attempts to tighten his grip on Angel, Guadalupe encourages Angel to make informed decisions through introspection; prayer to God and the Virgen de Guadalupe; and consulting someone who knows the vocation intimately, Angel's confessor at seminary school. When Angel is in crisis, she visits him at seminary and speaks to him in a loving but serious tone:

> piénsalo detenida y friamente, hijo mío, que te va en ello tu dicha temporal y la salvación de tu alma tal vez. Pero si te convences de que no te llama Dios para su ministro, arróstralo todo y abandona el Seminario sin vacilar

> [think about it carefully and coolly, my son, for your worldly happiness, and perhaps the salvation of your soul, is on the line. But if you become convinced that God does not call you to his ministry, face everything and leave the Seminary without hesitation]
> (Quintero *ca.* 1920, 123)

By invoking the higher power of God, she puts her husband's pressures into a wider perspective, giving Angel the vision to look past his uncle and consider his place in a larger world order.

Guadalupe essentially encourages Angel to fail, acknowledging and making room for failure as part of Angel's development. He must face the difficult reality that he is not called to be a priest and muster the strength and courage to go against Joaquín. Aleksandar Stević has written about the underappreciated role of "falling short" or failure in the *bildungsroman* as a genre. According to Stević, the process of coming of age for the *bildungsroman* protagonist is not a linear or smooth progression; rather, it "is always contested, invariably caught up in fundamental and often irresolvable disputes about the available ways of living." Thus "the defeat of the aspiring hero tends to reveal a broader crisis in the very assumptions that govern the processes of individual development and social integration" (Stević 2020, 2). Angel's failure to become a priest is more than a personal or individual crisis; rather, it represents a crisis brought on by modernity in early twentieth-century Spanish society.

Joaquín and his mother, Lucía, cannot envision a feasible path for Angel in their small Asturian village outside of the church. Because of his education in the city, Angel has become too cosmopolitan, too much of a modern subject, to have a future in his hometown. Lucía expresses this in a conversation with Guadalupe, asking timidly "¿qué va ser ... de este pobrín si tu marido no quiere ayudarle? Porque ya no podrá cultivar el campo, hízose muy señoritín ..." ["What will be ... of this poor little boy if your husband does not want to help him? Because already he will not

Espinas y rosas   125

be able to farm the land, he's become very much the little gentleman ..." (Quintero *ca.* 1920, 135). The privileges Angel had been afforded by his uncle, in terms of travel and education, have compromised his potential for finding belonging among his immediate family members and Asturian rural community, leaving him almost no options as a "señoritín" ["little gentleman"] in the countryside. As a protean subject on a journey toward adulthood, Angel was already a bit monstrous, in the sense of being not fully formed. Without the validation of the church or even Joaquín's support, Angel will be illegible to his mother and those around her. He will be caught between social classes: too educated to cultivate the soil, but too poor to live a life of leisure. Neither Joaquín nor Lucía can envision the possibility of a secular, educated middle class in the countryside, although in the end this is exactly what Angel achieves as a professor at a teachers college.

Choose Wisely: Education, Good Character, and Wealth

An important point of connection between both Gutierrez's and Quintero's *bildungsromane* is that their young protagonists are self-conscious and at times anxious about the role of their respective social classes in achieving the promises of adulthood. Although conversations about social mobility take place between the characters, that mobility means more to the characters than simply advancing to a higher economic class. In both books, talent, education, and virtue are idealized insistently over wealth. In Quintero's *Espinas y rosas*, Angel's immediate family is poor and has very little education. In Gutierrez's novel, although Leonor and Clotilde's social class is not totally clear, it is likely they were in the middle or upper class given that they had time for leisure activity and their uncle was a man of means. Gutierrez herself had day jobs. She went from being a domestic to a Spanish instructor, meaning she climbed from the working to middle class. The fact that both Gutierrez sisters were published shows their aptitude for writing and makes clear they had some education. Since in the *roman à clef*, Leonor acts as the author's double, it is possible her character can also be read as fairly well educated and middle class.

The differences between European and American class stratification help account for some of the differences in these novels. In her analysis of the history and qualities of the *bildungsroman*, Sarah Graham notes that European *bildungsromane* often depict middle-class male protagonists, while American ones focus on working-class male protagonists.[9] Building on this idea, she writes that

> the wider range of class positions in the American Bildungsroman not only implies a higher level of class mobility than in Europe, but seemingly also affirms the power of the American Dream ... working-class boys have far more reason to invest themselves in an ideology

126   *Vanessa Ovalle Perez*

that offers liberty, happiness and prosperity. Nevertheless, male protagonists of all classes implicitly or explicitly censure American society, querying the validity of the pledges it makes to its citizens.

(Graham 2019, 122–123)

Graham's insights resonate with both Gutierrez's and Quintero's novels. The lack of class mobility in Europe is at the heart of many of the anxieties expressed about Angel's future in his Asturian hometown. Gutierrez's novel breaks from the typical American *bildungsroman* in that it is written in Spanish and centers on female protagonists and Latinx characters. Leonor and Clotilde, however, have a complex relationship with the American Dream. They are invested in its ideology, while at once questioning and expressing disillusion with it from a uniquely Latina perspective.

The disenchantment the young ladies feel with American social and cultural values is embodied by their opinions of the Anglo-American character Mr. Plumb. The narrator describes Mr. Plumb as having a figure resembling a stalk of asparagus and a personality *"sui generis."* This Latin expression implies that he was in a class of his own, in this case a negative one. Mr. Plumb is so skeptical, cold, and indolent "que apenas pueden encontrarse entre las brumas de un Lóndres" ["that one scarcely could find the like amid the fogs of London"]. This derisive comment emphasizes Mr. Plumb's connection to a lineage that traces back to England, particularly the capital of its colonial empire, London. The narrator's tone undercuts any presumption of superiority for having the stereotypical personality traits of an English person. Mr. Plumb's wealthy economic status and resulting arrogance are also critiqued:

Ocupa en la sociedad un puesto elevado por su dinero, y por esta misma circunstancia, siempre está rodeado de amigos que le adulan, elogiando sus barbaridades. Le han dicho que tiene brillantes dotes para la literatura, y el buen Mr. Plumb en su torpeza, lo ha creido, hasta el grado de imaginarse inspirado á cada instante; siendo esto causa de que siempre ande provisto de una multitud de manuscritos que se pone á leer al infeliz que tiene la desgracia de manifestar simpatía por la literatura; porque, qué mayor desgracia puede haber que estar obligado á oir necedades una tras de otra y sin esperanza de que concluyan?

[He occupied a high position in society because of his money; and due to this circumstance, he was always surrounded by friends who flattered him, praising his nonsense. They told him that he had brilliant endowments when it came to literature, and the good Mr. Plumb, in his obtuseness, believed it, to the extent that he fancied himself being inspired every moment—this being the reason he always went about supplied with a multitude of manuscripts, which he began reading

Espinas y rosas   127

to any poor soul who had the misfortune of expressing an interest in literature. For what greater misfortune can there be than being obliged to listen to idiocies, one after another, without any hope that they might end?]

(Gutierrez 1877, 1)

Gutierrez is expressing a kind of *ars poetica* through her characterization of Mr. Plumb, vilifying him as the embodiment of all that is wrong with the literary culture around her. It is wealthy Anglo-American men who gain readers and are praised for their *barbaridades*, "nonsense" or "barbarities." The narrator expresses frustration not only with Mr. Plumb's lack of literary talent but with the fact that his writing can have such little merit, yet still be imposed unabashedly upon all those who cross his path. His race; gender; and, most of all, money combine to fuel his sense of arrogance, exceptionalism, and entitlement. For Gutierrez, achieving success and recognition as a writer are at the core of her American Dream. Thus, her characterization of Mr. Plumb expresses disillusionment and frustration with the democratic ideal that she might have a fair shot at pursuing literary prosperity, compared to a wealthy, Anglo-American male writer—no matter how idiotic he might be.

Gutierrez's *Espinas y rosas* insists that wealth is a poor measure of a person's worth or success. In addition to writerly talent, education is overtly valued over wealth. This focus on education is expressed further by way of character description. Leonor and Clotilde return with their uncle from their carriage ride and discover the calling cards of Sra. J... de C... and Sra. C... de M.... Asked about these ladies, Don Próspero says they belong to high society and are said to be very proud. This is because they have high standards when it comes to who they associate with, only granting their friendship to

> aquellas personas que por su educacion y buenas cualidades saben meecerla [*sic*, merecerla], y como hay varias que teniendo dinero creen con esto esto [*sic*] tener todas las cualidades requeridas nos on [*sic*, no son] honradas ni con las miradas de estas señoras.

> [those people who, due to their education and good qualities, they know to deserve it; but as there are some people who, having money, believe that with this they possess all the required qualities, they are not honored with even a passing glance from these ladies].

Once again, there is an emphasis that belonging to a higher economic class does not denote worthiness of character. It is education and goodness that count. The lesson Don Próspero wants to impress upon his nieces is not only that they mind the company they keep, upholding high standards like Sra. J... de C... and Sra. C... de M... but also that they understand what it is to be a person of good character. Rather than faulting them

128 *Vanessa Ovalle Perez*

for being too proud, he upholds his distinguished lady friends as models of virtue and praises their discerning attitudes. Furthermore, he respects these ladies for being "muy inteligentes, de fina educacion, sumamente amables, y francas y sinceras con sus amigos en general" ["very intelligent, well educated, extremely amiable, and frank and sincere with their friends in general"] (Gutierrez 1877, 2). As the mentor figure to his nieces, Don Próspero articulates the model they should aspire to. He encourages them to value and cultivate their intelligence and education but also to be mindful of the way they treat others. Striking a balance between being friendly, frank, and sincere with those around them is stressed as an important aspect of social education.

The insistence that education and character are more important than money is echoed throughout Quintero's *Espinas y rosas*. It is a driving theme of the plot, representing a central flawed predisposition within Angel that he is forced to overcome in his journey toward adulthood. Struggling to survive poverty, at times hungry, Angel's parents sometimes fantasize about the wealthy Joaquín returning to Asturias and ending all their troubles with his riches. Upon discovering that Joaquín is married, the first response of Angel's mother is to bemoan the fact that her children will not stand to inherit a large portion of Joaquín's assets. Angel also falls prey to fantasies of riches, envisioning himself going to America and becoming wealthy. Although it pains him to think of how his mother, childhood sweetheart, and sister would cry in his absence, he thinks, "¡Bah, consolaríanse luego y bien contentas se pondrían cuando viéranle volver trayéndoles arracadas de plata y coral y collares más guapos que los que tenían las hijas del señor alcalde!" ["Bah, later they would be consoled and very happy when they saw him return with gifts of silver-and-coral earrings and necklaces even more beautiful than those of the mayor's daughters!"] (Quintero *ca.* 1920, 25). In Angel's fantasy, valuable gifts would be enough to mend the emotional pain of female figures in his life. He also equates the adornment of these female loved ones with power, implying that he would be an even greater man than the mayor for being able to decorate his ladies in more precious finery. Angel's sexism is twofold: first, he minimizes their feelings by thinking he can stifle grief with commodities; and second, he objectifies the women in his life to bolster his manhood and a sense of superiority. These sexist ideas that Angel harbors are critiqued when he is forced to abandon them in his quest toward adulthood.

Quintero portrays how a combination of the protagonist's childishness and the fact that he grew up in poverty contribute to these problematic attitudes; but eventually, after education and many trials, Angel's pursuit of wealth evolves into a pursuit of knowledge. After being disowned by his uncle, Angel lives in Madrid and tries to sustain himself with odd jobs. Throughout this time, he reads voraciously and spends all his money on books. There are nights when he does not have a bed to sleep in or bread to eat "porque prefirió soportar hambre y dormir sentado en el quicio de una puerta antes que vender los libros de texto que adquiriera con tanto trabajo, a costa de tantas privaciones" ["because he preferred to endure hunger and sleep sitting in a doorway rather than sell the textbooks he had acquired with so much work, at the cost of so many hardships"] (Quintero *ca.* 1920, 146). Like Leonor's notebook in Gutierrez's novel, Angel's textbooks are tethered to a new sense of identity that he is coming into awareness of in his journey toward adulthood. At this point in the plot, it is not clear where all this education will lead, but for Angel, education for its own sake becomes a guiding light. The textbooks are a space where Angel can lose himself in learning, and they provide an escape he values over the creature comforts that wealth can provide. Just as Leonor can fashion herself through writing, Angel can find self-direction in reading.

Quintero's novels and stories have been read, in the context of Spanish children's literature, as educational tools; thus, their function is inextricably linked to the genre of the *bildungsroman*. Sánchez Pinilla refers to Quintero under the heading of "educadora en valores," as a female teacher of values or morals. Although Quintero's fiction is not overtly labeled an instruction manual, Sánchez Pinilla (2015, 124) observes that her stories always have some kind of moral function. In the case of *Espinas y rosas*, the moral that Angel learns is informed not only by his own social class but by that of Quintero as an author as well. As Quintero's father was a lawyer, journalist, and newspaper director who pushed her from a young age to publish her work, she grew up in a family where education and writerly talent were valued highly. It is unclear if her family was wealthy, but based on her father's profession, it does not seem they were impoverished or personally experienced the deprivations that she portrays Angel's family suffering in her novel. This might speak to a certain bias that she had in crafting the moral of her *bildungsroman*. By portraying the fantasies of upward economic mobility that Angel and his family members had as unevolved and in need of correction, she fails to validate their suffering and desire for long-term economic stability. Both Quintero and Gutierrez share a blind spot and inner contradiction when it comes to the idealization of education and values over wealth, in that their mentor characters, Don Próspero and Guadalupe/Joaquín, insist upon this moral code, while appearing to be affluent themselves. Thus, despite saying otherwise, the mentor characters inevitably reaffirm that riches bring social authority and that the rich are natural role models.

Overall, there are many similarities between these novels beyond their shared title, a couple of character names, and the *bildungsroman* genre. By placing them in conversation as discursive doubles, key connections and differences can be ascertained when it comes to the delineation of cultural and social values. Central female characters, particularly Leonor and Guadalupe, add complexity and recast the typical all-male dynamic of the mentor/mentee *bildungsroman*. Leonor's notebook and Angel's textbooks further complicate the mentor and mentee relationship,

130 *Vanessa Ovalle Perez*

undoing its binary nature by interjecting the possibility of self-fashioning and self-direction. The valuing of education and good character over the pursuit of riches, while central to both novels, evolves differently in each case. Important distinctions in terms of the structuring of social class in Spain versus the United States inform this element of the story. Understanding the novels as intertwined in a colonial legacy and reading the biographies of these women together—Gutierrez from the perspective of a working woman and Mexican immigrant in California and Quintero as a child prodigy from Spain—helps to contextualize and render visible a transnational literary conversation between these women, one that may or may not have been intentional. Read together, the *Espinas y rosas* novels provide a window into the social, cultural, and literary entanglements between the United States, Mexico, and Spain at the turn of the twentieth century from the often-underappreciated perspectives of Latina and Spanish women writers.

Notes

1 All translations are mine. Unless indicated, original quotations and names from nineteenth- and early-twentieth-century sources have not been edited for spelling or grammar.
2 In addition to misspellings and editorial liberties with Gutierrez's prose, the pages of the novel also appeared in an unusual order at the bottom of the newspaper page. On the front page of *La Sociedad*, pages 79, 82, and 83 of the novel appeared from left to right. On page two of the newspaper, 80, 81, and 84 were printed from left to right. Perhaps there was some logic to this, for example, in terms of stitching the pages together to make a booklet. For the casual reader, however, it probably made following the story confusing and tedious.
3 I read the editorial from *Las Dos Repúblicas* at face value here, assuming that the subtitle is not a sardonic joke. While it might seem to outrageous to modern sensibilities, I would not be the least bit surprised if the subtitle were real, judging by other ways in which nineteenth-century editors undermined female authors. Since there are no other issues of *La Sociedad* that I have been able to recover in which *Espinas y rosas* is published, I cannot confirm, one way or another.
4 I refer to Gutierrez as a "Latina" in this study but acknowledge that this is an identity term of today rather than a term she would have likely used herself. Likewise, uses of "Latinx" in reference to the literature and community of former Alta Californians and Latin American immigrants in the nineteenth-century United States is meant to express a contemporary set of gender-inclusive concerns and associations, rather than what identity term members of this group would have used historically.
5 To distinguish between sisters Guadalupe Gutierrez and Carlota Gutierrez, I refer to Carlota by her first name only throughout this chapter. For more on Carlota and her poetry, see my article: Ovalle Perez (2020).
6 *Espinas y rosas* is the only piece of writing by Gutierrez that I have record of, to date. It is possible that she published other writings, and I will continue searching.

7 For more on the *brindis* genre as it relates to Latinas of nineteenth-century California generally, and this editorial in particular, see my article: Ovalle Perez (2017).
8 Angelín is the Spanish diminutive of Angel.
9 Sarah Graham is building on the insights of Franco Moretti when she makes this distinction between European and American *bildungsromane*.

Works Cited

Bell, Michael. 2007. *Open Secrets: Literature, Education, and Authority from J-J. Rousseau to J.M. Coetzee*. Oxford and New York: Oxford University Press.

Bezhanova, Olga. 2014. *Growing Up in an Inhospitable World: Female Bildungsroman in Spain*. Tempe: V Premio de Critica Victoria Urbano.

Clark, Priscilla. 1984. "The Metamorphosis of Mentor: Fénelon to Balzac." *Romanic Review* 75, no. 2: 200–215.

Consuelo. 1876. "El programa de la noche." *La Crónica*, September 23, 1876.

De Célis, Pastor. 1877. "Al Cesar Lo Que Es Del Cesar." *La Crónica*, May 23, 1877.

Doub, Yolanda A. 2010. *Journeys of Formation: The Spanish American Bildungsroman*. New York: Peter Lang.

Fernández-García, Andrea. 2020. *Geographies of Girlhood in US Latina Writing: Decolonizing Spaces and Identities*. Cham, Switzerland: Palgrave Macmillan.

Graham, Sarah. 2019. "The American Bildungsroman." *A History of the Bildungsroman*, edited by Sarah Graham. Cambridge, UK, and New York: Cambridge University Press, 117–142.

Gutierrez, Guadalupe. 1877. "Espinas y Rosas." *La Sociedad*, October 27, 1877.

Las Dos Repúblicas. 1877. "Espinas y Rosas." *La Crónica*, December 1, 1877.

Lazo, Rodrigo. 2020. *Letters from Filadelfia: Early Latino Literature and the Trans-American Elite*. Charlottesville: University of Virginia Press.

Ovalle Perez, Vanessa. 2017. "Toasting *México* in the American West: *Brindis* Poems and Political Loyalties of Women's Mexican Patriotic Clubs." *Letras Femeninas* 43, no. 1: 60–77.

———. 2020. "Voicing a Transnational Latina Poetics: The Dedication Poems of Amelia Denis and Carlota Gutierrez." *J19: The Journal of Nineteenth-Century Americanists* 8, no. 2: 295–319.

Quintero y Escudero, María Berta. 1920. *Espinas y rosas*. Madrid: Madrid Biblioteca Patria.

Sánchez Pinilla, Francisca. 2015. *La narración para niños: autoras, circuitos y textos en el cambio del siglo XIX al XX*. Ph.D. Dissertation, University of Valencia.

Šnircová, Soňa. 2017. *Girlhood in British Coming-of-Age Novels: The Bildungsroman Heroine Revisited*. Newcastle upon Tyne, UK: Cambridge Scholars Publishing.

Stević, Aleksandar. 2020. *Falling Short: The Bildungsroman and the Crisis of Self-Fashioning*. Charlottesville: University of Virginia Press.

8 Spain, U.S. Whiteness Studies, and María Amparo Ruiz de Burton's "Lost Cause"

Melanie Hernández

As much as we, Chicano/a scholars and our allies, would like to read Ruiz de Burton as a prototypical Chicana feminist, resistance fighter, in-your-face Abraham Lincoln basher, and go-to-hell Supreme Court critic, she was none of these.

(José F. Aranda, Jr., "Contradictory Impulses")

María A. Ruiz de Burton wrote a protest novel not from a general Mexican American point of view but, rather, from an aristocratic Mexican American point of view—and this contrasts sharply with protest novels written later during the Chicano movement.

(Manuel M. Rodríguez)

Chicanx studies scholars struggle to reconcile the northern Mexican landed gentry within a field that, since its inception, has been invested in working-class and mestizo identity politics. The matter is how to create a literary genealogy that includes nineteenth-century Mexican American writers who self-identify as neither working class nor mixed race. What do scholars of Chicanx studies—and American studies more broadly—gain by studying antecedents whose claim for national inclusion is based on the insistence of their pure white [Spanish] bloodlines and good breeding, but whose disenfranchisement nevertheless helps give rise to the field? María Amparo Ruiz de Burton's 1872 novel, *Who Would Have Thought It?* presents such a problem.

Since its recovery and republication in 1995, scholars rightly place *Who Would Have Thought It?* within the context of U.S. nationalist and expansionist imperial projects. However, the extent to which this novel protests these projects while being simultaneously complicit within them is up for debate. Ruiz de Burton criticizes the U.S. nation-building machine that affected her personally: the legal and pro-monopoly economic policies that protected the rights of Anglo-American squatters who overran her property, crippled her business ventures, and engaged her in expensive, decades-long legal battles over the legitimacy of her land titles. Ultimately, she died penniless and dispossessed of her land holdings, Rancho Jamul, nearly 1000 acres in San Diego Country. For

DOI: 10.4324/9781003219460-8

Spain, Whiteness Studies, and "Lost Cause" 133

these reasons—and while still recognizing the complicated position from which Ruiz de Burton wrote—many foundational scholars in the field of Chicano studies represent her writing as partaking in an anti-racist, subaltern, anti-capitalist, or proletarian protest poetics (Sánchez and Pita 1995; Saldívar 1997; M. González 2009). I believe that these depictions are inaccurate insofar as: (1) they suggest a filial claim to Ruiz de Burton as a precursor to twentieth- and twenty-first-century Chicanx political struggles (instead of figuring her as part of the problem), and (2) they invalidate her claim to whiteness and, as a result, elide the source of the ever-widening internal rift between modern-day left-leaning and center-right U.S.-based Mexicans over assimilation politics within U.S. culture wars.

My analysis of *Who Would Have Thought It?* is more in line with scholars who position Ruiz de Burton not as a subaltern subject but as a woman of elite status who advocated within the United States' highest social and juridical circles in defense of her privilege, even as she was gradually being stripped of it (J. González 1996; Rodríguez 1996; Aranda 1998, 2004; Alemán 2004, 2007). She does not protest the incorporation of California into the United States so much as she decries the United States' inability or obstinate refusal to recognize California's preexisting race and class stratifications, which diminish her social rank under U.S. governance. I argue that rather than contorting her into a progenitor of Chicanx struggles and a spokesperson for all nineteenth-century Mexican Americans—which is how she may ultimately be remembered despite her objections to being lumped in with non-white *Californios*—it is important to recognize that she occupied a nebulous space in late-nineteenth-century society that was marginalized, yet privileged, racialized, yet racist.

In an effort to bridge these two views of Ruiz de Burton, Marcial González (2009) uses a Marxist framework to place her, as a *Californiana*, within a Chicano literary genealogy as a victim of capitalist accumulation and the proletarianization of Mexican Americans after 1848. M. González writes,

> if a Californio-Chicano literary genealogy exists, it does not emerge exclusively from a common "resistance" to racism and class exploitation, but equally, and in some cases perhaps more so, from a common desire to be included within the democratic institutions of American capitalism.
>
> (2009, 56)

González recognizes Ruiz de Burton's privileged class position and suggests that by all indications she operated *within* a system of capital, not in opposition to it. However, he also suggests that, like modern-day Chicanos, she shared a common resistance "to racism and class exploitation." By contrast, I argue that race and class exploitation formed the

134　*Melanie Hernández*

foundation of Ruiz de Burton's privilege, formed within the Spanish colonial *sistema de castas* and geo-specifically carried over through annexation from the California mission and hacienda systems.

What González inadvertently describes here is Ruiz de Burton's desire to assimilate into the upper tiers of U.S. social and economic systems after the United States' acquisition of formerly Mexican territories—which is a major divergence from most twentieth-century Chicano protest narratives. While González argues that her novels protest the proletarianization of Mexican Americans, I warn readers not to conflate all nineteenth-century Mexican American peoples into a monolith, but instead to recognize that any protest her novels offer is solely for the benefit of her class. She advocated for the inclusion of elite *Californios* based on their fitness to participate in civil society as cultivated, *gente de razón*, and for herself in particular as a "Spanish American." Indeed, many in this group claimed unadulterated white bloodlines. Her argument does not extend to laboring *mestizos*—and certainly not to *indios*, whether classified as *de razón* or *sin razón* (Saldaña-Portillo 2004, 145–146)[1]—both of whom would have ranked beneath her in status, prior to the conquest of California, and whom she largely ignores in her novels unless it is to insult them by oppositional gesture.

Put differently, her resistance to the proletarianization of Mexican Americans extended only far enough to protest the inclusion of elite *Californios* like herself within the post-1848 racialization process that turned most Mexican Americans into a race-based laboring class by the turn of the twentieth century. As José Aranda reminds us, "she represents a group of elite individuals who resisted their social and class demotion after 1848 but nevertheless had more in common with their conquerors than they were willing to acknowledge" (1998, 555). Although it is tempting to read Ruiz de Burton's corpus of work through the lens of U.S. territorial occupation, it is perhaps helpful to reimagine this moment—at least from her perspective—as the "merger" of two colonial forces.[2] Her novel does not concern itself with the fates of all *Californios*; it depicts the *Californio* aristocracy's attempt to vie for their positions under "new management," and the cultural terrain on which she waged this battle through her novels. Whereas Aranda suggests a discomfort of a too cozy alignment between *Californios* and Anglo-Americans, any actual discomfort is likely on the part of Chicanx scholars trying to retrofit Ruiz de Burton into a resistance fighter. My analysis predicates her resistance strategy entirely upon acknowledging her similarity to her conquerors and forcing them to recognize their likeness to her, which she achieves by galvanizing for her own use the same literary tools long familiar to a U.S. readership.

Ruiz de Burton stands at the center of an ongoing debate within Chicanx studies that resurfaces when conceptually attempting to map the Spanish colonial elite—whether *peninsulares* or *criollos*[3]—and their descendants away from a *sistema de castas* and onto a binary U.S. color

Spain, Whiteness Studies, and "Lost Cause" 135

line system. The recovery of a figure like Ruiz de Burton, according to Aranda, has "reactivated a long-standing debate about the heterogeneity of Mexican American culture and history and its relation to left-activist politics, and questioned anew the idea that Mexican Americans have always been proletarian in character" (1998, 553). When González makes the broad, conciliatory attempt to demonstrate Ruiz de Burton's protest against the "proletarianization of Mexican Americans," and to place her within a Chicano literary genealogy as a result of her shared protest, he discursively situates her at the end of the racialization process instead of at the beginning of it. To suggest that she shared political sympathy with modern-day Chicanos solely because both suffered under the same disenfranchising processes implies an anachronistic essence-based identification that she would likely not have appreciated.

The descendants of Spanish *Californios* ultimately would become Mexican American as we understand this ethnic category today; however, at the time of her writing, this process was not yet complete. In fact, at the time she was writing, there are multiple racial and class formations occurring simultaneously, and how her work figures into these processes is quite complicated. The "proletarianization" process is both a racial formation (the browning of Mexicans into a monolith within the Anglo-U.S. imaginary) and the relegation of this newly formed monolith to the "colored" side of the U.S. color line and into a laboring economic underclass. Her novels actually show little inclination to protest the proletarianization of Mexican Americans assuming this category is comprised exclusively of *mestizo* ex-Mexican nationals. Her effort, instead, is to prevent the racialization of elite *Californios* alongside *mestizos* into non-white Mexican Americans so that *Californios* would not be included as part of the proletarianization process. Curiously, the burning question that undergirds these analyses, but is not blatantly asked, is whether or not Ruiz de Burton was "actually" white, and on what grounds this might be determined? By her own account, the terms that she used to describe *Californios* were "Spanish," "Spano-Americans," and "native Californians" (M. González 2009, 47). In this light, Ruiz de Burton's work ought to be read within the context of U.S. whiteness studies, but rather than telling the story of how a particular group consolidated into whiteness, her work tells the story of a group that was weeded out during the same process.

These debates point to a problem of dissonance: *how* and *by whom* are Mexican Americans imagined in the nineteenth century versus a vastly different twenty-first-century readership with disparate identity categories available to mediate their interpretations? Readers run the risk of reifying a racial logic that comes at the end of the process González describes; however, we cannot place Ruiz de Burton as a member of a group that has not yet come into being, especially when her inclusion within this racial formation is the very process she is fighting to prevent. I argue that this second vantage—that which, based on its own political investments,

136   *Melanie Hernández*

attempts to depict her as a proto-Chicana—denies Ruiz de Burton's persistent claim to whiteness. To use concepts such as the "Spanish fantasy heritage" (McWilliams 1990, 37), "hacienda syndrome" (Paredes 1982, 52), or the "Caucasian cloak" (Gross 2006–2007, 340) to infer that she was not actually white ignores the nineteenth-century racial ontologies that would have recognized her ethnic Iberian whiteness and permitted Ruiz de Burton's 1849 intermarriage to a high-ranking Anglo-American military officer as a tolerated form of amalgamation (Almaguer 1994, 58).[4] Chicanx studies scholars are well aware of the legal maneuverings that the Spanish fantasy heritage enabled in the twentieth century and have rightly demonstrated that these concepts, like Ruiz de Burton's novels, ultimately functioned by sustaining white supremacist logics. However, dismissing her Spanish (white) racial identification ignores the different temporally and regionally specific racial formations that she negotiated in her own day. Moreover, interpreting her protest through a twenty-first-century racial analytic misconstrues rapidly changing racial formations that her writing participates in. As whiteness studies scholars remind us, whiteness is not a static category; it undergoes turbulent cycles of cultural negotiation and violent backlash throughout the period that Ruiz de Burton writes and continues to shift well into the early decades of the twentieth century.

My analysis recognizes that a twenty-first-century vantage point readily accepts "whiteness" as a consolidated and generic racial category. Modern-day usage of the term abstracts Anglo-Saxon specificity even while continuing to privilege it and while incorporating and downplaying the specificity of the less desirable ethnic whites enfolded within its dominion. From a nineteenth-century vantage, Iberian whiteness would have been one of several white races, even if it carried far less prestige in the United States than Anglo-Saxonism. Unlike the multiple "white races" of the nineteenth century that survived that consolidation process into "whiteness," the same is not true for *Californios*. Despite the tenuous protections that their legal whiteness promised, Mexican-descended Americans across multiple U.S. geographical regions suffered under de facto racial segregation. This lived reality makes it hard to imagine that the occasional claim to Mexican whiteness could be deemed legitimate instead of merely a political ploy to leverage Mexican American legal status against black noncitizenship—but this is a history that has not yet fully unfolded at the time that Ruiz de Burton was writing. We therefore must not forget that she lived in a time that recognized multiple white "races," however unequal, and that a small segment of *Californios* clung dearly to the legitimacy of their *sangre azul* ([pure Spanish] blue blood) or their being *blanco puro* (pure white)—as opposed to having purchased their whiteness from the Spanish crown through a process called *"gracias al sacar"*—as the racial basis of their claim to social rank (Haas 1995, 31).

A modern-day Chicanx political positioning might have difficulty in receiving Ruiz de Burton on her own racial terms and might classify a

Spain, Whiteness Studies, and "Lost Cause"   137

text like *Who Would Have Thought It?* as a racial passing novel. To be clear, *Who Would Have Thought It?* is not a novel about racial passing so much as it is a novel that evokes the hallmarks of the racial passing novel toward a strategic recuperation of Spanish whiteness for Reconstruction-era readers. Put differently, Ruiz de Burton does not try to pass her protagonist, Lola, off as white so much as she argues that Lola genuinely *is* white—and a culturally superior form of whiteness at that—and, as such, she deserves to be incorporated into her rightful position of prominence within the U.S. body politic. The notion of Spanish supremacy (or even equality), however, would have been a tough sell to a nineteenth-century U.S. readership, given the prevalent understanding that Mexican-ness did not signify national belonging; rather, "Mexican" as a common-place was understood mostly in biological terms as a "mongrel" race. Racialized Mexican-ness, as a popular representation that did not include Spanish *Californios*, abounded in the 1830s and 1840s American literary imaginary through sensational pamphlet literature, military reconnais-sance expedition reports,[5] travelogues, and Mexican–American war correspondence, then taken up again in the 1860s by southern writers such as Augusta Evans to help the Confederacy gain cultural leverage in opposition to alien Mexicanness as just one more form of unassimilable racial otherness threatening U.S. white supremacy after the Civil War.

In order to write against these negative depictions that increasingly included *Californios*, Ruiz de Burton had to rely on the literary tools at her disposal to persuade her readers to recognize that Lola—reared in Indian captivity and first introduced in blackface—is actually white. While the boom in racial passing novels as a genre would not begin until the 1890s, by 1872 popular literature with passing-related storylines already existed. Many of these centered on abolitionist "tragic mulatta" storylines, including Harriet Beecher Stowe's *Uncle Tom's Cabin* (1852) and Lydia Maria Child's *A Romance of the Republic* (1867), but were used toward very different racial politics than Ruiz de Burton's fiction.[6] Nevertheless, the trope of passing is still useful in *Who Would Have Thought It?* in order to clarify Lola's racial makeup to an audience that has primarily been exposed to mongrelized representations of Mexicans. Rather than begin with the premise that the central figure is a person of color who passes for white, Ruiz de Burton begins with the premise that Lola *is* white, and that the other characters are deficient in their ability to recognize this. Ruiz de Burton then complicates the intentionality of the pass by emphasizing that Lola is only being passed off as non-white when, under Indian captivity, her skin is dyed in order to thwart any rescue efforts. She is a victim, but remains virtuous, as there is no decep-tive intent on her part. In this situation, like many *Californios*, Lola's racial composition is being misread because, unlike the *sistema de castas*, people in the United States have fewer categories available to concept-alize race. If Ruiz de Burton can establish Lola's whiteness, she can then define the proper place for this specific form of whiteness against the

138   *Melanie Hernández*

complex tapestry of race, ethnicity, class, and religion already present in New England society and in the United States more broadly.

This study takes a novel view by exploring Ruiz de Burton's composite use of literary genre as the vehicle to render visible the hypocrisies she sees in American society: its self-concept against its stratifications, expansionist bloodlust, and venality. From her vantage point as elite, yet racially dispossessed Spanish gentlewoman, in a strategic intermarriage to an Anglo-American Union officer, Colonel Henry S. Burton—and, thus, privy to multiple goings on, spanning California's land grab to Washington D.C.'s parlor society—Ruiz de Burton crafts scathing commentary by invoking and subverting popular genre expectations. She takes liberties with the conventions of the captivity narrative, the sentimental marriage plot, the "passing" novel, and sensational and gothic anti-Catholicism, while conspicuously avoiding the one racialized nineteenth-century genre that connects all the others: the slave narrative.

Through role reversal, she inverts the United States' narrative position against its imagined imperial foe, Spain, thereby juxtaposing Spanish good breeding against American crudeness. In addition to her manipulation of literary genre, Ruiz de Burton reaches into her transcultural bag of tricks, invoking racial logics remnant from Colonial Spanish rule—*gente de razón* (people of reason), *limpieza de sangre* (blood purity), and against essentialist Anglo renderings of Spanish cruelty within *la leyenda negra* (the black legend).[7] However, she deploys these logics within distinctly U.S. geopolitical and literary contexts in order to argue for the enfranchisement of California's landed gentry on the basis of their fitness to participate as virtuous citizens of a republic. She appropriates the genre conventions of popular fiction to define the terms under which her American readers must fully comprehend their imperial dispossession of elite Spanish *Californios*, who she casts as racially equal, if not culturally and morally superior. She then recasts the "unprotected" Spanish gentlewoman—her protagonist, Lola—as the ideal of white womanhood, suffering at the hands of her New England captors, the Norval family. In this case, however, Lola exerts *her* moral influence through her impending intermarriage to the Norvals' only son, Julian, and allegorically to the U.S. nation-state by extension. Ruiz de Burton redraws the geopolitical map and the color lines with which the United States reestablishes its class, racial, and cultural citizenship requirements to include elite *Californios* under the shifting terms produced by the Civil War and in the midst of Reconstruction.

ENTER LOLA: A 'Spano-American' on the Minstrel Stage

> I think that Lola, instead of being a *burden* to us, will be a great acquisition.
>
> (Dr. Norval, *Who Would Have Thought It?*)

Spain, Whiteness Studies, and "Lost Cause" 139

Set against the backdrop of the U.S. Civil War, *Who Would Have Thought It?* begins with the return of Dr. Norval, a traveling amateur geologist, to his New England home after a four-year expedition to the U.S. southwest. In addition to the mysterious wagon load of boxes that Dr. Norval brings back, he also returns with a more curious specimen: a young "nigger girl" named Lola, who he claims as his charge and new addition to the Norval household. In his telling of how Lola came to be under his care, he recounts the Indian captivity of Lola's mother—Doña María Teresa Almenara de Medina, a Spanish-Mexican gentlewoman, who was abducted from her family's Sonora hacienda during an 1846 Apache raid, sold to a Mohave tribe, and wedded to their chief. Although Doña María was "insulted" by savages, the narrative is clear on the point of Lola's parentage. Doña María was already pregnant at the time of her abduction, and Lola was born just five months into her mother's captivity; thus "pure Spanish blood" courses through Lola's veins, despite the appearance or her "blackened" skin (Ruiz de Burton 1995, 28). Dr. Norval then describes the contents of the mysterious boxes he brought back from his expedition: western gold and uncut precious stones—diamonds, emeralds, rubies, and opals—that Doña María collected from the banks of the Colorado River, and that she hid away to provide for Lola in the event of her rescue. Lola, it turns out, is a wealthy heiress. Thus, Ruiz de Burton begins her novel by removing ten-year-old Lola from Indian captivity and placing her in an ever more precarious captivity—that of a wealthy, unprotected, "black"-skinned, Spanish Catholic transported to New England, where she is surrounded by Protestant social climbers.

Ruiz de Burton weaves a convoluted and satirical marriage plot impelled by the question of Lola's fitness for "good" society—a dilemma ultimately remedied by the lightening of her skin and the deepening of her pocketbook. She begins her story by complicating the standard Anglo-American captivity narrative, placing a Spanish heroine in the role usually occupied by an Anglo woman within the U.S. captivity narrative tradition. Then, on the heels of this first captivity narrative, she inverts the racial casting in a second captivity narrative, transporting a "blackened" Lola off to cold New England peopled by vehemently racist abolitionists. This cultural inversion of the captivity narrative also carries over into religious discourse. Catholicism is directly invoked as the dark "other" by the Protestant "black legend," and as the uncanny precursor to Protestantism prior to the Reformation. What is most striking about Ruiz de Burton's narrative strategy is her use of these reversals to critique U.S. Anglo society while simultaneously deploying these tropes to form affiliation with *Californios*. Based on their shared whiteness and fitness to participate as full citizens, she makes her case for the inclusion of California's landed gentry into decent society. In the end, the question she really begs is whether vulgar New England hypocrites, despite their new money and military might, are worthy of Lola.

140 *Melanie Hernández*

Who Would Have Thought It? is particularly interesting because of its messy racial, class, and religious convergences. Unlike other nineteenth-century novels, this text does not fixate on one binary at a time. Rather, it converges many race-based identity formations into a single tableau. In this way, it demonstrates the ways in which multiple groups vied for social position and configured their political identities in opposition to one another. The novel already must contend with the issues of abolition, northern industrial labor, and the Civil War. Lola's arrival to the Norval home further complicates the narrative by inserting racialized manifest destiny and gender politics within the novel's already complicated lines of inquiry. The Norval household, operating as a microcosm of U.S. social upheaval, becomes a nexus of racial, religious, class, and political antagonism.

From the moment of Lola's arrival, Mrs. Norval frets over how and where to integrate Lola—that "horrid little black thing," as she is referred to—into the hierarchical structure of the household. This problem resonates with the so-called Mexican Question which, like so many of the other "questions" of the nineteenth century, must resolve how to integrate newly formed Mexican Americans into the social fabric of the U.S. body politic. Lola is immediately greeted as an object of curiosity and disgust. Never once is it presumed that she enters the Norval home on equal footing with the family. Within the opening pages, and under a single roof, Ruiz de Burton conjures and disavows the numerous racial categories with which Lola, as the daughter of Mexican nationals, would typically be identified by a U.S. audience. She is Mexican, but is that closer to black or Indian within the United States' available racial categories? Readers might be quick to assume that, judging by her looks, she certainly is not white. However, Dr. Norval immediately establishes that Lola is neither black nor Indian and leaves no room for question that she is highborn. He racially identifies her as "pure" Spanish (she actually turns out to be half Spanish and half Austrian).[8] This emphasizes her European pedigree, unadulterated by the taint of Indian and black admixtures within *mestizaje*. Moreover, it makes clear that Lola, even if not of Anglo stock, is not to be relegated to the status of black or Indian peoples.

Mrs. Norval, a staunch Presbyterian abolitionist who, by her own admission "[hates] foreigners and papists" (Ruiz de Burton 1995, 92), plans to supplement their modest household income by outsourcing Lola as a servant. Dr. Norval intervenes and asserts that Lola, based on her bloodline (and, presumably, her wealth), will rank equally with the family members. In his final attempt to disabuse Mrs. Norval of the notion that Lola is anything but white, he asserts:

> Once and for all, let me tell you that the blood of that child is as good as, *or better* than, yours or mine; that she is neither an Indian nor a

Spain, Whiteness Studies, and "Lost Cause"   141

negro child and that, unless you wish to doubt my word, my veracity, you will not permit yourself or anybody else to think her such.

(Ruiz de Burton 1995, 25)

The novel is clearly invested in establishing Lola's position once transplanted to New England and, by extension, in determining the position that *Californios* will occupy within the United States after 1848. In this regard, I agree with Rosaura Sánchez and Beatrice Pita's observation that while the novel addresses racism, slavery remains [unexplored] in the background (1995, xviii). From the earliest moments in the text, Ruiz de Burton invokes blackness and abolitionism; she deploys them as useful tropes, but the actual institution of slavery does not factor significantly into the novel. This observation is only problematic if one positions Ruiz de Burton as subaltern and assumes that her goal was to protest racism, as many twenty-first-century critics argue. The novel, however, does not suggest that this was her goal. On the contrary, all indications are that she used dominant U.S. racial discourse to her advantage, manipulating anti-black sentiment in order to gain entry, secure rank for her protagonist, and protect her own real-life social capital in the process.

Racism does not appear to be a problem in *Who Would Have Thought It?* unless *Californios* suffer because of it. In fact, landed *Californios* generally benefited from racialized labor practices begun during the California mission era and refigured under the hacienda system.[9] Critics frequently cite Mrs. Cackle's infamous line to suggest that the novel launches a broad anti-racist critique. Mrs. Cackle proclaims: "To me they are all alike—Indians, Mexicans, or Californians—they are all horrid" (Ruiz de Burton 1995, 11). Rather than conclude, however, that this is a criticism of Anglo-American racism in general, this line serves two functions, neither of which is anti-racist. First, it undermines northern abolitionism as a righteous cause by depicting Northerners as racist and hypocritical; it is further proof of their "low" quality that they do not live by their own espoused values. Racism is not the problem here—hypocrisy is. Second, Mrs. Cackle's statement simply indicates that she, like so many other war-profiteering *nouveau riche*, does not possess a developed taste sensibility that would enable her to distinguish between blue-blooded aristocrats and "savages" when confronted by either. Neither of these readings views Mrs. Cackle's statement as challenging the racism launched at Indians or Mexicans but as suggesting that Californians do not belong in the same category. White supremacy is still a functioning logic, but it challenges the hierarchical relegation of *Californios* to a status lower than the vulgar and perceptively blunt *nouveau riche* like the Cackles, despite their Anglo-Saxon roots. In both of these readings, white supremacy is never challenged; it is assumed. The question becomes which form of whiteness deserves the greater privilege. This juxtaposition is used as a tool to lower the social capital held by Protestant New Englanders in order to carve out

142 *Melanie Hernández*

a niche for Lola, and to display her cultural superiority, set in relief beside people like the Cackles and Norvals.

The opening scene in the Norvals' parlor places Lola in the position of the racialized object undergoing visual scrutiny. She does not speak. She is not directly engaged. Rather, she is viewed and regarded in the third person as the type of ethnographic showpiece that was so popular at the time of the novel's writing—she is literally staged as a piece of southwestern fauna retrieved during Dr. Norval's geological expedition. But before she "becomes" white later in the novel, she functions in the parlor as the screen onto which the Norval women project their racial fantasies—an ocular power play akin to Laura Mulvey's "scopophilia." In this case, the pleasure is derived by shoring up the Norvals' whiteness and class status through the viewing of a live "black" specimen in their very own sitting parlor. In this regard, Lola's blackface serves the same speculative function that occurs upon the minstrel stage when a white audience gazes upon a white blackface performer. It is no coincidence that Ruiz de Burton places Lola in blackface at the center of a visual tableau reminiscent of the minstrel stage when the purpose of the minstrel "mask" was to deride blackness in order to shore up the whiteness of the person under the mask.

Ruiz de Burton engages precisely this maneuver: she reaffirms Lola's whiteness in contrast to the blackface that Lola is forced to wear, while also raising Lola above the women in the Norval household. Lola judges the Norval women as too "low" to be worthy of direct address and, as a result, she remains silent. While this scene establishes Lola's superior breeding in contrast to the Norvals' unguarded speech, it also reveals the hypocrisy between the Norvals' demonstrated racism and their espoused northern abolitionism. Although Lola is too refined to engage overtly in these racial politics, the effect is nevertheless achieved through the visual staging and pleasure-inducing racializations produced through the viewing spectacle itself. While the Norvals attempt to affirm their rank and power as the spectators in the scene, Lola triumphs—even in blackface. By refusing to engage, she allows the Norval women to reveal their base qualities; Lola comes across as the most prudent and refined of the women present. This, in turn, emphasizes the prosthetic burden of the blackness that is foisted on her and amplifies the disparity between her temporary appearance and her rightful social position. As Ruiz de Burton creates this contrast between Lola's comportment and her blackened appearance, at no point does the novel challenge the predicate of U.S. anti-black sentiment.

This opening scene is not the only time in the novel that Ruiz de Burton invokes the blackface minstrelsy in order to destabilize Protestant New England and Anglo-Saxon privilege in the United States. Later in the novel, she invokes minstrelsy yet again through a familiar trope—the burlesque love triangle—but replaces the black stock characters with New

Englanders. This love triangle lampoons the unfettered male aggression of two rivals in competition for the same undesirable woman. For example, "Coal Black Rose," features Sambo (an illiterate *nouveau riche* Zip Coon figure) and Cuffee (working class, whose free status is questioned) who fights for the affection of Rose (Lott 1993, 133). In *Who Would Have Thought It?* the triangle involves Mrs. Norval's youngest brother, Isaac, whose "most lamentable penchant for gallantry" gets in the way of his professional advancement. Isaac and Congressman Le Grand Gunn engage in "a most ignominious fistfight" over the attentions of the lovely Lucinda, a quadroon "lady of the demimonde" (Ruiz de Burton 1995, 58–59). Like "Coal Black Rose" that mocks Sambo's airs and challenges Cuffee's free status, Le Grand Gunn uses his political clout to block Isaac's prisoner exchange after being captured by the Confederate Army, thus securing Lucinda's attentions for the time being. Again, moments like these appear tangential to the central narrative plot, but they perform heavy lifting in terms of the novel's racial politics. Ruiz de Burton renders ironic that Lola's fitness for good society should be questioned, or that she should be scrutinized like a slave on the auction block and held in captivity, while two of the north's "finest" gentlemen engage in public brawls over the attentions of a mixed-race prostitute.

From the moment of Lola's introduction, Ruiz de Burton engages in a black–white color line epistemology, and strategically uses anti-black tropes in order to unseat New England Puritan virtue at the core of our national myth. In so doing, she attempts to reinsert a viable form of *Californio* whiteness into the U.S. racial imaginary and to restore *Californio* privilege on the basis of the bloodlines and cultivation. At the end of the parlor scene, the family finally retires for the evening. Behind closed doors Dr. and Mrs. Norval continue to argue over Lola's placement within the household. Meanwhile, Lola has already been sent to spend her first night in the house with the Norval's two Irish Catholic maids. Again, this is an inconspicuous moment in the overall trajectory of the narrative, but it is quite telling in terms of the way the novel depicts its myriad and interrelated racial configurations. Although one might be tempted to imagine an automatic affiliation based on their shared Catholic faith and social marginalization by Anglo-Americans in the 1850s, this does not turn out to be the case. Instead, their relationship is akin to the mid-century racial antagonisms between working-class Irish immigrants who identified in opposition to free northern blacks despite their shared labor interests.[10] As Jesse Alemán notes,

> The narrative must still negotiate the anti-Catholicism of the Protestant Northeast, where the influx of Irish immigrants created a host of alternative Anglo American anxieties regarding "savagery." Thus, Ruiz de Burton must also work to distance white Mexican

144 *Melanie Hernández*

Catholics from the Irish Catholic maids Lola encounters in the Norval house.

(2004, 103)

This tension becomes apparent when readers learn that "Lola had refused to share the bed with either of the two servants, and both had resented the refusal as the most grievous insult" (Ruiz de Burton 1995, 30). At this moment, both Lola and the Irish maids mutually reject one another, each clinging to her class and racial superiority, but the novel supports Lola's claim. While the maids remain offended by the slight, Lola's objection is a result of her finely tuned sensibilities. Ruiz de Burton uses the maids' unrefined conduct and unwashed bodies in order to trigger Lola's revulsion of them. This distaste, as Elise Lemire reminds us, codes as a biological indication of Lola's racial difference. Her refusal to share intimate space willingly with her inferiors further signifies a proper upbringing. Not only does Lola run the risk of being mistaken as non-white—both as a Spanish-*Californiana* and in blackface—but she further runs the risk of social demotion by being cast among inferior whites or by being branded a "papist" and then being lumped in with the Irish on religious and class grounds.

At this moment, despite her blackened skin, Ruiz de Burton distances Lola from mid-century Irish Catholics and positions her as the servants' superior in breeding, education, and manner, even after a lifetime spent in Indian captivity. Ruiz de Burton further emphasizes the servile status of the Irish maids by contrasting Lola's perfect English to the maids' low dialect. For example, the cook says [referring to Lola], "Niggers ain't my most particliest admirashun, I can tell ye, no more nor toads nor cateypillars. Haith! I think, on the whole, I prefer the cateypillars, as a more dacent sorty of baste" (Ruiz de Burton 1995, 30). Even though the cook at this moment mistakes Lola for black and expresses *her* disdain, the readers' scorn is redirected at the cook because of her crude speech. In the end, Lola prefers to spend her first night under the Norval roof sleeping in the hallway with the family dog, rather than share a bed with the Irish Catholic maids, but likewise having also been rejected by the Irish maids for being perceived as black.

Despite their mutual rejections, again, Lola's superior breeding provides cover. Even in captivity, Lola's mother was careful to educate her daughter with the refinements of a gentlewoman, which Lola would require upon her return to "civilization." As a result, Lola feels disgust toward the Irish women and the many grimy and "blackened" objects that Lola associates with the Irish—black stockings, blackened pillows, and shoes "like two dead crows" (Ruiz de Burton 1995, 31). In the effort to reaffirm Spanish whiteness, Ruiz de Burton alludes to the northern working-class Irish's perceived status alongside free blacks. Popular amalgamated terms such as "smoked Irishman" (Lott 1993, 95) to refer

Spain, Whiteness Studies, and "Lost Cause"   145

to blacks and "white slaves" (Roediger 1991, 67) to refer to the Irish suggest as much. By bringing this comparison to the forefront, Ruiz de Burton reminds her reader that blackness, slave labor, and the Irish occupy a shared sphere, and in so doing, she positions Spanishness in opposition to all three. Ironically, in her second novel, *The Squatter and the Don* (1885), Ruiz de Burton calls for a "redeemer" who will emancipate the "white slaves of California" (1992, 344), but this only further supports the idea that slavery and racism are only problems insofar as they threaten *Californio* capital. One might consider this move alongside tragic mulatta narratives that are not so much pro-African American or anti-slavery as they are sympathetic to the plight of a well-bred white (appearing) woman who faces these trials.

While maneuvering to represent Lola's Catholicism as an advantage, Ruiz de Burton nevertheless manages to circumvent any low connection that is implied between Lola and the Irish Catholics on the grounds of her wealth and breeding. This comparison to the Irish also enables a strategic inversion of colonial Spain's *gracias al sacar* practices, which allowed mixed-raced colonial Mexicans to purchase their whiteness from the Spanish crown. As alluded to earlier, the so-called Caucasian cloak and Spanish fantasy heritage imply that Mexican American claims to whiteness were false or grounded in a tenuous claim to Spanish ancestry that, for convenience alone, allowed the United States to annex northern Mexico while technically upholding its pre-Fourteenth Amendment whites-only citizenship policies. This allowed the United States to sustain its belief that Mexico mongrelized its citizen-class, whereas the United States did not engage in such practices or that legal hypodescent safeguarded U.S. society when racial admixture did occur. However, as the novel demonstrates, despite her black-coded body, the revelation of Lola's wealth immediately secures her equal footing in the Norval household as a ward instead of servant. Furthermore, the money siphoned from Lola's inheritance enables the Norvals' entry into elite social circles. Lola's physical attractiveness and desirability as a potential mate continue to increase over the years as the skin dye eventually fades. The fact, however, that Lola's wealth alone secures her position in the Norval household suggests that the United States, like most empires, is willing to overlook an unfavorable taint when riches are concerned. Jesse Alemán states as much in his observation:

> Enacting in miniature the history of Spanish colonization of the Americas, Doña Theresa uses the wealth she gains from indigenous exploitation to rescue (*sacar*) Lola from the threat of Indian identity [...] Doña Theresa's Spanish/Mexican caste system allows Lola to 'purchase' her whiteness from Northern bankers rather than from the Spanish Crown, as was usually the case with the gracias al sacar process. In other words, Californio colonial mentality in the novel

146   *Melanie Hernández*

is akin to Anglo American colonialism when it comes to fashioning whiteness by racializing and oppressing others.

(2004, 103)

At this moment, Ruiz de Burton places her young protagonist within competing mid-nineteenth-century discourses undergirded by nativism and expansionist concerns over the fate of U.S. republican government— concerns about annexing Mexican territories and admitting members of a "mongrel" race lacking the civic virtue requisite for citizenship within a republic. However, she also demonstrates Lola's fitness by distinguishing her Spanish whiteness and class standing from the domestic U.S. Irish and black communities. Meanwhile, she simultaneously deploys Mexico's *gente de razón* (people of reason) criteria, which qualified Mexicans for citizenship on the basis of not being "savage" (Garza-Falcón 1998; Saldaña-Portillo 2004; Martínez 2008). Through these multiple oppositional formations, Ruiz de Burton restores Lola's footing as a white gentlewoman. Moreover, in her distancing of Lola from the vulgar masses, Ruiz de Burton goes a step further to position Lola above the New England Anglo-Saxon middle class, as represented by characters like the Norvals' eldest daughter, Ruth, who puts on airs despite the family's want of capital and rank. In an earlier scene, the narrative brings the two girls' breeding into stark relief when Lola refuses to engage Ruth. Ruth assumes that, as Mexican, Lola must not speak English—which permits Ruth to speak freely. Dr. Norval finally reveals that Lola does, in fact, speak fluent English, but that "not liking [Ruth's] manner, she disdains to answer [Ruth's] question" (Ruiz de Burton 1995, 20), thus demonstrating Lola's proud demeanor in contrast to Ruth's vulgarity. This conspicuous show of dignity clearly positions Lola as the better of the two girls. Once Lola's superior breeding is established, she becomes the novel's exemplar of feminine grace and propriety, the more suitable representative of the Cult of True Womanhood—and not despite her Catholicism, but, in part, because of it.

While the issue of slavery remains obscured in the text—unless it is alluded to as a ploy to evoke sympathy for white womanhood as in the parlor scene—racism is central to the novel's functioning. Ruiz de Burton intersperses minstrel tropes like Lola's temporary blackface and the love triangle in order to juxtapose Lola with her northern "superiors." Lola's refusal to mix with the Irish contrasts Isaac and Le Grand Gunn's eager miscegenation; Lola's pure bloodlines and chastity stand out against Lucinda's blood mixture and sexual availability. Riffing off Mulvey's "male gaze," Eric Lott playfully coins the term, "pale gaze," which he defines as "a ferocious investment in demystifying and domesticating black power in white fantasy by projecting vulgar black types as spectacular objects of white men's looking" (1993, 153). In the parlor scene, Ruiz de Burton ultimately produces a similar scopophilia for her readership by recasting the black role with New England players and the white role with Lola. She situates the Norval women among vulgar New

Spain, Whiteness Studies, and "Lost Cause" 147

England types as spectatorial objects for her readership's ridicule. In so doing, she demystifies the Puritan ethos at the center of the American creation myth.

A Scribbling Woman: Ruiz de Burton Reimagines Popular Literary Genres

> Where the domestic novel appears turned most inward to the private sphere of female interiority, we often find subjectivity scripted by narratives of nation and empire.
>
> (Amy Kaplan, "Manifest Domesticity")

It has become a critical commonplace to locate *Who Would Have Thought It?* within the genre of the captivity narrative. Given that the text literally begins with the abduction of Doña Theresa, whose harrowing Indian captivity is transcribed on her deathbed into a physical text, this frequent observation makes sense. It is not enough that Ruiz de Burton provides the oral telling of an Indian captivity to launch her novel; she then goes to lengths to provide a physical artifact—a textual captivity narrative to perform the political work of the genre and to launch the meta-analysis of her novel. Much of this work is done sentimentally, possibly sensationally, despite her narrator's ironic distaste for the "popular sort of *artifice* freely employed by '*sensational*' novelists" (Ruiz de Burton 1995, 155). That said, she nevertheless makes full use of the pathos and voyeuristic titillation inherent to the genre and then pushes the formal limits of the captivity narrative's imagined possibilities through dripping sarcasm. At the heart of the captivity narrative is the mandate to cohere national values through a religious framework and to articulate this budding "new world" identity through stories that threaten gendered reproduction (Tinnemeyer 2006, 4). Ruiz de Burton certainly achieves both in her reimagining of the genre while further managing to loosen New England's Protestant stronghold as the nation's moral core. The latter is no easy feat given the captivity narrative's intimate connections to New England Puritanism as one of the nation's earliest and most widely circulated literary forms.

A small handful of critics recognize that the remainder of *Who Would Have Thought It?* functions allegorically as Lola's captivity among Protestant New Englanders and have teased out the work that the genre performs in advancing Ruiz de Burton's satire when set in this specific geographical region. Fisher, for example, inverts the popular American stereotypes about Mexicans and notes Ruiz de Burton's use of familiar captivity narrative tropes to suggest that Mexico's northern frontier (the "civilized" culture in this allegory) is under attack by both Indian and Yankee "savages" (1999, 61). Anne Goldman further notes Ruiz de Burton's parody of the United States' mythic Puritan origins when Goldman draws attention to Ruiz de Burton's snarky treatment of American holidays:

148   *Melanie Hernández*

> It was the anniversary of some great day in New England [...] some great day in which the Pilgrim fathers had done some one of their wonderful deeds. They had either embarked, or landed, or burnt a witch, or whipped a woman at the pillory, on just such a day.
>
> (2006, 63)

In addition to mocking New England's celebration of its own anti-feminism and arrogant mundaneness, this passage becomes all the more interesting in conversation with Andrea Tinnemeyer's observation that,

> Tales of brutal torture and death, similar to [Increase] Mather's use of the black legend to distance the Puritan colonial project from its Spanish predecessor, were circulated to testify to the exceptionalism of the United States in its colonial endeavors to remove American Indians and to annex one third of Mexico.
>
> (2006, xiii)

It is not too much to suggest, then, given Ruiz de Burton's apparent awareness of captivity narrative tropes, that she would have recognized Puritan anti-Spanish propaganda as foundational to the United States' self-concept throughout its experiences forged as a frontier society.[11] Therefore, her inversion of the captivity narrative is, in part, reclamation of the Spanish colonial system that produced her. It also recognizes that the Puritan mythos in U.S. culture is the necessary site of her intervention—that she must deconstruct this privilege before she can hope to implement an alternative exemplar of female piety and decorum. If we factor out all we know in hindsight about the events affecting Mexican Americans since the turn of the twentieth century, this novel reads much less like a subaltern protest narrative than it does another installment of the centuries-long struggle between Anglo-Protestant and Spanish-Catholic imperialisms, joined together politically by the Treaty of Guadalupe Hidalgo but also culturally and militarily as a sort of imagined community forged by the shared nuisance of Indian raiders onto their frontier territories. In this instance, the case for social parity is being made by a descendant of Spain to an overwhelmingly Anglo-American audience and under the rule of a nation-state that uses the black–white color line as its dominant racial logic.

Ruiz de Burton's challenge, then, is not solely to undermine New England Protestantism and to carve a niche for Spanish Catholics within this U.S. body politic but to engage U.S. racial politics amidst the tumult of Southern Reconstruction. She makes no attempt to subvert the black–white color line; rather, her goal is to ensure that Spanish *Californios* end up on the "white" side of it. Her goal is to ensure that the United States, in its effort to place Mexican Americans along its binary racial spectrum, does not "brownwash" all of colonial Spain's racial categories

Spain, Whiteness Studies, and "Lost Cause" 149

under the *sistema de castas* into a monolithic Mexican race, and she will achieve this on cultural terrain: through showy performances of Spanish-*Californio* impeccable breeding, and by insisting on unadulterated white bloodlines as both a fact and a birthright for some *Californios*, not a "fantasy heritage."

Much of her narrative is vested in loosening Anglo-American women's stronghold on ideal womanhood and recasting Spanish Catholics Lola and Doña Theresa as alternative exemplars of female whiteness. For example, what readers of early captivity narratives found so terrifying yet titillating are the looming threat of miscegenation and the question of whether a woman, once held in captivity, can return to good society. As so often is the case in nineteenth-century fiction, the defiled woman, "fallen" and no longer socially viable dies as a result of her injury. Her inability to survive the affront functions as narrative proof of her delicate femininity. We see this structural parallel at the beginning of *Who Would Have Thought It?* with the honorable death of Doña Theresa, who languishes in a hut near the banks of the Colorado river rather than bring shame upon her husband and father by returning to Mexico in her "insulted" state. Through this sentimental death trope, Ruiz de Burton situates Spanish-Mexican womanhood within the same discursive terms established by the Victorian Cult of True Womanhood, and in opposition to black womanhood—like Lucinda, able to survive sexual degradation—as described by Hazel Carby's famous critique.[12] At the end of the novel, when Doña Theresa's husband and father in Mexico finally receive word of her death nearly twenty years after her abduction, the two bereaved gentlemen grieve beneath a painting of her that seems to utter: "Do not weep for me. Do not mourn. I am an angel now. I was always pure, for my soul did not sin, although I was insulted by a savage. I was a martyr; now an angel" (Ruiz de Burton 1995, 202). Through this sentimental tribute and conspicuous martyrdom, Ruiz de Burton is able to position Doña Theresa within a literary tradition of female respectability and to transmit the same noble qualities to Lola.

Inasmuch as *Who Would Have Thought It?* relies on gendered norms and genre convention, one cannot understate the extent to which female propriety, pride, and good taste undergird Ruiz de Burton's argument for *Californio* inclusion as fully participating U.S. citizens, replete with its protections and privileges. This method of displaying female respectability resonates with the uplift strategy deployed by the African American Clubwomen in the same time period. However, rather than attempting to demonstrate that womanly virtue is not an exclusive form of white social capital—"whiteness as property" to borrow Cheryl Harris' term—Ruiz de Burton works under the opposite premise. She uses propriety and good taste not only as proof of Lola's whiteness but as further proof that the noble blood that courses through Lola's veins is the stuff of natural-born aristocrats. As Anne Goldman notes,

150 *Melanie Hernández*

"America" in this text parodies Anglo American versions of "Mexico"; it is crude and uncouth. America is peopled by barbarians who don't care when they miss the spittoon bucket and social climbers whose first contact with high culture send them into a tailspin of uncontrolled sensuality. In Ruiz de Burton's novel, aesthetes belong in Mexico; New England, by contrast, is home for the vulgar.

(2006, 73)

Ruiz de Burton stages *Who Would Have Thought It?* on two domestic fronts where she engages in intra-white cultural politics, where Lola defeats Protestant New England on their turf, but her terms.

In this respect, Ruiz de Burton invokes the "domestic" in terms of feminized home spaces as well as within U.S. national boundaries. As a satirical novel of "manners," *Who Would Have Thought It?* operates squarely within the gendered poetics of what Amy Kaplan calls "Manifest Domesticity," but with one important distinction. The woman within the domestic sphere still reproduces citizens and domesticates foreign and "savage" peoples within her domain (Kaplan 1998, 588–591), but in Ruiz de Burton's telling, it is Lola who exerts her superior influence over coarse, scheming New Englanders instead of being the foreign element to be tamed by the Norval women. This is not to suggest that Ruiz de Burton depicts all Anglo-Americans as crass; she specifically treats New England Protestants in this manner—Bostonians and New Yorkers, particularly—as representative of the north in her novel set amidst the Civil War.

Ruiz de Burton represents *Californios* and Southerners alike as victims of northern barbarism and treats southern agrarian plantation societies analogously to her own hacienda system, both systems resting on a foundation of white privilege and racialized labor. Jesse Alemán suggests that the greatest irony of the novel's social critique is that it "comes back on itself, despite the novel's attempt to forget the neo-colonial history and racism of Hispanos in the Southwest" (2007, 16). I believe that the novel would only attempt a forgetting of this history if, in fact, it ever imagined *Californios* as a race-inclusive society across class and labor. Instead, the novel assumes that as U.S. nationals *Californios* would nevertheless uphold the racial stratifications inherited from the mission and hacienda systems even if *Californio* society previously allowed for a more nuanced and racially permissive understanding of whiteness.[13] Even after the Treaty of Guadalupe Hidalgo granted legal protections to Mexican Americans, as Tomás Almaguer points out, only the elite actually benefited from these rights:

Although technically entitled to these same rights, members of the Mexican working class were never viewed by Anglos as political equals of the old ranchero elite. Despite being eligible for citizenship

Spain, Whiteness Studies, and "Lost Cause" 151

rights, the Mexican working class was not afforded any better treatment than other racialized groups in the state.

(Ruiz de Burton 1995, 57)

Rather than Ruiz de Burton forgetting Hispanos' "neo-colonial history and racism" in the sense of erasure, the only forgetting here is in not stating the obvious—her presupposition of racial stratification as a common-sense given. That white *Californios* occupied a higher social position than *mestizo* laborers is less forgotten than never questioned since it is so commonplace that it does not warrant further scrutiny. This distinction only requires remembering decades later, after these groups eventually become racialized into a single proletarianized labor force. Instead, the "natural" race-based stratifications separating these groups provide a cultural link not with *mestizos* but between elite *Californios* under the hacienda system to southern plantation whites:

[Raymund] Paredes's "hacienda syndrome" is not a flippant analogy—it likens Mexican American writers to Southern whites, whose constructed position of white racial power rested on the reality and legacy of black slavery. The alternative georacial cartography Paredes invokes challenges the subaltern strain of Chicano/a studies by seeing whiteness as the link between the cultures of Southern slavery and the Spanish/Mexican colonial history in the Southwest.

(Alemán 2004, 97)

Ruiz de Burton writes in the middle of Reconstruction, when the goal is to enfold the ex-Confederacy back into the fabric of the nation. If whiteness provides the connecting thread between these two cultures, then Ruiz de Burton is using this connection to the south to enfold white *Californios* within the purview of Reconstruction and to resist the de facto racialization process of all Mexican Americans into non-whites. "By invoking its pre-1848 (genteel) class and (white/Spanish) racial and caste identities through its narrative recovery of hacienda community," Vincent Pérez argues, "the Californio elite at the same time imagines a future place for itself within the newly ascendant white nation of the post-Reconstruction period" (2006, 28).

Such comparisons complicate the notion that Ruiz de Burton considers herself as part of a non-white Mexican American racial group. Even though she and her descendants may ultimately have succumbed to the proletarianization process that Marcial González describes, we must remember that her class grew wealthy from the proletarianization of mestizos and *indios* already long underway before Anglo-Americans entered the scene, and that these race-based class stratifications fueled her sense of kinship with the occupied south. Moreover, as Ruiz de Burton attempts to privilege *Californiana* womanhood, she does so in direct reply to writers like Augusta Evans who attempt the same maneuver

152   Melanie Hernández

for southern womanhood in opposition to Mexican women (Bost 2003, 652). Rather than pit elite *Californianas* against southern women, Ruiz de Burton (who, as a side note, shared an intimate friendship with Jefferson and Varina Davis) uses their similarities as the grounds for enfranchisement under Reconstruction.

Lastly, these perceived similarities between the hacienda system and southern plantation culture might further explain Ruiz de Burton's conspicuous silence on the subject of slavery. As we have seen, she certainly had no qualms in expressing anti-black sentiment, but to invoke African American slavery or the slave narrative directly would undermine her goal of de-privileging hypocritical northern abolitionists and Anglo-Saxon Protestants by proxy. When she finally does directly bring up slavery in *Who Would Have Thought It?*, it is to suggest that white citizens are "slaves" to an oppressive federal government. Likewise, her rhetorical mention of the "white slaves" of California in *The Squatter and the Don* is, once again, a tactic that allows her to insist on the whiteness of *Californios* through allusion to the south, vanquished and enslaved by northern policies (Ruiz de Burton 1992, 344). Her inversions of popular nineteenth-century genres—direct invocation of the captivity narrative, passing narrative, sentimentalism and sensationalism alongside allusions to blackface minstrelsy, and careful avoidance of the slave narrative—while vast, are methodical, and always work toward affirming *Californio* whiteness and high culture at a period when multiple white races were beginning to consolidate in response to black freedom and rising immigration.

Finally, as one of her loftiest narrative inversions, Ruiz de Burton evokes gothic and sensational tropes with which her nineteenth-century readers would have been well versed. Inasmuch as *Who Would Have Thought It?* attempts to position Spanish *Californios* favorably within existing U.S. racial schemas, and distances *Californios* from the Irish of the 1850s on racial and class terms through pervasive anti-black theatrical tropes, Ruiz de Burton must recover *Californios* further still by addressing head-on the rampant anti-Catholic sentiment of the time. She had to debunk the myth that Catholics were unfit for a republican form of government since their allegiance is always to the Pope, which she accomplishes through a hyperbolic rewriting of the black legend—an essentialist Anglo-Protestant rendering of Spanish cruelty and treachery. However, as we have seen in her handling of True Womanhood, she similarly reverses the character roles, placing Spanish Catholics in the position of moral superiority and reassigns all loathsome attributes to New England Protestants, strict Presbyterians no less. These genre inversions provide the reader with what Jane Tompkins calls "cultural shorthand" (1985, xvi) providing the didactic cues needed to interpret the text according to the author's design. Specifically, she makes extensive use of the seduction plot by conjuring the familiar figure of the lascivious gothic

Spain, Whiteness Studies, and "Lost Cause" 153

monk, who she reinvents in the form of a minister, the Reverend John Hackwell.

Whereas gothic and sensation novels such as Maria Monk's 1836 *Awful Disclosures* reveal the lurid goings on behind monastery and convent walls—and spurred such popularity that, by 1860, its sales figures placed it second only to *Uncle Tom's Cabin* (Frink 2009, 238)—Ruiz de Burton's narrative inverts the religious roles, casting a Presbyterian minister (the most staunch descendants of New England's Calvinist doctrine) as the sexually predatory aggressor, while making Lola's convent boarding school her only place of refuge (Ruiz de Burton 1995, 101). Ruiz de Burton responds to popular depictions of Catholics in nineteenth-century conduct literature that sensationalized Catholics as depraved and dangerous to the moral fabric of the United States. Sandra Frink describes popular depictions of Catholic religious figures that helped reaffirm a Protestant-centered U.S. national imaginary. According to Frink, "these texts juxtaposed the sanctity of the Protestant domestic sphere, believed to be the bedrock of the nation's virtue and democracy, against that of the Catholic 'family,' deemed to be sexually deviant, tyrannical, and corrupt" (2009, 239). These novels accomplish this through storylines and stock characters as Frink describes in the following passage:

> Nuns rejected the proper role of women by refusing to marry and have children and by becoming active in the public sphere through their charitable institutions and schools. Far more dangerous, however, were the debased sexual activities presumably engaged in by nuns and priests. Celibate and ensconced within the walls of the convents and monasteries, they developed unhealthy, perverse, and licentious sexual appetites and practices.
>
> (2009, 245)

Well aware of these popular stereotypes, through a clever role reversal, Ruiz de Burton uses the "cultural shorthand" of these stock characters to cast Lola as the damsel threatened by a cleric who deliberately chooses to become a Presbyterian reverend instead of a Catholic priest because, in Hackwell's own words, " 'Imagine what a loss that would have been to the ladies!' " (Ruiz de Burton 1995, 44).

Through this reversal, and coupled with her earlier racial productions, Ruiz de Burton is able to wrest away Mrs. Norval's claim to ideal Protestant womanhood and transfer it to Lola. Ruiz de Burton still plays to the narrative conventions but uses them toward her goal of supplanting New England womanhood with *Californiana* womanhood. This comes to pass early in the narrative when Dr. Norval is forced to flee the United States at the onset of the Civil War because of the north's intolerance of his democratic political sympathies. During his extended absence, the family in error receives notice of his death, leaving Lola—already astonishingly

154 Melanie Hernández

wealthy and increasingly beautiful as the skin dye fades—without a male protector. Mrs. Norval thereafter assumes the role of Lola's guardian and steward over her finances, which Mrs. Norval spends freely on an ostentatious new mansion in New York, and the purchase of her own daughters' entry into society through a narrative *gracias al sacar* reversal that removes the taint of low birth from the Norvals' class pedigree.

At this point, the novel follows Hackwell's repeated attempts to trap Lola and her wealth by marriage. His most direct access to Lola is through her guardian, Mrs. Norval, the "stately madam" that he was sure he could make "tremble like a girl anytime he pleased" (Ruiz de Burton 1995, 123). Until this point in the narrative, Mrs. Norval has been the most self-disciplined, austere, and respected woman in her parish. Now, despite the unconfirmed news of her husband's death, and Hackwell's knowing that Norval is actually alive, Hackwell seduces Mrs. Norval and tricks her into a bigamous marriage. This plotline echoes another popular anti-Catholic literary trope: the husband–wife–priest love triangle (Griffin 2004, 23) that wedges Rome into the sacred marriage bed and recalls the novel's earlier illicit love triangle involving the quadroon, Lucinda. Hackwell continues to pursue Lola, even as he seduces Mrs. Norval. What is more, this seduction plot demonstrates that, unlike Catholics accused of unthinking loyalty to Rome, Mrs. Norval is actually the figure least able to participate in republican government because of her blind devotion to the ex-Presbyterian divine. Her reason no longer belongs to her. In other words, she ceases to behave as *gente de razón*.

Even while knowingly engaged in a bigamous marriage, Hackwell still plots until the end of the novel to abduct Lola and take her aboard a steamship to Cuba where he will force her to marry him. He ultimately fails in his pursuit when Isaac figures out that Lola is the child in Doña Theresa's manuscript, and helps Lola's father retrieve her from New York and take her back to Mexico—but not without a dramatic diversion to evade Hackwell's abduction scheme! The novel ends with Lola's return to Mexico, the Civil War in its final year, and the promise that Julian will rejoin Lola within one month after the war's end. Lola's convent has cloistered her away from the illicit goings on under the Norval roof. Virtue intact, she emerges from her captivity as the exemplar of True Womanhood and with the prospect of a mutually beneficial cross-cultural match. Patriarchy is restored with the woman in her proper place, and the post-1848 transnational allegory is complete as dispossessed Lola resumes a dignified position within the familial structure spanning both nation-states.

By appropriating and inverting popular nineteenth-century genre conventions, Ruiz de Burton undermines much of the dominant political discourse used to disenfranchise U.S.-based Mexicans despite treaty protections (Pinheiro 2003, 77–78). She circumvents nativist discourse that questions whether a "mongrel" race can fully participate in a republican form of government by racially producing Lola as not being from that mongrel race at all. Lola is white, and her suitability for good society is evident through the breeding she displays in contrast to the Irish, blacks, and "savage" Indians. Moreover, Ruiz de Burton undercuts Protestant New England's imaginative stronghold on U.S. moral integrity by casting the Norvals and their surrounding community as hypocrites, simultaneously reimagining Catholicism in the morally superior position within gothic and sensational narrative structures. In the end, while Lola's racial identity remains problematic for critics hoping to place Ruiz de Burton as a progenitor of Chicanx anti-racist literature, this text demonstrates a fraught resistance strategy based entirely on the splicing of one colonial white supremacist model onto another. The tenuous claim to Spanish whiteness which enables the intermarriage of Lola to Julian, and metaphorically of northern Mexico to the patriarchal U.S. nation-state, in real life offered little protection to Ruiz de Burton. While U.S.-based peoples of Mexican descent ultimately were weeded out of the whiteness consolidation process, Ruiz de Burton's novel reminds us that this process was far from complete in 1872. Neither the "browning" nor proletarianization of U.S. Mexicans would be complete until after the turn of the twentieth century. If Ruiz de Burton's fiction is to be read as protest literature—if she is to be depicted as a resistance fighter against U.S. domination— then clearly her work's loudest protest is against the Anglo-American misidentification of Spano-American *Californios* as anything other than white, genteel, and fit for assimilation into the most privileged tiers of U.S. society.

Notes

1 To be *gente de razón* (people of reason) was a requirement for citizenship within Colonial Mexican society and subordinated race to the possession of reason. For example, Afro-Mexicans if free, and while always lowest on the racial hierarchy, could nevertheless be citizens based on their recognition of Spanish sovereignty and their being neither heathen nor savage.
2 In 1799, Francisco Goya published a collection of prints, *Los Caprichos*, which depict eighty comic and grotesque sketches of eighteenth-century Spanish folly. Among them is print number sixty-two, *¡Quién lo Creyera!* (*Who Would Have Thought It?*), that depicts two witches battling to their death as they hurl down a vast, shadowy pit, oblivious that they are both about to be pounced upon by demons. This print allegorically mocks warring nation-states that are so engrossed in their feud that they cannot see that they are destroying themselves in the process. In this regard, one might read Ruiz de Burton's novel, *Who Would Have Thought It?*, as a critique of the human victims (specifically, the Spanish-descended aristocrats of New Spain's northern frontier) that have been left unprotected throughout the ongoing political clashes between the United States and Spain and then again between the United States and Mexico.
3 Both *peninsulares* and *criollos* within the Spanish colonial *sistema de castas* are pure-blooded Spaniards who differ by location of birth: *peninsulares* are born in Spain and transplanted to New Spain, whereas *criollos* are born in New Spain.

156 *Melanie Hernández*

4 Almaguer notes the anti-miscegenation statutes in California that permitted ethnic intermarriage between Anglos and elite-class Mexican Americans but still prohibited intermarriage between Anglos and blacks, Indians, or Asian immigrants.

5 Lieutenant William H. Emory, *Notes of a Military Reconnaissance* (1848), documents his topographical survey of the southwestern territories during the U.S.–Mexican War, and in addition to his scientific measurements of the climate, he also provides his observations of the native peoples, their customs, and shortcomings.

6 See Raimon (2004) and Zackodnik (2004) for analyses of the political uses of the tragic mulatta figure in literature and for a historiography of legal racial discourse around miscegenation and racial admixture.

7 For further reading on colonial Mexican racial ontologies and qualifications for citizenship or social mobility, see Garza-Falcón (1998), Martínez (2008), Saldaña-Portillo (2004), and DeGuzmán (2005).

8 This Austrian admixture explains Don Luis Medina's support in chapter XLIII of Austrian Prince Maximilian monarchical claims to colonial rule over Mexico and the narrative attitudes in favor of paternalistic hierarchical structures, both racial and class based (which are not entirely separate within a *sistema de castas*).

9 Haas (1995) describes labor stratifications that varied by race under the hacienda system. While she describes some opportunity for mobility within this system and the occasional outlier, occupations tended to be determined racially.

10 For additional research on race relations between the Irish and northern African Americans, see Roediger (1991), Ignatiev (1995), Jacobson (1998), and Lott (1995).

11 See Slotkin (1973, 20–21) for additional background on the "improvements" that Puritan religious leaders made to captivity narratives for use in jeremiads and revival sermons.

12 Compare to Carby's (1997) argument which describes an oppositionally related, racially gendered logic. Carby critiques the narrative implication that slave woman are less refined than white women and better suited to hard manual labor because slave women do not die from sexual assault, as is regularly depicted in sentimental narratives about fallen white women.

13 Haas (1995, 30–31) describes whiteness as a category in California that originally meant "Spaniard" as a signification of whiteness but grew into a wealth- and comportment-based gradient system between aristocrats and laboring *indios*. While whiteness could encapsulate people with some blood mixture, it was very much a class dependent. She nevertheless emphasizes that those who could still claim *limpieza de sangre* (blood purity) would still rely on that as part of their claim to rank.

Works Cited

Alemán, Jesse. 2004. "'Thank God, Lolita Is Away from Those Horrid Savages': The Politics of Whiteness in *Who Would Have Thought It?*" *María Amparo Ruiz de Burton: Critical and Pedagogical Perspectives*, edited by Amelia María de la Luz Montes and Anne Elizabeth Goldman. Lincoln: University of Nebraska Press, 95–111.

Spain, Whiteness Studies, and "Lost Cause" 157

———. 2007. "Citizenship Rights and Colonial Whites." *Complicating Constructions: Race, Ethnicity, and Hybridity in American Texts*, edited by David S. Goldstein and Audrey B. Thacker. Seattle: University of Washington Press, 3–30.

Almaguer, Tomás. 1994. *Racial Fault Lines: The Historical Origins of White Supremacy in California*. Berkeley: University of California Press.

Aranda, Jr., José. F. 1998. "Contradictory Impulses: María Amparo Ruiz de Burton, Resistance Theory, and the Politics of Chicano/a Studies." *American Literature* 70, no. 3: 551–579.

Aranda, Jr., José F. 2004. "Returning California to the People: Vigilantism in The Squatter and the Don." *María Amparo Ruiz de Burton: Critical and Pedagogical Perspectives*. Edited by Amelia María de la Luz Montes and Anne Elizabeth Goldman. Lincoln: University of Nebraska Press.

Bost, Suzanne. 2003. "West Meets East: Nineteenth-Century Southern Dialogues on Mixture, Race, Gender, and Nation." *Mississippi Quarterly: The Journal of Southern Cultures* 56, no. 4: 647–656.

Carby, Hazel V. 1997. *Reconstructing Womanhood: The Emergence of the Afro-American Woman Novelist*. New York: Oxford University Press.

DeGuzmán, María. 2005. *Spain's Long Shadow: The Black Legend, Off-Whiteness, and Anglo-American Empire*. Minneapolis: University of Minnesota Press.

Fisher, Beth. 1999. "The Captive Mexicana and the Desiring Bourgeois Woman: Domesticity and Expansionism in Ruiz de Burton's *Who Would Have Thought It?*" *Legacy* 16, no. 1: 59–69.

Frink, Sandra. 2009. "Women, the Family, and the Fate of the Nation in American Anti-Catholic Narratives, 1830–1860." *Journal of the History of Sexuality* 18, no. 2: 237–264.

Garza-Falcón, Leticia. 1998. *Gente Decente: A Borderlands Response to the Rhetorics of Dominance*. Austin: University of Texas Press.

Goldman, Anne Elizabeth. 2006. "'Who Ever Heard of a Blue-Eyed Mexican?': Satire and Sentimentality in María Amparo Ruiz de Burton's *Who Would Have Thought It?*" *Recovering the U.S. Hispanic Literary Heritage*, vol. 2, edited by Erlinda Gonzáles-Berry and Chuck Tatum. Houston: Arte Público Press, 59–78.

González, John M. 1996. "Romancing Hegemony: Constructing Racialized Citizenship in María Amparo Ruiz de Burton's *The Squatter and the Don*." *Recovering the U.S. Hispanic Literary Heritage*, vol. 2, edited by Erlinda Gonzalez-Berry and Chuck Tatum. Houston: Arte Público Press, 23–39.

González, Marcial. 2009. *Chicano Novels and the Politics of Form: Race, Class, and Reification*. Ann Arbor: University of Michigan Press.

Griffin, Susan. 2004. *Anti-Catholicism and Nineteenth-Century America*. New York: Cambridge University Press.

Gross, Ariela J. 2006–2007. "'The Caucasian Cloak': Mexican Americans and the Politics of Whiteness in the Twentieth-Century Southwest." *Georgetown Law Journal* 95: 337–392.

Haas, Lisbeth. 1995. *Conquests and Historical Identities in California, 1769–1936*. Berkeley: University of California Press.

Ignatiev, Noel. 1995. *How the Irish Became White*. New York: Routledge.

Jacobson, Matthew Frye. 1998. *Whiteness of a Different Color: European Immigrants and the Alchemy of Race*. Cambridge: Harvard University Press.

158 *Melanie Hernández*

Kaplan, Amy. 1998. "Manifest Domesticity." *American Literature* 70, no. 3: 581–606.

Lott, Eric. 1993. *Love and Theft: Blackface Minstrelsy and the American Working Class*. New York: Oxford University Press.

Martínez, María Elena. 2008. *Genealogical Fictions: Limpieza de Sangre, Religion, and Gender in Colonial Mexico*. Stanford: Stanford University Press.

McWilliams, Carey. 1990. *North from Mexico: The Spanish-Speaking People of the United States*. New York: Greenwood.

Paredes, Raymund. 1982. "The Evolution of Chicano Literature." *Three American Literatures: Essays in Chicano, Native American, and Asian American Literature for Teachers of American Literature*, edited by Houston A. Baker Jr. New York: MLA, 33–79.

Pérez, Vincent. 2006. *Remembering the Hacienda: History and Memory in the Mexican American Southwest*. College Station: Texas A&M University Press.

Pinheiro, John C. 2003. "'Religion without Restriction': Anti-Catholicism, All Mexico, and the Treaty of Guadalupe Hidalgo." *Journal of the Early Republic* 20, no. 1: 69–96.

Raimon, Eve A. 2004. *The "Tragic Mulatta" Revisited: Race and Nationalism in Nineteenth-Century Antislavery Fiction*. New Brunswick: Rutgers University Press.

Rodríguez, Manuel M. Martín. 1996. "Textual and Land Reclamations: The Critical Reception of Early Chicana/o Literature." *Recovering the U.S. Hispanic Literary Heritage*, vol. 2, edited by Erlinda Gonzalez-Berry and Chuck Tatum. Houston: Arte Público Press, 40–58.

Roediger, David. 1991. *The Wages of Whiteness: Race and the Making of the American Working Class*. London: Verso.

Ruiz de Burton, María Amparo. 1992. *The Squatter and the Don*, edited by Rosaura Sánchez and Beatrice Pita. Houston: Arte Público Press, 1992.

———. 1995. *Who Would Have Thought It?* edited by Rosaura Sánchez and Beatrice Pita. Houston: Arte Público Press.

Saldaña-Portillo, María J. 2004. "'Wavering on the Horizon of Social Being': The Treaty of Guadalupe Hidalgo and the Legacy of Its Racial Character in Américo Paredes's *George Washington Gómez*." *Radical History Review* 89: 135–164.

Saldívar, José David. 1997. *Border Matters: Remapping American Cultural Studies*. Berkeley: University of California Press.

Sánchez, Rosaura and Beatrice Pita. 1995. "Introduction." *Who Would Have Thought It?* edited by Rosaura Sánchez and Beatrice Pita. Houston: Arte Público Press, vii–lxv.

Slotkin, Richard. 1973. *Regeneration through Violence: The Mythology of the American Frontier, 1600–1860*. Norman: University of Oklahoma Press.

Tompkins, Jane P. 1985. *Sensational Designs: The Cultural Work of American Fiction, 1790–1860*. New York: Oxford University Press.

Tinnemeyer, Andrea. 2006. *Identity Politics of the Captivity Narrative after 1848*. Lincoln: University of Nebraska Press.

Zackodnik, Teresa. 2004. *The Mulatta and the Politics of Race*. Jackson: University of Mississippi Press.

9 Future and Past in Nilo María Fabra's Science Fiction Stories on Spain versus the United States

Juan Herrero-Senés

Most of the historiography on the Spain–United States relations at the end of the nineteenth century has focused on politics, diplomacy, the press, and travel experiences, leaving narrative, poetry, and theater largely understudied.[1] This chapter aims to analyze a body of what we now call science fiction related to this topic. Motivated by the events leading to the Spanish–American War of 1898, the Spanish writer Nilo María Fabra authored some futuristic stories to pass judgment on American society and politics, particularly on foreign policy and affairs with Spain. These fictions synthesized the official, prevalent, and conservative viewpoint on the United States, while simultaneously registering global geopolitical alterations.

Nilo María Fabra (1843–1903) is usually considered one of the most reputable journalists of his time. He is also one of the founders of Spanish science fiction, a genre that had been blooming in the West since 1870. The intertwining of these two forms of writing defines his literary output. Devoted to journalism since his youth in Barcelona, in 1865 Fabra founded a News Agency in Madrid with his name and tested the use of carrier pigeons to mitigate telegraphic interruptions. He traveled as a correspondent through France, England, Italy, Germany, and Portugal. For the *Diario de Barcelona*, he covered the Austro-Prussian War (he reunited his chronicles in *Germany and Italy in 1866* [1867]), as well as the Franco-Prussian War in 1870. That same year the Fabra Agency associated with Havas and Reuter, and since then Fabra sought to control the information in and on Spain to support the successive governments of the Restoration.[2] He went into politics twice, first as a deputy in 1876 and later as a senator in 1891. He collaborated with the Spanish Ministry of War in Paris and also wrote pieces for *La Época*, *El Correo de Ultramar*, *La Ilustración Española y Americana*, and numerous other publications.

Fabra began his literary career as a poet, and in 1861, he won an award with the epic chant *La batalla de Pavía* [*The Battle of Pavia*]. After some plays and a novel, *Balls Park* (1870), he earned recognition with short stories on life on other planets, alternate versions of history, future wars, prospections, dystopias, and the fantastic. They were published between 1882 and 1903 and compiled into three illustrated books: *Por*

DOI: 10.4324/9781003219460-9

160 *Juan Herrero-Senés*

los espacios imaginarios (con escalas en la tierra) [*Through Imaginary Spaces (With Stops on Earth)*] (1885a), *Cuentos ilustrados* [*Illustrated Stories*] (1895), and *Presente y futuro. Nuevas historias* [*Present and Future. New Stories*] (1897).

Most of Fabra's stories originally appeared in the prestigious *La Ilustración Española y Americana* side by side with news reports and scientific, historical, and cultural pieces. Fabra introduced his fictions as "articles" and adopted an objective, direct, and journalistic narrative style, which relied on data and obliterated obvious fictional marks, fundamentally, a plot around some characters. The reader had to be attentive to acknowledge that he was presented a prospect and not actual events.

In Jules Verne's wake, Fabra was fascinated with global innovations in transportation and communications. As Juan Valera (1901, 147) noted, Fabra added a strong prospective inclination, including sociopolitical speculations, thus making his ideological positions explicit, in the vein of influential works such as Edward Bellamy's *Looking Backwards: 2000–1887* (1888, Spanish translation *En el año 2000: fantasía novelesca*, 1892) or William Morris' *News from Nowhere* (1890, Spanish translation *Noticias de ninguna parte*, 1903). In Spain, this type of writing was called "sociological fiction," as it prompted the reader through plot and description to observe and evaluate the foundations of an alternate society. It offered an ideologically charged anticipation, not a prediction. Fabra's apologues are weak in narration and minimal in character development, focusing mainly on descriptive accounts of coming inventions, international conflicts, and political revolutions. For two decades, he populated the future with new events consistent and cross-referenced with previous ones so that his texts resonate with others. For example, the account of future history of "Viaje a la Argentina en el año 2003" ["Journey to Argentina in the Year 2003"], published in 1889, begins with the world war narrated in "El desastre de Inglaterra de 1910," printed in 1883.

Fabra established a solid link between technological advancement and the shaping of a better world that sometimes, as Nil Santiáñez-Tió (1994, 276) observed, bordered on utopia. As asserted in the story "El presente juzgado por lo porvenir" ["The Present Judged by the Future"] (1894), "Nada contribuye tanto a los adelantos morales de un pueblo como el progreso material" ["Nothing contributes as much to the moral advancement of a people as material progress"] (Fabra 1894a, 263). Fabra exhibited confidence in science, industrialization, and the exploitation of natural resources as the primary material civilizing forces. Technology, run by the defining energy of modern progress, electricity, improved the general conditions of living and boosted economic growth and social advancement, as it was instrumental in significant changes: spatial liberation through travel and wireless transmission, physical alteration through construction and machinery, and interconnectivity by drawing a dense network between individuals and territories. Fabra concluded:

Future and Past in María Fabra's Fiction   161

"Las invenciones constituyen la mayor gloria del siglo XIX" ["Inventions constitute the greatest glory of the nineteenth century"] (Fabra 1884a, 226). A paradigmatic example is again in the text "Un viaje a la Argentina ...," where a trip in an electro-aerial train and then in a submarine from Madrid to Buenos Aires is described under a continuous sense of wonder, as the narrator sitting in an air-conditioned room enjoys a multiplicity of gadgets resembling the television or the internet to make immediate transactions, search for information, and be updated on global events. In its excitement to overwhelm the reader, the story ends with the substitution of planes for trains.

Politically, Fabra stood for bourgeois liberalism, encouraging entrepreneurship, economic laissez-faire, and individualism. He was also deeply patriotic, Catholic, and scorned socialism and anarchism as agents of social unrest, which endangered progress, which was based on stability. When dealing fictionally with these revolutionary ideologies, Fabra turned to humorous dystopia something customary in conservative science fiction, drawing on satire to ridicule these ideologies as viable political alternatives. Thus, the story "El futuro ayuntamiento de Madrid" ["The Future City Council of Madrid"] (1895), written along the lines of Eugen Richter's bestseller *Pictures of a Socialistic Future* (*Sozialdemocratische Zukunftbilder*, 1891, Spanish translation 1896), chronicled the resounding failure of a socialist mayor in Spain's capital in the 1940s who was damaged by ineptitude, corruption, and dispute. Fabra, like conservatives of his time, was incapable of foreseeing the growing strength of the claims for social justice and blinded by panic and anxiety failed to offer a response to inequality and social demands other than condescension, disdain, or repression. In sum, as a man de rigueur fascinated by the latest technology, Fabra could be labeled a retro futurist, keener in predicting material progress than social change.[3]

Along with inventions and radical ideologies, Fabra's prospective fictions had a third area of interest: global geopolitics. He enjoyed speculation on the course of nations, their possible strategic alliances and conflicts, balances of power, and hot regions of the globe. His views were framed by three tenets of Spanish conservatism. First, Anglophobia; the UK—and later by extension the United States—disputed the idea that Spain held the title of the largest colonial empire in history. The UK was Spain's greatest enemy; was historically prone to work against Spain's interest; and, last but not least, held a colony in Spanish soil (Gibraltar). Next, the dream of an Iberian confederation between Spain and Portugal. As Fabra explained in "Dos naciones hermanas" ["Two Sister Nations"] (1883b), an initial fiscal treaty could develop into a much deeper union to block future colonial claims. And finally, through the formation of a commonwealth between the Latin American nations and their spiritual "mother" Spain that would politically sanction the existence of an alleged "Latin race." Fabra sought to make these premises credible by acting them out in the future.

162   *Juan Herrero-Senés*

In the late nineteenth century, a subgenre of science fiction became the preferred vehicle to speculate on national realities and potential geopolitical upheavals: future wars. The stories unfolded intuitions about weapons deployment and new combat forms and displayed plausible scenarios of tensions in international relations and power balance. They functioned fundamentally as cautionary tales, warning about possible threats, frictions, areas of conflict, interests and ambitions of the states, foreign armaments, and especially national military deficiencies.

As I.F. Clarke (1992) has shown, future wars enjoyed enormous success from the publication in 1870 of "The Battle of Dorking" to the First World War, with hundreds published mainly in the UK, France, Germany, and the United States. To my knowledge, the earliest examples in Spain date from 1883: Federico Arnaiz's novel *La Estrella Iberia* and Fabra's own "El desastre de Inglaterra en 1910," to which he added "La guerra de España con los Estados Unidos" ["The Spanish–American War"] (1896c, 1896d). Fabra enjoyed narrating a prominent feature of his time, international conflicts, and similar to most of his contemporaries, he patronized naval battles, as they offered the greatest spectacle while making apparent the evolution of warfare from people-fighting to machine-fighting. Fabra's war-writing (both fictional and not) never called into question the morality of war, nor what he considered its main goal: gaining or keeping territorial control. Under Fabra's colonial gaze, unexplored or unclaimed territories are appreciated solely as enclaves for the expansion of the Western economy, and the right of conquest is never questioned unless used against a possession effectively occupied by another European state because that "significaría un acto de guerra" ["It would amount to an act of war"] (Fabra 1884b, 270).

Prior to "La guerra …," Fabra had outlined his geopolitical standpoint in the stories "El desastre …" and "Viaje a Argentina …." The first narrates the war between Great Britain and Continental Europe for control of the Mediterranean Sea, while simultaneously tensions between the United States and Latin American countries unfold due to the United States intent to hog the Panama Canal (which, along with the Channel Tunnel, already exists). Spain is strongly involved with the war as an opportunity to recover Gibraltar, which happens after the final English defeat. The globe transforms into a game board for sea warfare with the Anglo-Saxons persisting in "una política de ambición y de conquista" ["a policy of ambition and conquest"] (Fabra 1883a, 79). The second text, set in 2003, includes an epilogue summarizing the most dramatic geopolitical changes of the twentieth century. Impelled by its enormous growth, the United States violated Mexican territory to occupy Central America militarily; "un grito unánime de indignación" ["a unanimous cry of outrage"] (Fabra 1889, 338) from all the countries of Iberian origin with Spain at the forefront followed, and their alliance inflicted a severe defeat on the enemy both by sea and by land. The peace negotiations called the United States to pay millions in compensation, to curtail its army, and to

Future and Past in María Fabra's Fiction   163

return to Mexico the territories annexed after the Treaty of Guadalupe Hidalgo.[4] The victory promoted the establishment of a permanent "Latin American Confederation" to stop any further Anglo-Saxon invasion, and a new era of prosperity followed.

In the 1890s, Fabra's interest in the United States sprouted. The article "La guerra de intereses" ["The War of Interest"] (1890) blasted the protectionist policy of the McKinley tariff, branding it "Tax Inquisition," while omitting any reference to European regulations against American imports. In 1894, while the United States suffered the worst economic recession since its birth, the piece "El socialismo en los Estados Unidos" ["Socialism in the United States"] deplored the extension of unionism and the rise of the Socialist Party of America (SPA) as a "cáncer" (Fabra 1894b, 295) corroding the nation with strikes and protests. Meanwhile, the government failed to protect businesses, the consumers suffered, and the great fortunes grew by speculation and fraud. Fabra exaggerated to undermine the American reputation as a land of commercial prosperity and concluded by recommending that investors shift to Latin America, where their initiatives would be welcomed and protected.

Then came the Cuban insurrection of 1895, the critical phase of a decades-long process. The Spanish policy to guarantee the sovereignty of Cuba was based on two principles: the concentration of all privileges in the peninsular elite, which caused the insurrection of 1868, and staunch repression of the locals by the military administration. The metropolis turned a blind eye to the administration's abuses to secure their support and simultaneously promoted trade deals with the United States to perpetuate the status quo. Cuba did not become an immediate problem until violence erupted. Spain's failure to contain the insurgency in February prompted American public opinion and many of the Cuban landowning elite to call for a U.S. intervention to restore order. Cubans, inspired by José Martí and commanded by Antonio Maceo and Máximo Gómez, gained ground in the following months, occupying all rural areas, although not Havana or Santiago. The Spanish government then reacted with brutal repression, reviving in the United States the old images of intolerance and cruelty of the Black Legend and putting Washington to the test. But President Cleveland declared neutrality and refused to give international recognition to the rebels.

Madrid had rejected from the start any U.S. mediation and indeed unsuccessfully sought an international warrant to the Triple Alliance and Britain against possible American intervention. In Spain, a growing nationalist atmosphere rekindled anti-American prejudices and fueled unfounded theories that the United States had conspired for decades to seize Cuba and instigate the rebellion. During the spring of 1896, hostility became palpable, with a wave of demonstrations before the American consulates, especially in the cities of Alicante, La Coruña, Bilbao, and Barcelona. Against this background and lacking popular support, the government would eventually prefer to sacrifice Cuba in an armed conflict

164 *Juan Herrero-Senés*

with the United States rather than facing the risk of a military coup-d'état in the event of a negotiated abandonment of the island. The Restoration was a regime entirely based on the consent of the military establishment, which fully refused to yield Cuba without a fight.

Fabra decided this was the time to take a stand. On February 22, only days after General Arsenio Martínez-Campos was replaced by General Weyler as Governor of Cuba, Fabra penned in *La Ilustración Española y Americana* an admonitory letter addressed to the United States simply called "España y los Estados Unidos" ["Spain and the United States"]. Betraying a century-long friendship, the United States interfered in Cuba by creating discord, giving to the rebels "apoyo moral y fuerza material" ["moral support and material force"] (Fabra 1896a, 107), and acting as an arbitrator. Fabra interpreted these actions as a challenge from an incumbent for influence on Latin America (something already implied in the formulation of the Monroe Doctrine) and responded with an imagined community. The United States had nothing to do with the countries south of its borders because they were Latins, a race opposite to Anglo-Saxons forged during four centuries with robust ties in language, beliefs, and customs.[5] This heritage validated the right to preserve colonies as footprints of Spanishness. Fabra was not original here; since the Latin American independences, some Spanish thinkers had sought to formulate a new identity and a new position of Spain in the international system based on the idea of a "spiritual" Spanish preeminence over the American territories as they all were part of a community of shared humanistic values (Ñíguez Bernal 1987, 80) and, Fabra stressed, a similarity in character: Latins were outgoing, passionate, idealistic, and joyous, while the Anglo-Saxons were introverted, rational, melancholic, and practicality driven. In contrast, the United States had no interest in promoting any kind of spiritual ascendancy on their territorial acquisitions. Fabra opposed Spain and American trajectories inside an evolutionary notion of history where the fight between races played a central role. A similar narrative was developed by the doctrine of Anglo-Saxonism, "the chief element in American racism in the Imperial era" (Hofstadter 1955, 155).

The letter contradicted itself swinging between pragmatism, which implied pessimism, and hopeful idealism. Fabra acknowledged in one paragraph that "desde el punto de vista del orden práctico, mi raza es de tal suerte inferior a la tuya que, puestas ambas en contacto, forzosamente resultaría la completa destrucción de aquella" ["In terms of practicality, my race is so inferior to yours that their touch would necessarily result in the complete destruction of the former"], but in patriotic pride, he responded that "me sobra aliento para reducir al silencio a los que turban el reposo de mi familia" ["I have enough breath to reduce to silence those who disturb the rest of my family"] (1896a, 108). The second position prevailed, and a month later, Fabra offered "La guerra de España con los Estados Unidos," a lengthy account of a war between Spain and the United States for Cuba where the former was victorious[6]: a future war

Future and Past in María Fabra's Fiction   165

(in an immediate but unidentified future) that in light of the subsequent events it almost reads as an example of alternate history.[7]

"La guerra ..." is divided into four articles that correspond to the following content: an explanation of the current United States–Spain relations regarding Cuba, the origins of the conflict, the description of the main battles, and the end of the war and its consequences. For fiction, Fabra changed gears in his criticism of the United States, as he set aside discussions of spirituality and directly embraced conspiracy theory. America was ruled by two extremist groups: the people, who imposed their demands, and businessmen, "el gobierno oculto" ["the secret government"] (Fabra 1896b, 174). They shared greed and strong racism against the African-American population, so eventually they recovered the old idea[8] of making Cuba a colony for the colored population: to annex strategically located Cuba and create a colony to concentrate the colored population. The suggestion gained momentum with the insurrection, so American "secret associations" supported it while slandering Spain in the press, hoping that once liberated, the locals, incapable of forming a stable government, would end up throwing themselves into the arms of the United States. The United States proclaims belligerence when it provides a ship, the *Estrella Solitaria* [*Lone Star*], to the insurgents[9] and sends a plenipotentiary representative, disguised as a mediator, to meet with their president. Both countries start preparing for war, while the European powers ask unsuccessfully for arbitration; the spark flies when the *Estrella Solitaria* scuttles a Spanish merchant near Puerto Rico and after a chase a Spanish torpedo boat sinks it. Spain refuses to pay reparations and the United States declares war.

Copious descriptions of the logistical preparations (number of ships and soldiers, strategic decisions) are followed by the two decisive battles, one on the sea and one on the ground, both won by the Spanish army despite the apparent numerical superiority of the enemy. During the epic narration, Fabra contrasts the heroism, patriotism, and "superioridad de una nación de tradicionales hábitos militares" ["superiority of a nation with traditional military habits"] to a nation "que entrega la defensa del símbolo de la patria a aventureros asalariados" ["that entrusts the defense of the symbol of the homeland to paid adventurers"] (1896e, 223) lacking discipline and instruction. The United States calls for an armistice, and the defeat causes a violent "revolución del proletariado" ["proletarian revolution"] (Fabra 1896e, 226) against the government and businessmen. Lastly, the revolt is suffocated, and Spain reconquers the island.

The story effectively rendered the prevalent opinion in Spain on the United States, including that of public representatives such as Minister Enrique Dupuy de Lôme, the principal Spanish ambassador in the United States during the 1890s. Other European countries, also frustrated at the relentless American rise, held the same conservative, aristocratic, prejudiced, and ignorant view (Corrales Morales 2017a, 554): The

166   *Juan Herrero-Senés*

United States was an uncivilized country whose egalitarian and populist tendency produced a vulgar and ordinary society.

Fabra's portrait also aimed at dismantling the virtues of the "model republic" for which an enlightened minority in Spain felt admiration, especially regarding politics and law (Hilton 1998; Neila Hernández 2008, 41; Niño 2005, 58–59; Fernández de Miguel 2012, 65–70). The narrator alludes to them as "cándidos e ilusos" ["naïve and fool"] (Fabra 1896b, 174) and vilifies their arguments. The supposed American virtues did not show on the ground. Against the claims of ethnic diversity and capacity of assimilation, Fabra underscored the problems generated by racial discrimination, religious diversity, and urban concentration. The ability to promote prosperity and innovation was contested with the growth of unionism and consequently social conflict. On public affairs, Fabra highlighted the cases of corruption that uncovered the venality of professional politicians while underscoring the most eccentric facets of politics, such as the stardom of presidential candidates or the spectacular nature of electoral campaigns. And he insisted on the pervasive lack of morality which subjected all decisions exclusively to economic criteria.

In a way, it could be argued that Fabra accepted the terms of Kagan's "Prescott paradigm" and flipped its value. He accepted the United States as a republican, egalitarian, rational, industrious, and futuristic nation, countered by a monarchical, indolent, snobbish, and fanatical backward Spain. Fabra cherished faith and emotions such as patriotism, so ultimately, he was willing to sacrifice material progress to delay a modernity that defied Spain's core values. The entities "Spain" and "United States" possessed contrasting symbolic capital: they represented two national entities, but also, as we saw, two races (the Latin and the Anglo-Saxon), two temporalities (a long history sifted in tradition versus a short future-oriented history), two sets of values (humanistic or spiritual versus chrematistic or material), and the clash of the old world against the new. Beyond a territorial issue, Fabra's fictional Spanish–American War epitomized a struggle between two incompatible worldviews. It is in this sense that "La guerra" constituted a cautionary tale for the Spanish people: not because it warned out of the dangers of a war assumed by many, and even desired by some, but because the American sociopolitical landscape of materialism, diversity, and revolution might extend to Spain unless it resisted the contemporary dissolution of values and defended its historical significance as "patria del espíritu" ["homeland of the spirit"] (Fabra 1896e, 226).

"La guerra" is not free of contradictions: Fabra stressed the bonds of a Hispanic spiritual community, but in the story, no Latin nation is willing to effectively help Spain. He criticized professional soldiers, while acknowledging that a true national army relied on the exploitation of ignorant rural masses "refractarias a las disolventes ideas actuales" ["refractory to the current dissolvent ideas"] (Fabra 1896e, 223). Fabra demonized the people's agitation in confronting the establishment but

Future and Past in María Fabra's Fiction   167

praised it when showing support for the government. Utilitarianism and practicality, proposed as the solution to the ills of Spain in the 1894 text "Lo presente juzgado por lo porvenir," were deprecated two years later. And last but not least, if talking political corruption, the entire political system of the Restoration stood on a pact of power alternation between the Liberal and the Conservative parties based on fraudulent elections, networks of despotic landowners or *caciques*, and the repression of urban proletarian movements, all of which prevented access to power to any other ideology.[10]

Regarding the specific issue of Cuba and the war, "La guerra" is also valuable as an expression of affects. The majority of Spaniards who cared about the conflict believed Spain could win, drawn by frivolous warmongering by the government and the press to see in the United States "una nación joven e inexperta que nada tendría que hacer frente al peso, la tradición y la experiencia colonial de la vieja España" ["a young and inexperienced nation that would have nothing to do with the weight, tradition and colonial experience of old Spain"] (Sánchez Mantero 1998, 294); the rulers and an informed minority recognized the slim chance of victory.[11] Fabra tried to reconcile both positions and unify public opinion by presenting the war as inevitable, taking advantage of the heated Anti-American context to feed a state of opinion favorable to the government's stances. In this sense, "La guerra" narratively fleshed out Prime Minister Antonio Cánovas' principles for status quo: Spain should not intervene in any warlike conflict due to lack of means; it should not expand but concentrate on preserving its possessions, deemed as inalienable. Honor was paramount, so in the event of aggression, Spain, in advantage or disadvantage, should respond in self-defense (Ñíguez Bernal 1987, 83–84). The plot of "La guerra" confirmed all these points: Pacific Spain, with no new colonial aspirations, was attacked in its honor and carried out its obligation to defend the island of Cuba as an inalienable national territory. The outcome then reinforced the popular conviction of victory. "La guerra" added to many reports that manufactured popular consent to war, finally, by praising the work of Spain in Cuba—leaving unmentioned many serious problems—and vindicating its Spanishness, while attacking American imperialism and opportunism.

When the story appeared in book form in 1897, some foreign reviewers echoed its success in Spain. For *Public Opinion*, its novel narrative procedure managed "to encourage the Spaniards with a representation of the ease with which the US can be whipped" ("Literary" 1897, 793).[12] Other critics were not so benevolent. For Eduardo Gómez de Baquero (Andrenio), the story betrayed the duty of future war texts, "denunciar defectos en la organización de las fuerzas militares" ["to denounce defects in the organization of the military forces"] (1897, 132), by falling into a self-fulfilling optimistic chauvinism.

Fabra's piece of prospective propaganda was shortly tested by reality. When President William McKinley entered office in March 1897, he

168   *Juan Herrero-Senés*

promised to solve the Cuban problem, mainly for humanitarian reasons.[13] Of course, as Hugh Rockoff (2012, 51–56) has detailed, some special economic interests pushed for the war: the yellow press, property owners in Cuba, the sugar industry, steamship owners, bankers, and the military. President McKinley stressed the need for Spain's resignation to sovereignty in the Antilles and did not rule out armed intervention. This was the last option until the end, but once decided, it entailed territorial expansion, hence the fight in the Pacific. A clear signal to the traditional powers that the United States had joined the colonial race.

The story is well known. The United States found the pretext to enter the war on February 15, 1898, when it concluded that the explosion that sank the USS Maine, sent to Havana harbor to protect United States citizens, had been perpetrated from outside the ship. Since no accord with Spain for reparations was reached, the United States signed a war declaration on April 25, as Fabra had predicted. He was wrong about everything else.

The Spanish government trusted the Fabra Agency to lead a pro-Spanish coverage of the conflict and communicate the official position, but the strategy fell short, because the Havas Agency exercised strict control over the amount, selection, and handling of the news to satisfy its clients and did not limit itself only to Spanish sources (Schulze-Schneider 1998, 111). The reports included the same stereotypes and exaggerations that Fabra had exploited in fiction. In short, the United States, a nation of racist merchants and mercenaries, went to war prompted by imperialist ideals[14] against all international laws. The Spanish navy was stronger, and the courage of its soldiers unmatched.

The war lasted four and a half months with a humiliating defeat for Spain. In the first battle on May 1, the U.S. Navy destroyed the Spanish fleet in Manila Bay, and the same thing in Cuba on July 3. The land campaign did not progress as easily, and the Spanish troops surrendered on August 12. The Treaty of Paris, signed on December 10, wiped out Spain's overseas empire, with the loss of Puerto Rico, The Philippines, and the West Indies, in addition to Cuba, where the U.S. military occupation started January 1, after the Spanish officials left.

All this time Fabra remained silent, most likely tormented by the events of the conflict and sore with the aftermath. Ten days before the peace agreement ceremony, Fabra published his last science fiction text ever, titled "La Yankeelandia. Geografía e historia en el siglo XXIV" ["Yankeeland. Geography and History in the 24th Century"]. It is entirely dedicated to the United States and never made it into a book. There Fabra simultaneously conceded and exorcised the defeat by acknowledging the advent of the United States as the new unrivaled world power; his deeply negative vision of America and an exalted patriotism that canceled any form of self-criticism remained untouched. Fabra changed the science-fictional strategy he deployed, moving from the immediate future of "La guerra" to a transcription of the entry "Yankeelandia" from a

Future and Past in María Fabra's Fiction 169

Compendium of Universal Geography published in the twenty-fourth century.[15] "Yankeelandia" was a country encompassing the entire territory between Alaska and Tierra del Fuego, plus numerous islands such as the Azores, Ireland, Cape Verde, and Polynesia. Several reasons explained this expansion. In addition to being a "pueblo más joven, robusto y vigoroso" ["younger, more robust and vigorous people"] (Fabra 1898, 310), the United States benefited from its geographical position, fertility, and land size, a steady increase in population, the lack of powerful neighbors, and the unresponsiveness of European nations, fixated on their rivalries. Yankeelandia was run as a corporation by executives with the only goal of profits. Its regions operated as branches, the army consisted of mercenaries and weapon inventors, legislation was based on force, and the guiding principle of the foreign policy read "La explotación del universo por el yankee" ["The exploitation of the universe by the yankee"] (Fabra 1898, 310).

After the entry, the transcriber referenced the foundational event of the new empire, the Spanish–American War, "la guerra más inicua e injusta del siglo XIX" ["the most wicked and unjust war of the nineteenth century"] (Fabra 1898, 310). The UK was to blame for the Spanish defeat, because for decades it had failed to restrain the United States' increasing strength and in 1898 rejected a joined intervention with Germany that would have prevented the war.[16] An improbable fictional future offered some symbolic compensation with the American annexation of Canada and the British West Indies.

"Yankeelandia" underscored the U.S. drive to expansion, patiently listing the dates of each annexation until the year 2100, while back in the United States, President McKinley was selling his decision to incorporate the Philippines. The United States shaded Europe and Japan in a "passage of power" (Schoonover 2003, 2) and expanded in both the Caribbean and the Pacific. According to Fabra, the United States would establish its hegemony primarily by imposing American businesses and economic interests in the name of freeing people, using military intervention only when necessary. Fabra was adjusting his thoughts, tied to colonial presence, amidst the changes in the structure of capital and power dynamics that Giovanni Arrighi defined as a contrast between "territorialism" and "capitalism." Under the logic of the former, rulers identify power with the extent of their domains, which makes wealth a byproduct of the pursuit of expansion; under the second logic, power equals the extent of command over scarce resources, and territory appropriations are considered as a byproduct. While the U.S. strategy was mainly capitalist, the Spanish empire may be considered mostly territorialist (Arrighi 1994, 33).

The termination of this old empire was simultaneously physical and mental. The highly praised supranational unity with Latin American nations condensed in the "Latin race" revealed a baseless sentimental construct, at least in political terms, as no American republic came to the

170   *Juan Herrero-Senés*

aid of Spain.[17] In fact, nobody did, proving Spain's isolation, a weak old power anchored in useless past glories. The same could be said of Fabra himself, unable to concede errors and inconsistencies. The emotional conclusion of "La Yankeelandia" demanded from Spaniards national pride: No regrets for defending Spanish territories, and no responsibility for the defeat; it was the victory of a ramping "materialismo utilitario" ["utilitarian materialism"] (Fabra 1898, 310) over the "culto del espíritu" ["cult of the spirit"] (Fabra 1898, 310). These abstractions and "premodern rhetoric" (Fernandez 2012, 79) reveal Fabra's lack of objectivity when Spain was at stake. Otherwise, he was more prudent. Take 1884: when writing about Germany, he admitted that in a conflict between a nation using the force, and "naciones que tienen derechos históricos y escasez de recursos materiales para hacerlos valer" ["nations that have historical rights and scarce material resources to assert them"] (Fabra 1884b, 271), the former was as a rule victorious.

Blind patriotism proved useless, and the Spanish debacle triggered introspection and fueled a regeneration. The Restoration started to crumble, regionalism boomed, the middle class reacted, socialism (opposed to the war both in Spain and the United States[18]) went on the rise, old values collapsed as new ones emerged, and young intellectuals and artists engaged in an obsessive analysis of the ills of the homeland with fierce criticism. Future lay ahead.

Notes

1 Some mentions can be found in Serrano (1984, 72–74) and Sevilla Soler (1986, 490). Bardavío Estevan (2018) has studied through this lens the short stories of Emilia Pardo Bazán.

2 According to Olmos (1997, 64–65), the Agencia Fabra was by 1900 the most important source of international information for Spanish media, with more than 55 subscribers, including 45 newspapers and organizations such as the National Bank of Spain.

3 That being said, "Un viaje …" describes a popular revolution in Russia at the start of the twentieth century where the crowds expel the tsars from power (Fabra 1889, 348).

4 In "Cuatro siglos de buen gobierno" ["Four Centuries of Good Government," 1883], Mexico never loses those territories to the US, as the latter refrains in fear of the Hispanic federation (Fabra 1883c, 60).

5 See Corrales Morales (2017b) for a survey of this debate on Latin and Anglo-Saxon races from 1898 until 1914. He does not take into consideration examples previous to the war.

6 It was originally published in four installments in *La Ilustración Española y Americana* between March and April 1896 and later included in the 1897 collection of stories *Presente y futuro* with minimal changes. I quote from the original publication.

7 Technically, it is not as it was written before the events. An actual example of alternate history about the Spanish–American War with a victorious Spain

Future and Past in María Fabra's Fiction   171

is *Fuego sobre San Juan* [*Fire on San Juan*, 1999] by Pedro A. García Bilbao and Javier Sánchez Reyes.

8 It was originally proposed in 1854 in the Ostend Manifesto by slaveholding expansionists.

9 According to Miller (2011, 7), since 1895, "more than seventy filibustering operations [that] sailed from the U.S. shores to supply arms to the Cuban revolutionaries." These trading practices had a long history, and Fabra might have in mind the Virginius Affair. Between 1873 and 1875, the *Virginius*, a fast ship flying an American flag but owned by Cuban rebels, was used to smuggle aid into the island. The Spanish Navy eventually captured the ship and executed 53 of its men (Ñíguez 1987, 82).

10 In fact, Paz Rebollo (1989, 362) pointed out that Fabra himself obtained fraudulently his deputy seat for Barcelona. Fabra had harshly criticized the Spanish political system in "El presente juzgado por lo porvenir."

11 Perceptions would change with time and according to Hilton (1994, 76), "by early 1897 many in Spain were apparently resigned to the idea that defeat by the American colossus, though painful, would at least be honourable, and would definitively end the Cuban war."

12 See also the reviews by A. Savine in *L'Humanité Nouvelle* (by A. Savine) and by Ephrem Vincent (1898) in *Mercure de France*.

13 For Matthew McCullough (2014), the circumstances around the Spanish–American War gave rise in the US to "messianic interventionism," the belief, articulated by an array of Christian leaders, that America could and should intervene altruistically on behalf of other nations. They mimicked Fabra's definition of Spain as the "homeland of the Spirit," by considering America the land of true Christianity. Bonnie Miller (2011) has shown how the media largely framed the war in plain idealistic terms.

14 On the influence of the British imperial model on US foreign policy and particularly in the case of Cuba, see Priest (2014).

15 Thirty years earlier, Fabra had composed an analogous book: *Compendio de geografía universal, extractado de los mejores de su clase* ([*Compendium of Universal Geography, extracted from the best of its kind*] 1867). There he concluded regarding the US: "Este coloso [que] no contento con dominar en el Nuevo Mundo procuraba ya influir de una manera directa en los asuntos de Europa" ["this colossus not happy with dominating the New World, was already trying to influence directly the European affairs"] (Fabra 1867, 172).

16 Fabra was wrong. De la Torre (1997) has traced the efforts of Sir Henry Drummond Wolff, the British ambassador in Madrid, to make Prime Minister Salisbury support Spain, And Robles Muñoz (1997) has meticulously analyzed the stand of the European powers on the war, proving Germany's disengagement.

17 See Quijada (1997) for a study of the reactions of the Latin American countries to the Spanish–American War, and their retelling of the topic of Latins vs Anglo-Saxons.

18 In the case of Spain, see Serrano (1979) for the position of the Socialist Party (PSOE) and Maestro (1998) for the response from the workers' organizations. Charles Quince (2017) has recently studied anti-imperialist positions in the United States during the Spanish–American and Philippines Wars.

172 *Juan Herrero-Senés*

Works Cited

Arrighi, Giovanni. 1994. *The Long Twentieth Century: Money, Power, and the Origins of Our Times*. New York: Verso.

Bardavío Estevan, Susana. 2018. "¡España Es También Aquí!": Nación e Imaginario Colonial En Los Cuentos De Emilia Pardo Bazán." *Castilla. Estudios De Literatura* 9: 176–203.

Clarke, I.F. 1992. *Voices Prophesying War: Future Wars, 1763–3749*. 2d ed. New York; Oxford: Oxford University Press.

Corrales Morales, David. 2017a. "Reflejos del futuro presente. Imágenes de los Estados Unidos en la prensa española de principios del siglo XX (1898–1914)." *Revista de Indias* 270: 551–583.

———. 2017b. "Latins Against Anglo-Saxons: Spanish Cultural Magazines as a Channel for Transatlantic Debates about Race (1898–1914)." *Journal of Transatlantic Studies* 15, no. 3: 273–283.

De la Torre del Río, Rosario. 1997. "1895–1898: Inglaterra y La Búsqueda De Un Compromiso Internacional Para Frenar La Intervención Norteamericana En Cuba." *Hispania* 57, no. 196: 515–549.

Gómez de Baquero, Eduardo. 1897. "Colección Elzevir Ilustrada." *La España Moderna* 1: 130–134.

Fabra, Nilo María. 1867. *Compendio de geografía universal*. Madrid: Rubio y Compañía.

———. 1883a. "El desastre de Inglaterra en 1910." *La Ilustración Española y Americana*, February 8, 1883: 79–82; later included in 1885a.

———. 1883b. "Dos naciones hermanas." *La Ilustración Española y Americana*, August 15, 1883: 86–87; later included in 1885a.

———. 1883c. "Cuatro siglos de buen gobierno." *La Ilustración Española y Americana*, November 30, 1883: 311–314, and December 6, 1883: 338–339; later included in 1885a.

———. 1884a. "Asuntos de la China." *La Ilustración Española y Americana*, October 10, 1884: 226–227.

———. 1884b. "Alemania en África." *La Ilustración Española y Americana*, November 8, 1884: 270–271.

———. 1885a. *Por los espacios imaginarios (Con escalas en tierra)*. Madrid: Librería de Fernando Fe.

———. 1889. "Un viaje a la Argentina en el año 2003." *La Ilustración Española y Americana*, August 8, 1889: 335–338; later included in 1895.

———. 1890. "La guerra de intereses." *La Ilustración Española y Americana*, October 22, 1890: 238–239.

———. 1894a. "El presente juzgado por el porvenir." *La Ilustración Española y Americana*, April 30, 1894: 263–265.

———. 1894b. "El socialismo en los Estados Unidos." *La Ilustración Española y Americana*, May 15, 1894: 295–296.

———. 1895. *Cuentos ilustrados*. Barcelona: Imp. de Henrich y Cía.

———. 1896a. "España y los Estados Unidos. Carta de Santiáguez a Jonathán." *La Ilustración Española y Americana*, February 22, 1896: 107–110.

———. 1896b. "La guerra de España con Los Estados Unidos. Los Estados Unidos y Cuba." *La Ilustración Española y Americana*, March 22, 1896: 171–174.

Future and Past in María Fabra's Fiction   173

———. 1896c. "La guerra de España con Los Estados Unidos. Orígen de la guerra entre España y los Estados Unidos." *La Ilustración Española y Americana*, March 30, 1896: 190–191.

———. 1896d. "La guerra de España con Los Estados Unidos. La guerra entre España y los Estados Unidos." *La Ilustración Española y Americana*, April 8, 1896: 206–210.

———. 1896e. "La guerra de España con Los Estados Unidos. El triunfo de España." *La Ilustración Española y Americana*, April 15, 1896: 223–226.

———. 1897. *Presente y futuro (Nuevos cuentos)*. Barcelona: Juan Gili.

———. 1898. "La Yankeelandia. Geografía e historia en el siglo XXIV." *La Ilustración Española y Americana*, November 30, 1898: 308–310.

Fernández de Miguel, Daniel. 2012. *El enemigo yanqui: Las raíces conservadoras del antiamericanismo español*. Zaragoza: Genueve Ediciones.

Hilton, Sylvia L. 1994. "The Spanish-American War of 1898: Queries into the Relationship between the Press, Public Opinion and Politics." *Revista Española de Estudios Norteamericanos* 5, no. 7: 71–87.

———. 1998. "Los Estados Unidos como modelo: los federalistas españoles y el mito americano durante la crisis colonial de 1895–1898." *Ibero-Americana Pragensia* 34: 11–29.

Hofstadter, Richard. 1955. *Social Darwinism in American Thought*. Boston: Beacon Press.

"Literary Notes." 1897. *Public Opinion*, June 27, 1897: 792–793.

Maestro, Francisco Javier. 1998. "La respuesta obrera: ¡O todos o ninguno!" *Viento Sur* 36: 15–20.

McCullough, Matthew. 2014. *The Cross of War: Christian Nationalism and U.S. Expansion in the Spanish-American War*. Madison, Wisconsin: The University of Wisconsin Press.

Miller, Bonnie M. 2011. *From Liberation to Conquest: The Visual and Popular Cultures of the Spanish-American War of 1898*. Amherst: University of Massachusetts Press.

Neila Hernández, José Luis. 2008. "Entre Cuba y las Azores: Imágenes y percepciones en las relaciones entre España y los Estados Unidos." *Estudios Internacionales* 160: 35–62.

Ñíguez Bernal, Antonio. 1987. "Las relaciones políticas, económicas y culturales entre España y los Estados Unidos en los siglos XIX y XX." *Quinto Centenario* 12: 71–134.

Niño, Antonio. 2005. "Las relaciones culturales como punto de encuentro hispano-estadounidense." *España y Estados Unidos en el siglo XX*, edited by Lorenzo Delgado and Maria Dolores Elizalde. Madrid: CSIC, 57–94.

Olmos, Victor. 1997. *Historia de la Agencia EFE: El mundo en español*. Madrid: Espasa Calpe.

Paz Rebollo, Maria Antonia. 1989. "Relaciones del poder político con los medios informativos: Nilo María Fabra y la Restauración." *Haciendo historia: Homenaje al profesor Carlos Seco*, edited by Teresa Martínez de Sas et alii. Madrid: Ed. Universidad Complutense, 357–366.

Priest, Andrew. 2014. "Thinking about Empire: The Administration of Ulysses S. Grant, Spanish Colonialism and the Ten Years' War in Cuba." *Journal of American Studies* 48, no. 2: 541–558.

174 *Juan Herrero-Senés*

Quijada, Mónica. 1997. "Latinos y Anglosajones: El 98 en el fin de siglo Sudamericano." *Hispania* 57, no. 196: 589–609.

Quince, Charles. 2017. *Resistance to the Spanish-American and Philippine Wars: Anti-Imperialism and the Role of the Press, 1895–1902.* Jefferson, North Carolina: McFarland.

Robles Muñoz, Cristóbal. 1997. "España y Las Alianzas Europeas En 1898." *Hispania* 57, no. 196: 479–514.

Rockoff, Hugh. 2012. *America's Economic Way of War: War and the US Economy from the Spanish-American War to the First Gulf War.* Cambridge and New York: Cambridge University Press.

Sánchez Mantero, Rafael. 1998. "El 98 y la imagen de España en los Estados Unidos." *Revista de Occidente* 202–203: 294–309.

Santiáñez-Tió, Nil. 1994. "Nuevos mapas del Universo: Modernidad y ciencia ficción en la literatura española del siglo XIX (1804–1905)." *Revista Hispánica Moderna* 47, no. 2: 269–88.

Schoonover, Thomas. 2003. *Uncle Sam's War of 1898 and Origins of Globalization.* Lexington: University Press of Kentucky.

Schulze-Schneider, Ingrid. 1998. "From Dictatorship to Democracy." *The Globalization of News,* edited by O. Boyd-Barrett and T. Rantanen. London: SAGE Publications, 108–24.

Serrano, Carlos. 1979. "El PSOE y la guerra de Cuba (1895–1898)." *Estudios de Historia Social* 8–9: 287–310.

———. 1984. *Final del Imperio. España, 1895–1898.* Madrid: Siglo XXI.

Sevilla Soler, Rosario. 1986. "La intervención norteamericana en Cuba y la opinión pública andaluza." *Anuario de Estudios Americanos* 43: 469–516.

Valera, Juan. 1901. *Ecos argentinos.* Madrid: Fernando Fe.

Vincent, Ephrem. 1898. "Lettres Espagnoles." *Mercure de France,* July: 304–308.

10 George Santayana's Transatlantic Literary Criticism and the Potencies of Aesthetic Judgment

David LaRocca

The specificity or ambiguity of George Santayana's national identity, like that of his contemporary Henry James, is a vexed and therefore fecund topic. If Santayana is understood to have been Spanish, if that claim feels legitimate, then it may not strain credulity to say he was the greatest, and now most enduring (if also strangely under-read) Spanish philosopher working in the nineteenth-century United States and the first decades of the twentieth century too. Such superlatives, if contested, only get us so far anyway. Still, they serve at least to stoke our thinking more generally about the presence of Spanish thinkers in the United States and their influence on American thought. Hard to fathom, then, that more than a half-century has elapsed since John Lachs commended to us that "the time is ripe for a thorough critical examination of Santayana's philosophy" (1967, 1). Since then, the character of Santayana's work hasn't changed, yet a time for our reckoning with his work remains unfinished business. While many fine studies have been conducted in the intervening years, including conspicuous interventions by Lachs, Santayana's particular relationship to Spain and to the United States, the nature of Spanish literature and its connection to American literature, the qualities of Santayana's identity as Spanish, his capacities for literary-philosophical expression, and his presence as a late nineteenth-century thinker who comes of age in the early twentieth century remain worthy topics, ones to return to, develop, and explore further. In the light of the prompt of the present volume, and in conversation with the way we might pick up Lachs' comment as an invitation for a renewal of our consideration of Santayana—more than fifty years in the making—we have an occasion to reflect on the relevance, if any, of Santayana's national and cultural identity/identities, of his "Spanishness" and his "Americanness," for thinking about literature, philosophy, and the transatlantic communion between two nations—one Santayana's birth nation and the other his fodder and sometimes foil.

Indeed, the very attempt to "nationalize" or "naturalize" thought (the second punning the philosophical naturalism that defines Santayana's five-volume *The Life of Reason*, 1905–1906) comes in for reassessment in his midst. *Can* we be confident in saying that Santayana is a Spanish

DOI: 10.4324/9781003219460-10

176   *David LaRocca*

philosopher? Or is it better to say he was (merely?) a Spanish philosopher working in the United States? Other permutations abound—all of them seemingly valid, if unsettling: a Spanish-national educated in Brahmin New England; one among the golden age of American Philosophy (Mink 1980) who happened to be Spanish. Referring to Santayana as "Spanish-American" sounds both inaccurate and a designation *avant la lettre*. What to make of the application of the now-familiar demographic census category Hispanic? Or the even more up-to-the-minute Latinx? We can be assured, at the least, however, to describe times and texts as well as locations, and lines of inheritance (for instance, that Santayana was a philosopher working in the United States who was of Spanish descent). The difficulty of giving names to Santayana's position in and out of the United States, within and without of the academy, being from a given nation and living in another, we also hit upon contemporary trends aimed to quash national identities altogether. On this line, there is much to trouble, but also to inform, in prevailing academic habits that suppress the appellation "international" in favor of the "transnational."[1] Indeed, we might say, as the prefix hints, that a contested politics of identity (underwritten by use of the national and international) has been traded for a transcendental signifier (viz., transnational). By these means, Santayana is neither Spanish nor American (even as a longtime inhabitant of the milieus that generate such attributions) but something more like a transnational figure, someone who—after further stints in Oxford and Paris and Rome—becomes a paragon of cosmopolitanism.

As the ancient Greek Cynics and Roman Stoics envisioned: the cosmopolitan is a citizen of the cosmos—yet lacking, or denying claim to, a particular place within it to call home (for he is said to be at home wherever he finds himself). Thus, as Kwame Anthony Appiah writes, there are "two strands" of thought "that intertwine in the notion of cosmopolitanism," and paradoxically so, as the Cynic's brand of skepticism was wont to cultivate: "the idea that we have obligations to others, obligations that stretch beyond those to whom we are related by the ties of kith and kind, or even the more formal ties of citizenship," and the other being "that we take seriously the value not just of human life but of particular human lives, which means taking an interest in the practices and beliefs that lend them significance" (2006, xv). Appiah's helical formulation befits Santayana's own circumstances, for he was, as Socrates before him, attuned to the general and the particular, the empirical claim and the spiritual fact. For no matter the extent of one's literate abstractions, a body that knows sense and sensibility is discoverable. It can seem that by living many places, one may dilute one's national affiliations—or perhaps one's desire for them or, as noted, one's claims to them. But can this be so? Hence, there may abide some resistance to the giving up of international borders and traits for the post-post-modern transnational.[2] We may be in need of something Stanley Cavell described as a "universal provincialism," a condition in which states of being are indicative of traits, the

Santayana's Philosophy and Criticism   177

collection of which come to form an identity.[3] Indeed, "American" itself can be treated as just such a pliable signifier: one that works for William James as well as his brother, Henry; William's Harvard colleagues, Hugo Münsterberg, Josiah Royce, and Alfred North Whitehead; and, of course, for the Spanish-born Santayana.

However one comes to categorize Santayana's national identity, one of the most surprising details of his life is the way—and the fact that—he abandons his prestigious academic affiliation at its height (i.e., from within the aforementioned golden age of Harvard philosophy, with numerous published works in circulation), choosing instead to spend the remainder of his life as a bachelor writer working out of the libraries, *pensiones*, and hotel rooms of Europe. And so famously, like Friedrich Nietzsche and Ludwig Wittgenstein, we have in Santayana a signal case of a leading world philosopher turning away from the conduct of philosophy in the academy. Of especial pertinence in this context is the further fact that like Santayana, both Nietzsche and Wittgenstein can be counted among the community of wandering philosophers.[4] Indeed, Nietzsche's troubling of nationality led to him being described after his own ideal as "the good European" (Krell 1999). Wittgenstein, for his share, left his native Austria (along the way abdicating a prodigious fortune) and made modest camps in Cambridge, Norway, and elsewhere (including his own sojourn to the United States, which included a quick passage through New York City, a stop in Northampton, and perambulation in Ithaca[5]).

The motif of the wandering philosopher finds literary form in Santayana's *The Last Puritan* (1936), which he described as "a memoir in the form of a novel." Not only should we be intrigued when a writer adopts fiction for the telling of facts—in the spirit of, say, the *roman à clef*, and the "thinly veiled autobiography" of autofiction[6]—we can also appreciate how Santayana sees his life in archetypical terms (e.g., the first pilgrimage, home, the last pilgrimage, etc.). These narrative frames call to mind M.H. Abrams' (1971) trenchant analysis of the "crisis auto-biography" but also bold works of metafiction—such as Cervantes' *Don Quixote*—understood, as it is, as a series of sallies and visitations interrupted by authorial intervention and related modes of *mise-en-abîme*. In thinking of this company of texts and methods, we may glean something of Santayana's transnational life: with the homeland, the pilgrimage, the adopted country, the arc of success beyond one's borders, the return (and various circuitous journeys), the prodigal son, and the habits of the endlessly itinerant, perpetual seeker (contrasting him, for example, with the comparatively domestic Henry David Thoreau, who "settled," remained local, ventured mostly to nearby ponds and rivers, and saw his profession as that of neighboring).

For these reasons, among others, the remarks known as "Tom Sawyer and Don Quixote" provide an invitation—and an impetus—for considering transatlantic literary criticism as mediated and moderated by Jorge Agustín Nicolás Ruiz de Santayana y Borrás, better known in

178   *David LaRocca*

the United States as George Santayana: born in Madrid, he summered in Avila, was educated in Boston and Cambridge, became a central part of the golden age of Harvard Philosophy, and retired from university life at forty-eight to Europe—especially Rome, where he died in 1952 in a world very far from his natality in 1863. The literary criticism on offer in his brief dispatch is characteristically, for Santayana, gestural and allusive, light on direct quotation and *explication du texte*. Rather, what we find is more in keeping with the second line of the piece: "And I had not read far in that book [*The Adventures of Huckleberry Finn* by Mark Twain, 1884] when a vague sense came over me that the ghost of Don Quixote stalked in the background" (Santayana 1952, 116). What follows thereafter is a series of peculiar comparisons and contrasts between the American boy, Tom Sawyer (made famous by Mark Twain), and his literary predecessor as found in *The Ingeniuous Gentleman Don Quixote of La Mancha* by Miguel de Cervantes Saavedra (1605–1620). According to Santayana, Quixote was "mad," where Sawyer's suffering is a function of "adolescence" (no doubt with its own native perturbations of sanity) (1952, 117, 122).

Santayana's coupling of iconic American and Spanish literary marvels amounts to only a handful of pages written in the final year of his life (published in the *Mark Twain Quarterly* in 1952, and at that, somewhat shamed into existence by the kindness of Mr. Cyril Clemens, a Twain relation who sent him the volume), and yet, not just the association but the literary analysis draws much interest. Indeed, I would like to make something rather concrete from Santayana's "vague sense," namely, an invitation to allow the specificity of Tom Sawyer (along with Huck Finn too) and Don Quixote to accompany (more than haunt?) the following notes on the nature of Santayana's literary criticism and the potencies of his aesthetic judgment—perhaps especially when those activities are couched in terms of national and cultural identities, as well as the specifics of Santayana's reading of the adventures (or romances) penned by Twain and Cervantes. Santayana's life in (at least) two nations—principally Spain and the United States, but also a career-long ex-academic retirement with stops in Oxford, Paris, parts of Spain, and at last Rome—makes his allegiances and the expressions of affiliation much more complex. So, it is perhaps fitting that we take inspiration from speaking of dreamers caught up in the romance of adventure (such as the narrative frames and genre characteristics that there abide in *Huckleberry Finn* and *Don Quixote*) to undertake an analysis of how, for Santayana, literary criticism gets done, what literary-critical methods are invoked, and to what ends aesthetic sensibilities are involved in the adjudication of literary merit and philosophical probity. Together these will be the lively ghosts who stalk me in what follows.

There is a constellation of texts and ideas to consider on Mark Twain and Cervantes, but Santayana himself does not quite provide the full study we may be seeking. In Twain's *The Adventures of Huckleberry Finn*, a

Santayana's Philosophy and Criticism   179

veritable transcription of Quixotic concerns is reimagined when Huck wonders how Tom can defend the existence of "Spaniards and A-rabs," whereupon Huck is told matter-of-factly that "if I warn't so ignorant, but had read a book called 'Don Quixote,' I would know without asking. He said it was all done by enchantment" (Twain 2005, ch. 3, 10). Some scholars suggest that Twain's loyalty to and preference for Huck appear coded in Tom's condescending use of the word "enchantment," but we can, given our intertext, consider as well the magical allusions of the term (Twain 2005, 277). To a better prosecution of the case, then, we would wish also to expand outward to Olin Harris Moore's (1922) "Mark Twain and Don Quixote," Edward L. Galligan's (1978) "True Comedians and False *Don Quixote* and *Huckleberry Finn*," Michael David MacBride's (2016) "The Quixotic Dream of Mark Twain's Jim," and Michel Foucault's remarks on Cervantes in *The Order of Things*. We have assessments by Harold Bloom (2003):

> But [Quixote] is neither a fool nor a madman, and his vision always is at least double: he sees what we see, yet he sees something else also, a possible glory that he desires to appropriate or at least share.

And for more on doubleness as literary construct, we can draw in Elif Batuman's (2007) dissertation—*The Windmill and the Giant: Double-Entry Bookkeeping in the Novel*, where she says "[c]ontrary to the Marxist claim that traces of labor are always effaced from the literary text, I show that many of the best-loved European novels include a running account of their own production."[7] And many invoke the very qualities and characteristics that catch our eye in the company of these texts, as when Dorothea Brooke, the heroine of *Middlemarch*, is described as having a "Quixotic enthusiasm" that no doubt couples nicely with her "affectionate ardor" (Eliot 1871–1872, Book Four, ch. 42). Not surprisingly, given its precedence and prominence, *Don Quixote* as early metafiction is a path of decided illumination.[8] I rehearse this rich bibliography as an exemplification of Santayana's productive literary-critical instincts: he recognized something about the transatlantic intimacies of Twain and Cervantes (of Tom and Huck and Alonso Quijano) early on, though not earlier than Moore, who published in 1922. Let us say, then, that Santayana's capacity to adjudicate literary thematics across temporal expanse and national provenance make for further generative reflections.

Another such occasion is Santayana's essay "Hellenism and Barbarism" (1963 [Santayana 1968a]), which at a glance echoes Matthew Arnold's earlier "Hellenism and Hebraism" (1869). Published posthumously, Santayana's comparative work here—not between author or text but something more like between styles of civilization or, in more contemporary parlance, contrasting mindsets—comes to the fore precisely because he sustains a concern with Cervantes' *Quixote* as a representative standard and thus a point of cultural reference. Indeed, Krzysztof

180 *David LaRocca*

Piotr Skowroński glosses the lexicon by saying that "barbarism" in Santayana's sense is *cultural* barbarism, something that

> can be discerned both in the ancient past, when "barbarian genius infused into Christianity"—the Gothic cathedrals having been an example of such an infusion—and in the modern era, when such optimal representativeness of the "poetry of barbarism" can be found, such as Walt Whitman and Robert Browning.
>
> (2018, 254)[9]

In this context, and in the ongoing spirit of using examples as a mode of clarification, Santayana contrasts Cervantes' *Quixote* with Goethe's *Faust* and Henrik Ibsen's *Peer Gynt*. Santayana claims that Quixote's "romanticism is archaic, an atavism in the midst of civilization" (1963, 26). At odds with Faust and Peer Gynt, Quixote "does not conceive, like those essential barbarians, that man has a vague soul to develop *ad libitum*" (Santayana 1963, 27). Santayana concludes: "the romanticism of Don Quixote is a madness, an accident; not like that of barbarians a beginning of experience that, with time, might lead to the discovery of nature and art" (1963, 27). Santayana diminishes Goethe's apparent "classism" as merely "retrospective," as "only a phase of romanticism," whereas "true classicism is the understanding that life is an art within natural limits" (1963, 27). To underscore the aesthetic bifurcation announced in his title, Santayana concludes:

> [Quixote—or more precisely, Alonso Quijano] was a civilized soul infected with barbarism; and his romantic folly was but a superficial misdirection of his natural reason and goodness. Faust and Peer Gynt, on the contrary, were barbarians infected with civilization.
>
> (1963, 27)[10]

Recall that Santayana said in "Tom Sawyer and Don Quixote" that the Spanish knight's affliction was an "artificial madness" (1968b, 122).

As Santayana was educated in the same institutions as Ralph Waldo Emerson, a generation after his death—Boston Latin School and Harvard College, indeed, residing in Hollis Hall (same as Emerson)—Santayana would also later come to be among the first inhabitants of Emerson Hall (dedicated in December 1905), a name for the home of Philosophy at Harvard agitated for by German émigré and fellow faculty member, Hugo Münsterberg (2013, 333–345). And so, at mid-century, as the leading lights of Anglo-American logical positivism would be required to pass by the bronze statue of a seated Emerson (created by Daniel Chester French), prompting some, like Stanley Cavell, to reconceive their philosophical relationship to the "repressed" founders of thought in the United States (along with Thoreau), as an occupant in that same building,

Santayana's Philosophy and Criticism   181

Santayana—whose Harvard years ranged from 1886 to 1912—made known his impressions of the Sage of Concord.[11]

I have sketched a very brief biography of Santayana's particular orientation to Emerson, aiming to highlight those moments when Santayana took the most trouble to say something specific and sustained about one of the "ghosts" that remain on Harvard Yard—apparitions that were already sensible to Harvard graduate, R.W. Emerson (1836), back in September 1836, in the aftermath of the College's bicentennial jubilee:

> Cambridge at any time is full of ghosts; but on that day the anointed eye saw the crowd of spirits that mingled with the procession in the vacant spaces, year by year, as the classes proceeded; and then the far longer train of ghosts that followed the company.[12]

Now then, and more briskly, we see that while Santayana's most famous statement on Emerson comes in a group portrait known as *The Genteel Tradition in American Thought* (presented in 1911 on the eve of Santayana's departure from the United States and published in 1913 after his arrival in Europe as a newly ex-academic and itinerant scholar [Santayana 2013b]), Santayana sounded a confident series of assessments of Emerson in 1900 (first published in *Interpretations of Poetry and Religion* [Santayana 2013b]) and returned to his subject for Emerson's centenary a few years later with "Emerson's Poems Proclaim the Divinity of Nature, with Freedom as His Profoundest Ideal" (1903 [Santayana 1967]). And continuing our temporal rewinding, it may come as something of a surprise to learn that Santayana—a young reader of Emerson, much like Nietzsche a continent away—submitted a senior thesis to Harvard College in 1886 titled *The Optimism of Ralph Waldo Emerson*.[13] Indeed, Santayana's affinities for Emerson, elective or prospective, were observed by John Crowe Ransom, who concluded:

> I imagine [Santayana] is what Emerson might have been if Emerson had had a philosophical instead of a theological background; in other words, if his Harvard had been the Harvard of today or yesterday. As an Emerson disturbs the theologians, a Santayana disturbs the philosophers—an admirable function.
>
> (1967, 403–404)

Though it has become something of a habit to believe (aside from notable exceptions made by exemplars such as Stanley Cavell and Cornel West[14]) that the American pragmatists, by and large, condescended to Emerson as antique or antiquated—as part of a prehistory that can be acknowledged but not recovered or reconceived for a new era— Santayana stands out as someone whose often strident statements about Emerson land as dismissive criticisms, yet, upon further reflection and

182   *David LaRocca*

re-reading seem to be not just informed by deep and cogent assessment but also by respectful, admiring, and productively critical admiration. It is true that after reading, say, Santayana's remarks in *Interpretations of Poetry and Religion*—work that limns the nineteenth and twentieth centuries, offering a brief moment of pause (or poise) to consider where Emerson brought us by 1900, only eighteen years since his death, and to what lay ahead in the new century—Emerson would appear to have been denied some membership or legitimation (as Cavell has famously said, "his thought is repressed in the culture he founded" [2003, 194]). Yet, that denial or repression obtains only if one takes at face value that one should want Emerson to have earned such associations in the first place; or, by extension, that it is worth the labor, individually and collectively, to claim new titles *ex post facto*, as if in his defense or his honor.

Take, for example, that definitively made statements such as "[a]t bottom [Emerson] had no doctrine at all" are followed quickly by Santayana's hewing supplement: "[t]he source of his power lay not in his doctrine, but in his temperament, and the rare quality of his wisdom was due less to his reason than to his imagination" (Santayana 2013a, 298). The Lord giveth and taketh away. Indeed, Santayana shares a measure of this fate, as Lachs adduces:

> Some think [Santayana] too poetic, others too deeply devoted to science. Positivists find him too metaphysical, metaphysicians too positivistic. Stern moralists condemn him for having embraced an aesthetic or spiritual life; religious people bemoan that he is not spiritual enough.
>
> (2014, 145)

For someone hoping to make a case for Emerson's doctrine, Santayana's claim can seem an affront and, worse, a nascent defensiveness that can blind and deafen one to all the qualities and qualifications Santayana does, in fact, bestow on his quarry. For instance, Santayana is very savvy to notice that of the transcendentalists, "Emerson hardly regarded himself as a member of that school," and "passed for its spokesman"—an achievement that Emerson himself did not aspire to effect (Santayana 2013a, 299). Take another instance, when the "German romantic or idealistic philosophers" are noted as "great system-makers," and Emerson is contrasted—"he cannot rival them in the sustained effort of thought"—which, again, would seem an insult until one reads Santayana's addendum: "But he surpassed them in an instinctive sense of what he was doing" (Santayana 2013a, 300). A catalogue of such give-and-takes once adduced may yield insight (or provocation) by the care of their formulation: "Emerson [...] was not primarily a philosopher," since it "was not Emerson's vocation to be definite and dogmatic in religion any more than in philosophy" (Santayana 2013a, 300, 303). Emerson was primarily, by this reading, a poet, and "[s]o long as he is a poet [...], we can blame this

Santayana's Philosophy and Criticism   183

play of mind only by a misunderstanding. It is possible to think otherwise than as common sense thinks; there are categories beside those of science" (Santayana 2013a, 301). Again, the denial of membership in "common sense," the attribution of his "play of mind" may scan as derogatory, and yet they are meant to be clarifying, even marks of praise, setting Emerson in his proper location. Admittedly, after the schema is laid out, we may find Emerson in a place where we do not recognize him (or, as our own).

This volume takes as a constitutive point that nationality or national identity or national character is something that may be said to travel, to become a vector for transmission of ideas, to serve as a context or pretext for translation, and most literally can travel by some means across the ocean—hence the figuration of a transatlantic liaison between Spain and the United States, the Spanish and the American. There are many cases that conform to this structure, but our present one is complicated by Santayana's own expression or embodiment of transatlanticism—the way he travels from Spain to the United States and back iteratively throughout his adolescence; but also the way he leaves the United States—one wants to say forsakes it, for prominent European capitals of learning (Oxford, Paris, and finally Rome). All this to say, in what sense are we prepared, if at all, to claim that he offers us a *Spanish* take on Americans and the United States; on philosophy, on *American* philosophy? He has, for example, a clear vision of Emerson as a product of his New England roots and the English traits that seeded them ("a Puritan mystic with a poetic fancy and a gift for observation and epigram, [...] he saw in the laws of Nature, idealized by his imagination, only a more intelligible form of the divinity he had always recognized and adored" [Santayana 2013a, 303][15]). But in what sense—even if the facts are there to apply— are these evaluative pronouncements made as if from a transatlantic reader from Spain? To sustain Santayana's own sensibilities: the question haunts the proceedings.

In the return to Santayana on Emerson ventured—and occasioned by the present collection—and given what I have sketched about the dialectic between the Spanish-born and American-educated Santayana, I find myself dwelling more insistently on the way Santayana is an insider-outsider (or outsider-insider, depending on your emphasis), that is, a Harvard-educated Harvard professor who nevertheless (perhaps like his colleagues Münsterberg and Whitehead) remained perpetually a visitor. Yet for that invited and welcomed status, he may yield especially poignant accounts of the native insiders—the born-and-bred Brahmins of the Boston firmament.

What interests me on this occasion is not whether Santayana is accurate in his descriptions, one way or another (as if we have been inadvertently charged, for example, with debating Emerson's true nature as a thinker, poet, philosopher, American, "Psyche of Puritanism" or "old-fashioned divine" [Santayana 2013a, 303–304], etc.), but rather, in Santayana's position as an interpreter of culture. Is it not a truism that

184 *David LaRocca*

the outsider has clearer eyes for what is admirable or fallible in a given context? Indeed, is not the margin—even if just a mile or two from the center of town—enough, as it was for Thoreau's experiments in living on Emerson's land at Walden Pond, to activate a perspicuity lacking in the "mass of men" leading lives of "quiet desperation," suffering from a "secret melancholy" (Emerson 1844b; Thoreau 1854)?[16] Thus, it is precisely Santayana's capacity as a *critic* that makes his encounters with Emerson, American thought, American literary expression (e.g., Twain) so salient in the company of this volume, where we are asking after the relation or interrelationship of sensibilities of or for aesthetic judgment.

There is something salutary about exposing oneself to a close encounter with accomplished writers as they assess other esteemed writers. Indeed, this was a presentment of *Estimating Emerson*, a project inspired from keeping company with none other than John Lachs, himself a legendary interpreter of Santayana.[17] The idea Lachs and I mulled over was and remains that by becoming an audience to this communication—in our case, as the phrasing goes, Santayana "on" Emerson[18]—we achieve the necessary distance from, or lack of selfish implication in, the proceedings and that we, in the end, come away with a bit of an insight about both figures, their writing, their ideas, and if we are lucky a revitalized sense of our own stakes in the undertaking. As I put it in my introduction to *Estimating Emerson*: "No matter what is said, *that* these many excellent writers said anything at all [about Emerson] seems in itself a sufficient impetus to explore their common subject" (LaRocca 2013a, 1). Indeed, the question that opens the volume:

> Why have so many notable writers taken their interest in Ralph Waldo Emerson's work beyond private admiration—or irritation— and chosen to write essays, critical remarks, and other forms of prose as well as poetry that name, engage, correct and clarify, and often celebrate his writing?
>
> (LaRocca 2013a, 1)

One reply, to be sure, comes with the territory of literary-philosophical inheritance: that we are obliged to contend with what Cavell calls "monsters of fame."[19] And yet, notoriety only goes so far. Being well known does not always betoken influence—or, at least, of the sort one intended. Indeed, Santayana's own fortunes as a fellow "monster of fame," to the chagrin of many beloved readers, seem to be regularly constrained to the single dictum "those who cannot remember the past are condemned to repeat it" (Santayana 1905–1906). Ironically, of course, those who cannot remember what Santayana actually wrote are condemned to repeat paraphrases, some more passable than others, such as: "those who cannot learn from history are doomed to repeat it." (In a book title, Masha Gessen seems to have ably condensed the wary sentiment into a handy distillate: *The Future Is History*.) Still, for a person

Santayana's Philosophy and Criticism 185

such as Santayana, who wrote several books while an academic (including the five-volume *The Life of Reason* 1905–1906) and nearly twenty more books while in exile, it is astonishing, is it not, that Santayana's notoriety can seem to hinge on a single line, more often misquoted than not? Such a fate seems to nip at Emerson's legacy as well—with misquotations and misattributions becoming a careful scholar's unpleasant fever dream. Even when the words are correct, the application may be skewed—from a "shot heard 'round the world" to a "foolish consistency is the hobgoblin of little minds" (often quoted *without* "foolish," thus undermining and inverting the point), and "I shun father and mother and wife and brother when my genius calls me" (used as a cudgel for a stripped-down, egoist take on self-reliance). Perhaps it is a function of the epigrammatic and aphoristic nature of certain notable writers—Montaigne, Emerson, Nietzsche, Santayana—that their prose often feels quotable (made into extracts of digestible, memorable size) and yet, for the specificity of their grammar and diction, their remarks are as commonly butchered and therefore divested of their original meaning.

There is a sense, after spending some time dwelling in and absorbing Santayana's particular readings of Emerson—as a person, as a thinker, as a temperament for our consideration—that this figure "Emerson" may be held in company, if not with the children Tom and Huck, then with the "madness" of the Quixote—what might be deemed, in Santayana's lexicon, a strain of mysticism. Does this homology do service to Santayana's assessment of Emerson; and by extension, does that coupling do Emerson any favors in our ongoing attempt to understand him, his works, and his situatedness in the history of ideas? In reply, one thinks first of various fashions of reading texts, which appear with as much variability as they do periodic and emphatic expression: from John Crowe Ransom's (1937) "Criticism, Inc." to Robert Holub's (1992) work on reception theory; from Stephen Best and Sharon Marcus' (2009) "surface reading" to Andrew Kopec's (2016) "Digital Humanities, Inc." The temporality of a textual encounter seems highly consequential for what one can conjecture or find in the work itself. Our reading, like our literary criticism, is conditioned by metaphilosophical and methodological parameters. Thus, even a gloss on what we mean by "madness" will depend on a frame of reference—for instance, Santayana's philosophical appreciation of mysticism or Foucault's analysis of the institutional regimes set upon disciplining the body.

As a quick case study, consider how the type of "madness"—or mental derangement—that we find, time and again, in works of philosophy may travel under several names: iconoclasm, nonconformism, anti-authoritarianism, and anti-institutionalism, and these forms may be embodied and enacted in dynamic ways. Some figures aim to "awaken and persuade and reproach" citizens of the polis; as gadfly, Socrates is the Western emblem of this brand of irritation to the slumbering masses of humanity.[20] But is he taken to be mad or sane—the fool or the wise

186   *David LaRocca*

one? While history may have judged him the epitome of the sage, in his own time such pronouncements forced him to choose between exile and execution. Thus, when Santayana asks of Emerson "Was not the startling effect of much of his writing due to the contradiction to tradition and to common sense?" we may think as well of Socrates ... and perhaps also the dreamy visions of the Quixote. Indeed, Santayana, whose first volume of *The Life of Reason* is dedicated to "Reason in Common Sense," says that "Common sense, we are allowed to infer, is a shallow affair: true insight changes all that" (2013a, 301). And Santayana sees that when "imagination invades the sphere of understanding and seems to discredit its indispensable work," we stand on the cusp of "true insight." "When so applied, poetic activity is not an unmixed good," Santayana concludes, so it is, we might say, tainted or tainting (2013a, 301). With the Quixote in mind, but recalling that it is of Emerson Santayana speaks:

> It is possible to think otherwise than as common sense thinks; there are other categories beside those of science. When we employ them we enlarge our lives. We add to the world of fact any number of worlds of the imagination in which human nature and the eternal relations of ideas may be nobly expressed. So far our imaginative fertility is only a benefit: it surrounds us with the congenial and necessary radiation of art and religion. It manifests our moral vitality in the bosom of Nature.
>
> (2013a, 301)

And yet? "Poetic activity" leads to, or at least allows for, a certain kind of detachment, which in turn courts a diminishment or degradation of sensuous impressions and "the atrophy of his whole nature":

> It loosens our hold on fact and confuses our intelligence, so that we forget that intelligence has itself every prerogative of imagination, and has besides the sanction of practical validity. We are made to believe that since the understanding is something human and conditioned, something which might have been different, as the senses might have been different, and which we may yet, so to speak, get behind—therefore the understanding ought to be abandoned. We long for higher faculties, neglecting those we have, we yearn for intuition, closing our eyes upon experience. We become mystical.
>
> (Santayana 2013a, 301)

After navigating Santayana's not always forthcoming analysis, we nevertheless arrive at a definitive—and crystal clear—claim ("We become mystical"). And yet, such a definitive pronouncement is not an "unmixed" liability, since it can as much be taken as an attribute that yields further insight. Indeed, Santayana is moved to constrain the instinct to too quickly brand Emerson a mystic, once and done. For Emerson's "diffidence,"

Santayana's Philosophy and Criticism   187

"the same constant renewal of sincerity which kept [his] flights of imagination near to experience, kept his mysticism within bounds." To be sure, "[a] certain mystical tendency is pervasive in him," Santayana admits, "but there are only one or two subjects on which he dwells with enough constancy and energy of attention to make his mystical treatment of them pronounced" (2013a, 301). Once again, Santayana seems to couch a compliment with an insult: Emerson's mysticism while "pervasive" was not "pronounced" because he could not remain sufficiently concentrated on more than a couple of topics at a time or even over time! Once again, we wonder about the nuanced reading that Santayana's often-recondite prose demands, for it first requires that one determines one's own commitments to his terms (e.g., is being a mystic or mystical attributions what one wants for Emerson? Or, despite personal interpretive preferences, are they defensibly ascribed to him?); and second, we are compelled to adjudicate the "mixture" of Emerson's traits, intellectual and otherwise.

Some of the same necessary adjudication attends the reading and reception of Cervantes' *Don Quixote*, for the reader—as much as the character and his compatriots—is forced to consider the bounds of reason and the nature of common sense. Cervantes further complicates (and wonderfully enriches) the diegesis by innovating metafictional attributes, encouraging the reader to contend with the status of the work as a fiction along with layers of reality and representation.[21] (Not incidentally, *The Adventures of Huckleberry Finn* begins with the narrator invoking an author named Mark Twain who wrote a book called *The Adventures of Tom Sawyer*—so the metafictional gambit familiar in *Don Quixote* plays itself again in Twain's sequel.) As we know, Cervantes commences his tale with a moment of literary legerdemain, claiming that what we are about to read was taken from "the archives" of La Mancha, and moreover, that some of the material had to be translated from Cide Hamete Benengeli's Arabic text. Still more, we know that it is Alonso Quixano's *reading* that appears to disquiet him, to set him upon the notion of becoming one of the characters he reads about in his story books. In our contemporary popular culture, Quixano is often figured as a madman or dreamer (and either way, problematical for others), when, in fact, he is inspired, troubled by literature, by the chivalric romances he reads. His hallucinations, we might say, are virtuous idealizations of a literary mind: perhaps taken up now as a cognitive precursor to technologically achieved augmented, mixed, or virtual reality.

Quixano's "madness" conjures Quixote; it is a function of the blending or bleeding categories of fiction and fact, of artifice and reality, of on-page and off-the-page, since he "reads the world in order to prove his books," as Foucault (1970, 47) puts it. And such hermeneutic practice is, of course, what Cervantes sets up as the crux of *his* literary project called *The Ingenious Gentleman Don Quixote of La Mancha*. Whether, as Foucault says, Don Quixote "transform[s] reality into a sign" or Don Quixote takes literature as a sign he can transform—by means of (literary)

188   *David LaRocca*

imagination—in reality, we are addressing the same phenomenon. Prompting our remembrance of the *ouroboros*, Foucault writes in *The Order of Things*: "Cervantes's text turns back upon itself, thrusts itself back into its own density, and becomes the object of its own narrative" (1970, 48). Foucault's conclusion—that the character Don Quixote is "the book in flesh and blood" proposes a performative, embodied semiology that has a decidedly Emersonian cast, as in the rhetorical question: "What is a farm but a mute gospel?" (Emerson 1860, 42).[22] Quixote's adventures, as Foucault writes, "will be a deciphering of the world: a diligent search over the entire surface of the earth for the forms that will prove that what the books say is true" (1970, 47).

Metafictional tactics and tricks abound as when Quixano is beaten (for real, not in a dream) and lies unconscious while his local community (his niece, the housekeeper, a priest, a barber!) takes it upon itself to burn some of his books—the reading of books, again, being the apparent source of his ill-temper and choleric humor. Cervantes puts his own work (such as his first book *La Galatea*, 1585) up for (re)assessment (it is saved), while using the opportunity to unpack the literary merits or shortcomings of works by others (such as predecessor Melchor de Ortega's *Felixmarte de Hircania*, 1556, which is sent to the flames—under the just-barely altered title *Florismarte de Hircania*).[23] Cervantes takes a rest between Quixano's first and second sallies, in which the latter's mental state is a central point of concern, to provide us with chapters devoted to literary analysis of other books, real and imagined. Hence, Cervantes' own authorial assessments are mixed and matched with those of his literary characters, creating metafictional hybrids that cannot be undone. And as Cervantes has already provided evidence enough that reading books can be a cause of mental malady or distress or agitation, so, by extension, he provocatively, playfully, that is satirically, exhibits that like a plague, the sources of such causes should be burned. Thus, destroying books (in the midst of a novel based on apparently historical texts) is understood to be an antiseptic and thus a curative. So, doubtless, as the ironies accrue, we read on in *Don Quixote*, our capacity for maintaining our own sanity thereby endangered by the deliberate, immersive, world-creating act, as it was for our hero.

When Santayana writes about *Don Quixote* in the company of *The Adventures of Huckleberry Finn*, our ongoing deliberations about madness and mysticism, common sense and imagination, as seen above, come in for further comment:

> There had been the same disinterestedness in *Don Quixote* and the same romantic lead of the imagination [as found in *Huckleberry Finn*], overruling legality and convention, as well as common sense, in the name of the inner man, heroically autonomous.
>
> (Santayana 1952, 117)

Santayana's Philosophy and Criticism   189

As Santayana continues, this mood or temperament of "disinterestedness"

> [...] in Mark Twain's young heroes, is chiefly boyish play and love of mischief; yet in the case of Tom Sawyer it goes with a curious respect for superstitious prescriptions and ceremonies, often involving vigils and labours of the most exacting kind, with pain and wounds cheerfully accepted. All this, at least in the romances that had turned Don Quixote's head [a lovely turn of phrase for the books Quixano read and led to his apparent mental derangement], contained a mixture of belief in witchcraft and magic, with something of Christian penance and martyrdom.
>
> (1952, 117)

Santayana tells us that this "mixture was essential to chivalry" that "united the principle of honour, essentially the voice of the inner man, romantic, personal, and independent, with the principle of charity, bound to relieve all suffering, and to protect innocence against corruption" (1952, 117). The "voice of the inner man" travels under many names—from Socrates' daemon to Emerson's self in aversion to conformity, but here tethers Quixano's flights of fancy to protocols of conscience. Perhaps not surprisingly, "Don Quixote, who was mad, could confuse this Christian charity with honour, and could sally forth on his own authority to right wrongs everywhere" (Santayana 1952, 117). Yet this misidentification could be as easily said of the propitious lessons of mysticism. As Santayana wrote of Emerson:

> The faculty of idealization was itself what he valued. Philosophy for him was rather a moral energy flowering into sprightliness of thought [...]. He secured the freedom and fertility of his thought and did not allow one conception of law or one hint of harmony to sterilize the mind and prevent the subsequent birth within it of other ideas, no less just and imposing than their predecessors. For we are not dealing at all in such a philosophy with matters of fact or with such verifiable truths as exclude their opposites. We are dealing only with imagination, with the art of conception, and with the various forms in which reflection, like a poet, may compose and recompose human experience.
>
> (2013a, 300)

As we trade time registers along with factual or fictional identities— Twain's Tom and Huck for Cervantes' Quixano as well as Emerson's "Puritan mystic"—we encounter the child's "native courage and the cry of the oppressed" (herewith chattel slaves in the antebellum United States); the *hidalgo*'s morally motivated adventure, if by madness; and

190   *David LaRocca*

depictions of the poet's literary, interpretive, and ideational powers. In these vignettes, we are given reason to link such pursuits of justice and happiness to the aspirations of what Cavell titled Emersonian moral perfectionism.[24] Given the melioristic nature of such endeavors, we are pressed to consider whether they are by nature, or by definition, quixotic. Taking steps in the direction of freedom and liberation puts each of us on a "quest"—indeed, "in quest of the ordinary"—since what marks all three scenarios is the way each finds the fantastical (if not also the fanatical) in the everyday, the adventure in every step. In the company of Cervantes, Cavell's punning mastery here—in quest/inquest—of course yields uncanny variations on the fact and legacy of the *Quixote*, including the more notorious Tribunal of the Holy Office of the Inquisition (*Inquisición española*), it being a venture (not an adventure) established in 1478, inspired and enforced by imaginative fits of religious fervor, and thereafter sustained in its dominion and full force onward through the composition and publication of the *Quixote* (1605–1620) and concluding only on a summer's day, centuries later, when Emerson happened to be camping in Maine, still very much in the midst of his youthful vocational discernment (July 15, 1834).

If crusades can be holy, then they can also be bloody. And it is merely a trait of historical frameworks that we may articulate the difference between the moral justification of one and the evil of the other. Santayana concludes without equivocation:

> When, at the end of his history, Cervantes represents his hero to have recovered his sanity, and to have confessed the folly of his imaginary knight-errantry, the dying man retains all his dignity; for his sanity washes away, so to speak, only the mud from his armour, only the ridiculous claims from his generous aspirations.
>
> (1952, 117)

That is, his *return* to sanity washes away the mud—and blood. In concluding remarks, however, Santayana complicates a simple restoration of sanity and the propinquity of righteousness: "The Christian order," he notes, "which [Quixano] now recognizes to be alone authoritative is, after all, itself, like romantic heroism, an imagined fulfillment of the inner man's demands." And so the "native courage" that motivates Tom, the dream of righting wrongs in Quixano, and the in/quest of the ordinary that we apprehend in the poetical and mystical as well as in moral perfectionism confess their shared "romantic heroism" and the presentments of an inhering "inner man" (*daimon*, self, conscience, *eidos*, moral law, etc.) that would disclose sense that is anything but common. As Emerson attests: "common-sense is as rare as genius" (1844a, 67).

Just as the names and categories of our investigation get mixed together—fictional characters and historical figures, dreams and daily life, transcendental claims and scientific results, literary gleanings and

Santayana's Philosophy and Criticism   191

philosophical musings—we should find ourselves crossing back and forth between the realms on offer: the mystical and metaphysical as well as the ordinary and the uneventful. For "romantic heroism" is an attribute of life as we find it even as, in *Huckleberry Finn*, "Tom immediately takes the case in hand and devises all the details that must be set 'right,' according to the rules of romantic fiction [...]" (Santayana 1952, 118). The scare quotes around "right" are meant to remind us that "it appears that [Tom] knew from the beginning that the fugitive slave was no longer a slave at all"—that "[h]is mistress had died, leaving him a free man in her Will" (Santayana 1952, 119); knowledge of history's conditions upbraids the contours of imagined intentions and the literary events that might follow them. And so it is at precisely such a cleave point when a reader of *The Adventures of Huckleberry Finn* will also share in Santayana's "vague sense" that "the ghost of Don Quixote stalked in the background" (Santayana 1952, 116). As with Quixano, "[f]or Tom, it had all been private theatricals, done to the life of the other deluded actors, and by his own irresistible love of make-believe." When the vague sense is converted to specifics, however, a bold contrast emerges, since "Tom Sawyer, young as he was, was not mad like Don Quixote. He was aware of the futility of his stage setting, and the serious trouble it caused" (Santayana 1952, 116). In translating the contrast and finding conceptual categories, we could do worse than say that Don Quixote is sincere while Tom is cynical. Still more, we could say that despite his delusions, Don Quixote pursued a righteous cause, whereas Tom's adventure was a hoax.

As I looked to John Lachs to gain momentum for this study, I would also like to draw from his remarks on Santayana as I wind it down, since Lachs is among the inheritors of Santayana who is most attuned to the way philosophers conduct their labors—in terms of their selected texts, points of references, and the problems they deem worthy of extended attention as well as, not incidentally and indeed quite consequentially, the metaphilosophical methods they deploy, most especially the prose styles they mount to explicate these texts, references, and problems. As Lachs writes, with Santayana in mind,

> [i]f the philosopher who attempts precision and rigor is often misunderstood, the fate of the thinker who writes as though he were a poet is still worse. A picturesque style rich in metaphor invites misapprehension not only of its content and detail but also of the author's general intention.
>
> (2014, 47)

Let us call this observation Lachs' lament, for the suspicion he references has invaded and obscured the reception of many fine prose stylists whose work would otherwise have made more pronounced contributions to the history of philosophy, that is, if only philosophers would have had ears and eyes for such offerings—which is to say, in large

192 *David LaRocca*

measure, a capacity for coupling logical acumen with aesthetic sensibility. "In precisely this fashion" of disregard or marginalization, Lachs notes, Santayana "has long been celebrated as a consummate stylist, a poet, and a literary psychologist, while"—and here we brace for the outcome—"the view that his philosophy does not warrant serious study has been gaining ever wider acceptance" (2014, 48). Some readers will take the observation as an opportunity to double down on abandonment (John Crowe Ransom complained that Santayana remains "imprisoned with all his graces in the net of his intellectualism" [1967, 404]), while others will lean in to question the ongoing prevalence (and expansion!) of the ancient quarrel between poetry and philosophy. Where, for some, "[t]he result of such misunderstanding and of the frustration attendant upon the attempt to explicate poetry in prose is disdain and eventually the total neglect of the thinker's work" (Lachs 2014, 48). As we sidestep the charges against Santayana's "courageous naturalism" and "the vague and almost mystical things he said about the realm of spirit," we have aimed to imitate Santayana's mode of literary criticism as philosophical enterprise. Perhaps Santayana's appreciation for Don Quixote, and for Emerson, stemmed from a certain fellow feeling—a recognition of kindred spirits, thinkers and scribes who fathom the symbolical character of nature (and the humans who inhabit it) and the need to treat them all as interpretable objects, however inscrutable they may at first, and even second, glance seem.[25] These are translations, transatlantic and otherwise, that call our attention now and onward to further, future occasions.

Notes

1 See LaRocca and Miguel-Alfonso (2015, 1–28).
2 See LaRocca and Miguel-Alfonso (2015, 3).
3 See LaRocca (2020b, 20–29).
4 On the scene of walking and thinking, see, for example, Kagg (2018) and Bouwsma (1986).
5 See Pinch and Swedberg (2012) and Bouwsma (1986).
6 See LaRocca (2017b; 2017c; 2020a).
7 For more on Elif Batuman, see Kirsch (2010).
8 See LaRocca (2017c).
9 For Santayana on "barbarian genius," see Santayana (1922, 99–126); on "the poetry of barbarism," see Santayana (1905, 166–216).
10 See also Moreno (2015, 141).
11 For more from Cavell on the notion that the United States' founders of thought are "repressed," see Cavell (2003, 60–61, 114, 171, 194). Intriguingly, on another occasion, when Cavell writes of "repression," he contrasts it with a word of distinctly Santayanian association, namely, the "genteel" (Cavell 2004, 80). For epistolary coverage of these years, see Santayana (2001).
12 A longer excerpt from this day's entry is inscribed on the gate that surrounds Harvard Yard, above Cambridge Street, on a wall facing Annenberg Hall.

13 See my header introduction to Santayana's essays in LaRocca (2013c). See also LaRocca (2005; 2017a).
14 See again Cavell (2003) and West (1989), where Emerson is figured as the "root" of the pragmatist tradition in American thought, its essential "prehistory."
15 For more on Emerson's English traits and *English Traits* (1856), see LaRocca (2013d). See also remarks on varieties of inheritance in LaRocca (2020b).
16 See also LaRocca (2013f; 2020b, 32–33).
17 For more on this line of thought, see LaRocca (2013b).
18 As it happens, and pertinent to this phrasing, Lachs is the author of *On Santayana* (2006) and I am the author of *On Emerson* (LaRocca 2003), both in the Wadsworth Philosophers Series.
19 For more on this topic, see Rhu (2020) and Cavell (2004, 5).
20 See Plato (1979, 30eI–31a7).
21 For more on metafiction, see LaRocca (2017c).
22 See also LaRocca (2013d, 127–133). See also my dissertation, *The Fate of Embodiment* (LaRocca 2000) and LaRocca (2013e).
23 See Reichenberger (2005).
24 See esp. Cavell (2004) op cit.
25 For more on the symbolical, see LaRocca (2015).

Works Cited

Abrams, M.H. 1971. *Natural Supernaturalism: Tradition and Revolution in Romantic Literature*. New York: W.W. Norton & Company.

Appiah, Kwame Anthony. 2006. *Cosmopolitanism: Ethics in a World of Strangers*. New York: W.W. Norton & Company.

Batuman, Elif. 2007. *The Windmill and the Giant: Double-Entry Bookkeeping in the Novel*. PhD Dissertation, Stanford University.

Best, Stephen and Sharon Marcus. 2009. "Surface Reading: An Introduction." *Representations* 108, no. 1: 1–21.

Bloom, Harold. December 13, 2003. "The Knight in the Mirror," *The Guardian*.

Bouwsma, Oets Kolk. 1986. *Wittgenstein: Conversations 1949–1951*, edited by J.L. Craft and Ronald E. Hustwit. Indianapolis: Hackett Publishing Company, Inc.

Cavell, Stanley. 2003. *Emerson's Transcendental Etudes*, edited by David Justin Hodge. Stanford: Stanford University Press.

———. 2004. *Cities of Words: Pedagogical Letters on a Register of the Moral Life*. Cambridge: Belknap Press of Harvard University Press.

Eliot, George. 1871–1872. *Middlemarch*. Boston: Houghton Mifflin Company.

Emerson, Ralph Waldo. September 13, 1836. *Journals and Miscellaneous Notebooks*.

———. 1844a. "Experience." *Complete Works*, vol. III.

———. 1844b. "New England Reformers." *Complete Works*, vol. III.

———. 1860. "Fate." *Complete Works*, vol. VI.

Foucault, Michel. 1970. *The Order of Things: An Archaeology of the Human Sciences*, translated by Alan Sheridan. New York: Vintage.

Galligan, Edward L. 1978. "True Comedians and False *Don Quixote* and *Huckleberry Finn*." *The Sewanee Review* 86, no. 1: 66–83.

194 *David LaRocca*

Holub, Robert C. 1992. *Crossing Borders: Reception Theory, Poststructuralism, Deconstruction*. Madison: University of Wisconsin Press.

Kagg, John. 2018. *Hiking with Nietzsche: On Becoming Who You Are*. New York: Farrar, Straus and Giroux.

Kirsch, Adam. February 24, 2010. "A Comedian in the Academy." *Slate*.

Kopec, Andrew. 2016. "Digital Humanities, Inc.: Literary Criticism and the Fate of a Profession." *PMLA* 131: no. 2, 324–339.

Krell, David Farrell. 1999. *The Good European: Nietzsche's Work Sites in Word and Image*. Chicago: University of Chicago Press.

Lachs, John. 1967. "Introduction." *Animal Faith and Spiritual Life*, edited by John Lachs. New York: Appleton-Century-Crofts, 1.

———. 2006. *On Santayana*. Belmont: Thomson Wadsworth.

———. 2014. "A Community of Psyches: Santayana on Society." *Freedom and Its Limits*, edited by Patrick Shade. New York: Fordham University Press, 145–158.

LaRocca, David. 2000. *Fate of Embodiment*. PhD Dissertation, Vanderbilt University.

———. 2003. *On Emerson*. Belmont: Thomson Wadsworth.

———. 2005. "Una traduzione transatlantica: Fato e libertà in Emerson e nel giovane Nietzsche" ["Transatlantic Translation: Young Nietzsche Writing Toward Emerson"]. *Nietzsche e l'America*, edited and translated by Sergio Franzese. Edizioni ETS, Nietzsceana Saggi 2, 83–105.

———. 2013a. *Estimating Emerson: An Anthology of Criticism from Carlyle to Cavell*, edited by David LaRocca. New York: Bloomsbury.

———. 2013b. "A Conversation among Critics." *Estimating Emerson: An Anthology of Criticism from Carlyle to Cavell*, edited by David LaRocca. New York: Bloomsbury, 1–25.

———. 2013c. "George Santayana." *Estimating Emerson: An Anthology of Criticism from Carlyle to Cavell*, edited by David LaRocca. New York: Bloomsbury, 297–298.

———. 2013d. *Emerson's English Traits and the Natural History of Metaphor*. New York: Bloomsbury.

———. 2013e. "Performative Inferentialism: A Semiotic Ethics." *Liminalities: A Journal of Performance Studies* 9: no. 1: 1–26.

———. 2013f. "Reading Cavell Reading." *Stanley Cavell, Literature, and Film: The Idea of America*, edited by Andrew Taylor and Áine Kelly. New York: Routledge, 26–41.

———. 2015. "'Eternal Allusion': Maeterlinck's Readings of Emerson's Somatic Semiotics." *A Power to Translate the World: New Essays on Emerson and International Culture*, edited by David LaRocca and Ricardo Miguel-Alfonso. Hanover: Dartmouth College Press, 113–135.

———. 2017a. "Emerson Recomposed: Nietzsche's Uses of his American 'Soul-Brother.'" *Nietzsche and the Philosophers*, edited by Mark T. Conard. New York: Routledge, 211–230.

———. 2017b. "The European Authorization of American Literature and Philosophy: After Cavell, Reading *Bartleby* with Deleuze, Then Rancière." *Melville among the Philosophers*, edited by Corey McCall and Tom Nurmi with an afterword by Cornel West. Lanham: Lexington Books, 189–212.

———. 2017c. "Translating Carlyle: Ruminating on the Models of Metafiction at the Emergence of an Emersonian Vernacular." *Religions* 8, no. 8: 1–26.

Santayana's Philosophy and Criticism   195

———. 2020a. "Autophilosophy." *Inheriting Stanley Cavell: Memories, Dreams, Reflections*, edited by David LaRocca. New York: Bloomsbury, 275–320.

———. 2020b. "Must We Say What We Learned? Parsing the Personal and the Philosophical." *Inheriting Stanley Cavell: Memories, Dreams, Reflections*, edited by David LaRocca. New York: Bloomsbury, 1–48.

LaRocca, David and Ricardo Miguel-Alfonso. 2015. "Thinking Through International Influence." *A Power to Translate the World: New Essays on Emerson and International Culture*. Hanover: Dartmouth College Press, 1–28.

MacBride, Michael David. 2016. "The Quixotic Dream of Mark Twain's Jim." *The Mark Twain Annual* 14: 93–103.

Mink, Louis O. 1980. "The Golden Age of the Golden Department," a review of *The Rise of American Philosophy. Cambridge, Massachusetts, 1860–1930*, by Bruce Kuklick. *History of Education Quarterly* 20, no. 2: 189–195.

Moore, Olin Harris. 1922. "Mark Twain and Don Quixote." *PMLA* 37, no. 2: 324–346.

Moreno, Daniel. 2015. *Santayana the Philosopher: Philosophy as a Form of Life*, translated by Charles Padrón. Lewisburg: Bucknell University Press.

Münsterberg, Hugo. 2013. "Emerson as Philosopher." 1900. *Estimating Emerson: An Anthology of Criticism from Carlyle to Cavell*, edited by David LaRocca. New York: Bloomsbury, 333–345.

Pinch, Trevor and Richard Swedberg. 2012. "Wittgenstein's Visit to Ithaca in 1949: On the Importance of Details." *Distinktion: Scandinavian Journal of Social Theory* 14, no. 1: 2–29.

Plato. 1979. *Plato's "Apology of Socrates": An Interpretation, with a New Translation*, edited by Thomas G. West. Ithaca: Cornell University Press.

Ransom, John Crowe. 1937. "Criticism, Inc." *The Virginia Quarterly* 13, no. 4: 586–602.

———. 1967. "Art and Mr. Santayana." 1937. *Animal Faith and Spiritual Life*, edited by John Lachs. New York: Appleton-Century-Crofts, 403–404.

Reichenberger, Kurt. 2005. *Cervantes and the Hermeneutics of Satire*. Barcelona: Kassel.

Rhu, Lawrence F. 2020. "Monsters and Felicities: Vernacular Transformations of the Five-Foot Shelf." *Inheriting Stanley Cavell: Memories, Dreams, Reflections*, edited by David LaRocca. New York: Bloomsbury, 161–178.

Santayana, George. 1905. *Interpretations of Poetry and Religion*. New York: Charles Scribner's Sons.

———. 1922. *The Life of Reason, or the Phases of Human Progress: Reason in Religion*. New York: Charles Scribner's Sons.

———. 1967. "Emerson's Poems Proclaim the Divinity of Nature, with Freedom as His Profoundest Ideal." *George Santayana's America: Essays in Literature and Culture*, edited by James Ballowe. Urbana: University of Illinois Press, 85–96.

———. 1968a. "Hellenism and Barbarism." 1963. *The Birth of Reason and Other Essays*, edited by Daniel Cory. New York: Columbia University Press, 23–30.

———. 1968b. "Tom Sawyer and Don Quixote." 1952. *The Birth of Reason and Other Essays*, edited by Daniel Cory. New York: Columbia University Press, 116–122.

———. 2001. *The Letters of George Santayana: Book One, 1868–1909*. Vol. 5 of *The Works of George Santayana*, edited by William G. Holzberger and Herman J. Saatkamp, Jr. Cambridge: MIT Press.

196 David LaRocca

———. 2013a. "Emerson." 1900. *Estimating Emerson: An Anthology of Criticism from Carlyle to Cavell*, edited by David LaRocca. New York: Bloomsbury, 298–304.

———. 2013b. "The Genteel Tradition in American Thought." 1911. *Estimating Emerson: An Anthology of Criticism from Carlyle to Cavell*, edited by David LaRocca. New York: Bloomsbury, 305–318.

Skowroński, Krzysztof Piotr. 2018. "Santayana's Philosophy of Education against Fanaticism and Barbarity." *The Life of Reason in the Age of Terrorism*, edited by Charles Padrón and Krzysztof Piotr Skowroński. Leiden: Brill-Rodopi, 245–260.

Thoreau, Henry David. 1854. *Walden; Or, Life in the Woods*. Boston: Ticknor and Fields.

Twain, Mark. 2005. *Adventures of Huckleberry Finn*. 1884, edited by Amber Reed and Lisa M. Miller. Clayton: Prestwick House.

West, Cornel. 1989. *The American Evasion of Philosophy: A Genealogy of Pragmatism*. Madison. University of Wisconsin Press.

Index

Abrams, M. H. 177
Adorno, Rolena 12, 18, 27, 84
Alhambra 17, 37, 83, 88
American colonies 24
Anda y Salazar, Simón 67
Appiah, Kwame Anthony 176
Arnaiz, Federico 162
Arrighi, Giovanni 169

Barlow, Joel 59
Bartosik-Vélez, Elise 25
Bellamy, Edward 160
Biblioteca Nacional de España 112
bildungsroman 113, 119, 122–25, 129
Bates, General John C. 67
Belknap, Jeremy 59
Biography 10–12
Black Legend (Leyenda negra) 138, 163
Böhl von Faber, Johann N. 84
Boudinot, Elias 36–37
Bryant, William Cullen 2
Burstein, Andrew 10–11
Bushman, Claudia 23

Calderón de la Barca, Frances 79–95; Life in Mexico 80, 81, 85, 90, 92; The Attaché in Madrid 81–95
Calderón de la Barca, Pedro 83
Californio(s) 6, 132–45, 148–52, 155
canon 1, 2, 8
captivity stories 29–54
castas (system of) 107, 134, 137, 145, 149, 155, 156
Castro, Américo 32
Catholic/Catholicism 30, 35, 43, 52, 54, 76, 81, 89, 138, 139, 143, 145, 146, 153, 155, 157, 158, 161
Cavell, Stanley 176, 180, 181, 190

Célis, Pastor de 114
Cervantes, Miguel de 30, 34, 35, 87, 177; Don Quixote 38, 49, 60, 83, 177–80, 185–87, 191
Cheetham, James 2
Child, Lydia Maria 137
Clark, Priscilla 117
Columbus, Christopher 18–26, 57, 59, 65, 68
Conrad, Joseph 39
Cooper, James Fenimore 1, 2
Coronado, Raúl 8, 29, 49
Cowdery, Jonathan 42
criollos 107, 134, 155
Cuba vii, 62–64, 76, 90, 91, 154, 163–68, 171
Cushing, Caleb 2

DeGuzmán, María 23–24, 103
De las Casas, Bartolomé 39
Dickens, Charles 80
DiCuirci, Lindsay 10
discovery of America 19, 57
Dulce Nombre de María (catedral) 67

Emerson, Ralph Waldo 180–84, 190
empire (American) 1, 10, 31, 40, 48, 57–62, 64, 67, 71, 145, 169; empire (Spanish) 1, 3, 4, 8, 16, 17, 20, 24, 29, 55, 58, 63, 65, 84, 168
Escorial (Palace) 88
Espartero, Baldomero 92
Everett, Alexander Hill 10–12, 60
expansionism 84, 91, 157

Fabra, Nilo María 159–74
Federalist Party 64, 173
Ferdinand and Isabella (see also Reyes Católicos) 17, 19, 26, 60, 87

198   *Index*

Fernández de Navarrete, Martín
  10–11, 60
Florida 11, 31, 39, 52, 65, 70
Foucault, Michel 187–88
Franchot, Jennie 43
Freneau, Philip 59
frontier 30–33, 39–44, 46–49, 147
  148, 155
Fuchs, Barbara 33

Giles, Paul 10
Glass, Navy Captain Henry 66
Golden Age (Spanish) 30
Gómez de Baquero, Eduardo 167
González, Marcial 133
gothic 88, 89, 138, 152–55, 180
Granada 32, 34–36, 83
Gruesz, Kirsten Silva 8
Guadalupe Hidalgo (Treaty of) 43–44,
  148, 150, 163
Guam 57, 65, 66–69, 70
Gutierrez, Guadalupe 111–31

Hamidullah, Mohammed 13
Havard, John C. 58
Hazlett, John 23
Henry, General Guy Vernon 64
Hispanism (in the U.S.) 61, 67, 69, 70

Irving, Washington 1, 10–22, 37–38,
  43, 58, 59–61, 82, 84, 91; *Tales of a
  Traveller* 10, 82; *Life of Columbus*
  11–15, 19, 20, 21, 37, 60, 83; *Tales
  of the Alhambra* 1, 26, 38, 60, 75,
  82–84, 86, 88, 95; *Chronicle of the
  Conquest of Granada* 60–61, 83;
  "Rip Van Winkle" 91; *The Sketch
  Book* 91–92

Jaksic, Iván 58
James, William 177
Jáudenes, Fermín 55
Jefferson, Thomas 107

Kagan, Richard 29, 58, 103, 166
Kaplan, Amy 150

Lazo, Rodrigo 8, 102, 113
Leary, Captain Richard 66
Lepanto (Battle of) 34
Longfellow, Henry Wadsworth 1, 2,
  84, 84, 86
López de Legazpi, Miguel 67
Los Angeles 111, 114, 118, 120–23

MacKenzie, Alexander S. 2
Madrid 37, 55, 60, 81, 83, 85, 86, 87,
  90–94, 116, 118, 128, 159, 161,
  163, 171, 178
Magellan, Ferdinand 65, 67, 68
Malcolm, George A. 69
Martí, José 163
Martínez de Rozas, Juan 97
McKinley, President William 57,
  63, 167–69
Matar, Nabil 42
Mather, Cotton 106
McElroy, John H. 21
McLamore, Richard 23
Mediterranean Sea 31
Melville, Herman 84; "Benito
  Cereno" 96–110
Merritt, General Wesley 55, 66
Mexican-American War 62, 82, 91
migration 44, 49, 61, 152
military orders (Spanish) 31
Monk, Maria 43, 153
Mormonism 30, 42, 44–48, 50–54
Morris, William 160
Morrison, Toni 103
Muley Boabdil 18, 20, 26

Native Americans 24, 25, 30, 34, 42,
  46, 47, 106, 107, 140, 148
Nelson, Dana 102
New England 30, 98, 99, 139, 141,
  142, 147, 148, 152, 176
Núñez Cabeza de Vaca, Alvar
  34, 39, 41
Núñez Muley, Francisco 37

O'Donnell, Leopoldo 92
O'Sullivan, John L. 84

Pérez, Juan 20
Pestana, Carla 30
Pettigrew, James 2
Pfitzer, Gregory 21–22, 24
Philippines 66–69, 168
Prescott, William H. 2, 43, 49, 58,
  61–62, 79, 80, 85, 103
Puerto Rico 57, 63, 64, 67, 168

Quintero y Escudero, María
  Berta 111–31

racial passing 137
racism 105, 141, 164
Ransom, John Crowe 181

Reconquista (Spanish) 10, 15–18, 29, 32
Reeve, W. Paul 47
Reyes Católicos (see also Ferdinand and Isabella) 15–18, 20, 32
Revolutionary War 1, 56, 59
Riley, James 42
roman à clef 119–20
Rowlandson, Mary 30, 40–42
Royce, Josiah 177
Rubin-Dorsky, Jeffrey 82
Ruiz de Burton, M. Amparo 132–58

Sánchez Albornoz, Claudio 33
Santayana, George 7, 175–96; *Interpretations of Poetry and Religion* 182; *The Last Puritan* 177; *The Life of Reason* 175, 185, 186
Schlegel, August 84
Silk Road, the, 14
Shurr, William 25
Slotkin, Richard 48

Soulé, Peter 90
Spanish-American War 1, 55, 56, 57, 62, 65, 68, 168–69
Stowe, Harriet Beecher 137

Ticknor, George 2, 43, 61–62
Toledo 32
Trans-Atlanticism 4, 8, 12, 14, 25, 27, 29–31, 49, 53, 57, 60–64, 92, 96, 105, 172, 176–79, 179, 183, 192
Tryal affair 5, 96–99, 104, 107
Turner, Frederick Jackson 31
Twain, Mark 178–82, 187–89, 191, 195

Urdaneta, Andrés de 67

Valera, Juan 160
Verne, Jules 160

Ward, Maria N. (pseudonym) 45–48
Warren, John Esaias 82, 84, 86, 89, 95

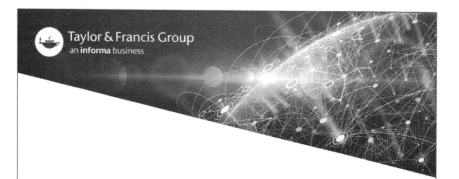

Taylor & Francis eBooks

www.taylorfrancis.com

A single destination for eBooks from Taylor & Francis with increased functionality and an improved user experience to meet the needs of our customers.

90,000+ eBooks of award-winning academic content in Humanities, Social Science, Science, Technology, Engineering, and Medical written by a global network of editors and authors.

TAYLOR & FRANCIS EBOOKS OFFERS:

- A streamlined experience for our library customers
- A single point of discovery for all of our eBook content
- Improved search and discovery of content at both book and chapter level

REQUEST A FREE TRIAL
support@taylorfrancis.com

Printed in the United States
by Baker & Taylor Publisher Services